Short Log & Timber
BUILDING BOOK

A Handbook for Traditional and Modern Post and Beam Houses

JAMES MITCHELL

Hartley & Marks
PUBLISHERS

In dedication to Grant and Laurel
and in special memory of Terry

Produced by
Hartley & Marks, Ltd.

Published in the U.S.A. by
Hartley & Marks, Inc.
P.O. Box 147, Pt. Roberts
Washington
98281

Published in Canada by
Hartley & Marks, Ltd.
3663 West Broadway
Vancouver, B.C.
V6R 2B8

Printed in the U.S.A.

ISBN 0-88179-010-9 paper
ISBN 0-88179-009-5 hardcover

If not available at your local bookstore,
this book may be ordered from the publisher.
Send the cover price plus one dollar for
shipping to the above address

Contents

Preface

The Short Log and Timber Building Book is based on ten years of study, practice, and teaching the architectural forms of log blockwork, post and beam work, and timber frame work. It deals specifically with the craft of log and timber post and beam building because, in my experience, it produces the most realistic and practical form of owner-built housing attainable by novice builders—whether living on the fringe of civilization or in the heart of a suburb. Furthermore, though log post and beam building is an integral part of the North American heritage, its history and methods remain largely unknown. Thus, this is the first book to exhaustively describe and teach traditional and contemporary log and timber post and beam construction. It is also my hope that in using this book the reader and builder will gain in understanding, appreciation, and respect for that most natural and alive of building materials—wood.

The work of researching and organizing the material for this book has been greatly furthered by the assistance of a grant from Canada Mortgage and Housing Corporation (CMHC) under the terms of the External Research Program. The views expressed are those of the author and do not necessarily represent those of the Corporation.

Lastly, I would like to express my gratitude to the illustrator, Bob English, whose artistic talents have given substance to my drawings.

Introduction

Snow fell on me,
Rain beat down on me,
Dew fell on me,
Long I seemed dead.

A stanza from the Viking Edda.

This ancient passage could well be heralding the revival of the wood building method whose roots reach deep into its Viking past. It is a method which served northern Europe during the Middle Ages and became the stepping-stone between log blockwork and timber framework construction. While being used temporarily in seventeenth century America, through diverse routes it became Canada's first traditional building form, being used across the entire New World, from the Atlantic to the Pacific coasts and north to the Beaufort sea. Yet for a time it was destined to be forgotten and buried by a modern society whose sweeping doctrine of progress led to a disowning of traditional ways. This building method is called "post and beam." Throughout its transition and migration it was understood by a variety of names, notably "pièce-sur-pièce." For years the method "long seemed dead." Indeed, had it not been for the ability of these sturdy structures to withstand centuries of snow, rain, and "dew," we would have no surviving models from which to learn. And that would be a sad loss, for today more than in any other period of history we are in need of ways to regain our intimate contact with nature. How much knowledge, I wonder, have we let die with no fragment left to nurture back to life?

I have studied the ancient crafts of solid wood joinery—blockwork, post and beam, and framework, and these studies have taken me around the world. While building with those traditional methods, I have had the opportunity to pass on my limited knowledge to northern Inuit (Eskimo) and Dene (Indian) peoples living on the edge of the Canadian treeline, and to build as far south as the oak hills of Arkansas. I have found, no matter where we live, we are all alike in that, as human beings, we all require shelter for our physical protection and our psychological well-being. Obtaining this human necessity should not have to lead to a mortgaged life. It never did for our ancestors, who bequeathed us their traditional methods locked inside the buildings they constructed —methods which utilized natural materials, reaffirming our bond with nature. If we wish to free ourselves from the bonds of a mortgage we must adopt an owner-builder attitude and learn to use nature's materials. For our psychological well-being we must strive to link progress with tradition, connecting past with present and humankind with nature. Thus, in this book I have endeavored to combine valuable methods from the past with others from the present, in order to develop practical methods for creating beautiful wooden structures in as simple a manner as possible.

This, therefore, is a practical book about post and beam construction methods. This method should not be confused with braced timber framing, for although it has often been subjugated under this term, it is a method which bridges and unites timber framing (framework) and notched corner log building (blockwork). Framework only includes techniques for vertical braced framing, and blockwork involves only horizontally layered building with interlocking notched corners. Post and beam construction, however, combines these two methods with a unique simiplicity. The post and beam house can duplicate the fundamental forms of blockwork and framework or it can be used purely as its own form, depending on the builder's preference.

There are great advantages in this method for the novice owner-builder. Such a builder must rely on modest tools, with a minimum of assistance, limited skills, and a tight budget. A feasible building method for the owner-builder must be adaptable to these limitations. It must also possess design flexibility so as to appeal to a variety of tastes, and permit construction in a variety of geographic regions, permitting use of local building materials. The post and beam method meets all these requirements, while other building methods do not. It is for such reasons as these that the Canadian government supports a program in the Northwest Territories in which the sole method of construction is post and beam. It is the only viable method for such remote areas, where the cost of shipping stud frame components is prohibitive, and the region's tree sizes permit neither blockwork nor framework.

In this book, construction procedures for five different post and beam houses are explained, allowing for a wide range of personal tastes and geographic practicality. They vary from one another in the amount of material preparation required, in their degrees of difficulty, and in the use of alternative materials. Log post and beam buildings, for example, require a minimum of material preparation, their appearance and simplicity are ideal in a rural or vacation home. Another method includes notched corners for those who like the appearance of blockwork architecture but have neither access to long poles nor the lifting machinery and sufficient help to build one. A third approach for the traditionally oriented builder explains timber post and beam construction, employing traditional joinery techniques. For areas where wood materials are scarce, or the builder simply prefers its appearance, a method using either a log or timber frame with stackwall infills is explained. For those who like framework architecture but do not possess the skill to execute a braced frame, there is a method for a stucco plaster finish with a post and beam frame. This method is particularly well suited for urban locations, since conventional siding, glass, rock, etc., can also be used as infills, allowing such a house to blend in with its neighbors. A variety of roof systems are explained, from conventional stud frame truss and rafter structures to log gable ends with longitudinal beamed roofs.

CHAPTER ONE

Evolution of Post & Beam

The structure and style of mankind's dwellings have always been closely linked to regional climate and the availability of suitable building materials. It is not a coincidence then, that cultures living in similar regions have come to similar solutions with respect to their housing needs. In a sampling of characteristic dwellings around the world, author-architect Jean Dollfas found houses of heavy timber with beam construction in cold northern forest and mountain regions. These ranged from the North American northwest to Scandinavia, the Himalayas, and beyond to Japan. In the Middle Ages vast forest regions stretched from northern Scandinavia through northeastern Europe and extended to Asia and the Pacific Ocean. During this period these regions excelled in the three wooden building methods, blockwork, post and beam work, and framework, and the development of one method over another was directly related to each area's forest reserves. In this book my concern is with cultures which have contributed to our North American construction methods, therefore discussion will be limited to the European communities.

Figure 1–1 shows the areas in northern Europe during the Middle Ages where the different methods of wooden architecture became prominent. In eastern Europe and Russia, forest reserves were plentiful, while the available tools were very rudimentary. Saws and drills were inaccessible for most people up to the nineteenth century and the common axe had to be relied upon for all manner of construction. As a result, the blockwork method was developed above others, since trees could be felled and stacked in horizontal tiers with the ends notched together using a simple woodsmanm's axe. Russian mastery of the blockwork method is exemplified in the monastic Church of Transfiguration in Figure 1–2.

In contrast to eastern Europe and Russia, the forest reserves of western Europe were rapidly diminishing with increased population, and regulations were created to conserve wood supplies. In these more populous regions there were, however, numerous craftsmen's guilds and access to specialized woodworking tools which led to the development of framework architecture. The braced frame required less wood and allowed

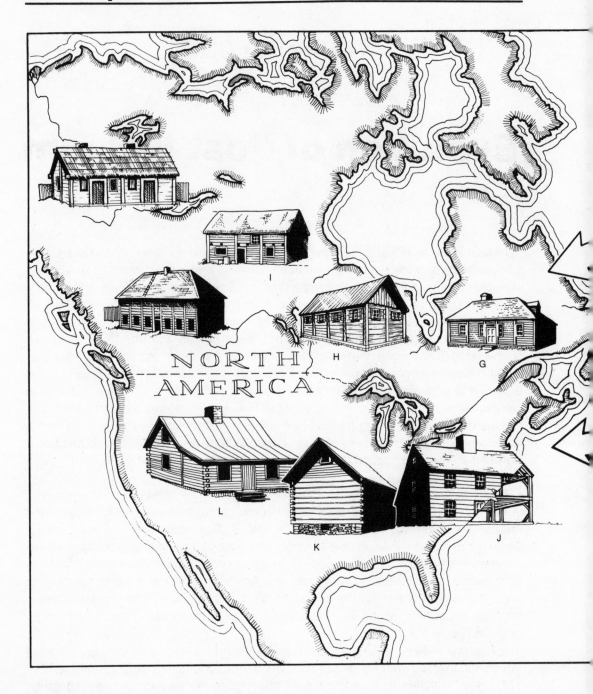

Figure 1-1 Early wooden architectural forms of northern Europe and the New World of North America.

MAP KEY

EUROPE

A Blockwork church, northwestern Russia (1400 A.D.), using notched corner log construction called "laft" in Norway.
B Framework building, western Europe (1500 A.D.), using braced timber frame construction.
C Stav church, Norway (1000 A.D.), using post and beam construction with plank infill between the posts.
D *Stav og laft* farmhouse of Norway and Sweden (1400 A.D.), combining stave and laft construction forms.
E *Stav og laft* church, western Russia (1400 A.D.), merging stave and laft construction to form true post and beam.
F Log posts and walls of earliest known post and beam structure, Poland, (700 B.C.)

NORTH AMERICA

G French (1600 A.D.) *piece-sur-piece* house.
H English (1600 A.D.) Red River frame house.
I Hudson's Bay (1800 A.D.) trading fort.
J Timber (framework house), New England (1800 A.D.).
K Standard dovetail long log (blockwork) building.
L Round notch long log (blockwork) building, western United States (1800 A.D.).

Figure 1-2. Russian blockwork church (Church of the Transfiguration) 1400 A.D.

infills such as stick wattle clay surface daubing or simply rock rubble between the open frames. (See Figure 1-3.) By the sixteenth century the scarcity of forest reserves in England and France forced buildings to be constructed almost entirely of stone.

The cultures between western Europe and Russia were fortunate in that they had the forest reserves, tools, and the geographic position to benefit from their neighbors' architectural influences. The result was a unique blending of both blockwork and framework to form the post and beam method. Post and beam construction did not demand the lengthy procedure of squaring the timbers, nor the intricate joinery of the braced framework bents, while the wood infill was substantially warmer than rock or clay. In addition, this method did away with restrictions to a building's size and the difficulty of handling the heavy, large materials used in blockwork construction.

The question remains whether post and beam architecture developed as a result of the influences of blockwork and framework or if it developed independently. We know that during the Middle Ages the Vikings had an advanced understanding of shipbuilding and frame and skin structure. On their expeditions of conquest they learned of new cultures and architectures, and were able to apply their shipbuilding skills to create new variations of post and beam construction. Consider the famous stave churches of Norway of which over 700 were built between 1000 A.D. and 1300 A.D. (Figure 1-4.)

Figure 1-3. English Tudor
framework building.

Figure 1-4. Norwegian (reiswerk)
stave church, 1000 A.D.

Figure 1-5. Norwegian farmhouse, 1400 A.D., showing the "stav og laft" method.

"Stave" refers to the vertical stave or post used in this construction method, which they called "reiswerk," "reise" being the verb to place something upright (i.e., the post). The use of natural log corner posts and the absence of individually braced frame bents sets it apart from the framework methods of western Europe, though undeniably these are Christian churches which reflect the Gothic architectural influence of Christian Europe. In a similar way, Russian and Swedish blockwork methods influenced their Norwegian domestic structures. A merging of the two methods is seen in the typical Norwegian farmhouse in Figure 1-5. The Norwegian word for the horizontal notched corner blockwork construction method is "laft," while the name for this combination of the two forms is "stav og laft" (a vertical post and horizontal beam). A fine example of totally integrated stav og laft, or post and beam, construction is shown in the Russian Church of Lazarus in Figure 1-6. Examples of post and beam construction can also be found in Denmark, where it is called "bulhuse" construction, "bul" or "bole" referring to the trunk or wood of a tree, and "huse" to house. In his book "Architecture in Wood," Hans Jürgen Hansen refers to more than a hundred dwellings in Biskupin, Poland from the year 700 B.C., constructed of vertical posts with horizontal log infill joined in tongue and slot fashion.

The standard log cabin, using notched long logs, was first built in Pennsylvania by Scandinavian settlers. But despite its Viking beginnings, it is the French and British who brought the solid wood post and beam method to the New World. Sixteenth century colonialization of North America was begun by the French in Quebec, Canada (New

Figure 1-6. Russian Church of St. Lazarus (ca. 1300 A.D.) which combines true post and beam with notched corner building methods.

France), and by the British in Maine and Massachusetts (New England). In "The Log Cabin Myth," author Harold Shurtleff describes the construction of these early New England post and beam buidlings. "Their walls, instead of presenting the horizontally corrugated surface and projecting ends at the corners by which the true log cabin is universally recognized, were squared off smoothly by broadaxe; and the corners were either formed by posts into which the wall timbers were mortised, or else the timbers were evenly and neatly joined by some form of dovetailing."[1] In New England this construction method was very soon replaced by braced framework with clapboard siding, due to diminishing wood reserves and the advent of more efficient tools and sawing methods. (Figure 1-1.)

1. Shurtleff, Harold R., *The Log Cabin Myth* (Gloucester, Mass.: Harvard University Press, 1939).

In early Canada, however, post and beam became the primary building method from the Atlantic to the Pacific coast, and north to the Beaufort Sea. In 1664 Pierre Boucher wrote of the houses built in Canada, "Some are built entirely of stone, and are roofed with pine boards or shakes; others are of colombage, that is, framed and then filled with masonry between the timbers; others still are built wholly of wood and are roofed, as I have said, with boards."[1] But by the second half of the seventeenth century, the solid wood post and beam house became the most distinctive construction method in Quebec. It made little sense to use stone or rubble when wood was a better insulator against the cold and was in plentiful supply. The French called the post and beam framing technique "poteaux sur sole," meaning post on sill. The method of wood infill between the posts was called "pièces de bois sur pièces de bois," meaning wood pieces on wood pieces. Soon, the common name became shortened to pièce-sur-pièce," by which name it is still known today throughout Canada. Conventional pièce-sur-pièce houses in Upper Canada had wall timbers fully squared with a tenon or tongue at each end fitting into a vertical groove in the upright post of the frame.

Enticed by news of a rich fur trade, the British were drawn to early Canada and into competition with the French. As established historical rivals, the only thing they did not disagree on was the use of the all wood post and beam construction method for their houses and forts. However, instead of using the French name, the English preferred to call the method "Red River frame" after the river of the same name in Manitoba, or "Hudson Bay corner," presumably after the Hudson's Bay Company, which built most of its fortifications with this method. Post and beam forts were built throughout Canada across the continent from the Atlantic to the Pacific ocean, and north to the Beaufort Sea, in a concerted effort to exert dominance over the New World, and to collect valuable furs from the natives. In all, over two hundred forts were built by the North West and Hudson's Bay fur trading companies between the seventeenth and nineteenth centuries, making the log and timber post and beam method Canada's first building method. Indeed, the plaque commemorating the building of Fort Langley in 1827 records it as "... the first Trading Post on the Pacific Coast of Canada" and the "Birthplace of the Colony of British Columbia".[2] (Figure 1–7.)

The next flood of immigrants to the New World came largely from Sweden. And as the blockwork method was their primary construction technique, it is this form which was brought to the vast, unpopulated, heavily forested northwestern United States and western Canada. In contrast, in the northeastern United States the framework method was again practiced as a result of high population demands in a less heavily forested region. The building patterns of northern Europe in the Middle Ages appear to have been replayed in North America. And quite possibly the post and beam method which "once seemed dead," with it's special advantages is destined once again to play the role of bridge between two methods.

1. Moogk, Peter N., *Building a House in New France* (Toronto: McClelland and Stewart, 1977).
2. Cullen, Mary K., *History of Fort Langley, 1827–1896* (Ottawa: Natural Historic Parks and Sites Branch, 1979).

Figure 1-7. Fort Langley, Canada, 1800.

Figure 1-8. Short log post and beam house, 1985.

Figure 1-8 shows a recently constructed rural ownerbuilt post and beam house which required only a minimum of expertise, tools, and lifting equipment to build. Note the design flexibility which permits the incorporation of rock, solid wood, or glass infill between the posts.

From the seventeenth to the twentieth centuries post and beam and timber framing continued to grow into what we know today as stud frame construction. This latest method relies on numerous smaller dimensional pieces wire-nailed together to form a framework which is then sheathed with interior and exterior finishing materials. Here the strength of the structure is dependent upon the sheathing. But though solid wood post and beam construction remained dormant again until the mid 1960s, a social up-

heaval in North America challenged many accepted values. Individuals began search-
ing for methods to reaffirm their severed bonds with nature. They began to question the
notion of a mortgaged society and sought alternative means of housing. As a direct
result, traditional skills were rediscovered and combined with modern technologies to
produce a new breed of owner-built housing. Not only have cultures living in similar
regions come to similar solutions in creating their houses, but the passage of time
seems to have made little difference, and the method which was developed in the
Middle Ages, is as practical today as it was then.

Figure 1–9. "Reiswerk" Viking stronghold in the Netherlands (Zeeland) ca. 1000 A.D.

Figure 1–10. An 1854 "Red River frame" house in Manitoba.

CHAPTER TWO

Design

If we are to be successful in our pursuit of truly personal owner-built housing, it is not enough to simply combine traditional skills with modern technology. The end product may be an affordable house, but unless we understand that personal housing must be an expression of ourselves, of our environment, and of the materials which constitute its structure, the owner-built house will become just another unit, devoid of character and self expression. Personal housing begins with personal design. Good design is not a fancy, geometric configuration which only a professional architect can conjure up. On the contrary, only the persons who are to occupy the dwelling are qualified to make the value judgments and decisions necessary to create a real home. For this reason I have included a discussion of the fundamental elements of design as they relate to the building's structure and materials, its environment, and inhabitants.

The Building

In the post and beam construction method, a series of vertical posts unite with horizontal beams to form a structural framework. This frame defines the total building and the individual rooms. Consequently, posts will be located at each corner of the building and at every major interior partition. Since the weight of the roof will be transmitted through the posts to the foundation, load bearing roof trusses and tie-beams should be placed directly over vertical posts. Although this is not a requirement, doors and windows are more easily installed between two posts than set in a horizontally laid log or timber wall, and their appearance will then also be more pleasing. The distance between vertical posts should not exceed eight feet (2.4 meters) for the following reasons. The first is structural. A dimensional top plate (supporting the roof weight) would overtax its strength if made to span too long a distance. Secondly, it is harder to construct solid wood infill panels if they are longer than eight feet. Lastly, the house will look better if the posts are not too far apart. Post spacings should be as homogeneous as possible to achieve the most attractive appearance. Equal post thickness and spacings will permit prefabrication of infill panels *and* interchangeability of these components from one house design to another, if desired. Figure 2–1 shows a design with equal post spacing.

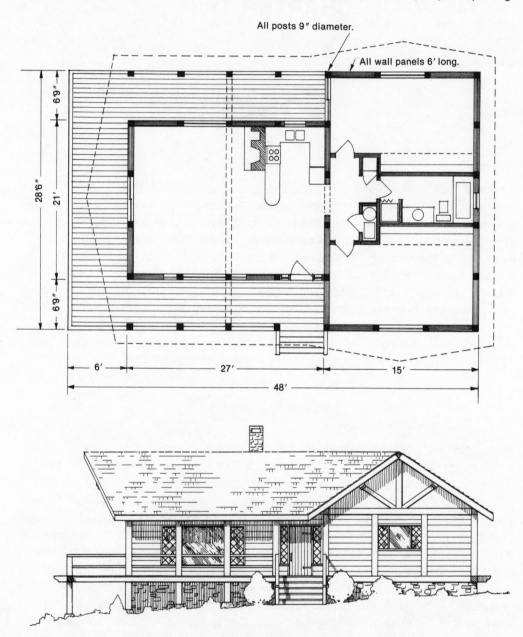

Figure 2–1. House designed with equal post spacings.

The infill between the posts can be of log or half timber, and can also include notched corners. An additional advantage of this method is that the structural framework can incorporate large floor-to-ceiling glass areas without shrinkage or settling problems. In regions where wood materials are at a premium, stackwall, rock and mortar, or other infill types which afford adequate thermal and weather projection can be substituted. The house's strength is achieved with solid beams and posts, leaving partition walls to act more as room dividers than as structural units. As a result, interior living spaces can now be opened up or conveniently curtained with nonstructural fabrics. The Japanese artfully rearrange room sizes and shapes in their post and beam homes to suit the occasion by simply shifting rice paper walls. The design possibilities in this type of building are numerous.

Roof design should incorporate a wide eave overhang of sufficient distance (i.e., 3 feet/1 meter) to protect the solid wood walls from repeated rain soaking.

The Material

Since the construction methods in this book use wood as the primary building material, it follows that the wood will play a key role in the house's design. When logs are used for construction, the material undergoes an abrupt transition from a natural freeform round to geometrically straight edges at the joinery points. Surviving examples of historic Swedish log work show how craftsmen made this gradual transition by shaping the logs back from the joinery intersection with axe and drawknife. (Figure 2–2). Figure 2–3 shows an example of such a transition with the added benefit of a support. Here kneebracing connects the vertical post and horizontal beam while adding supportive strength to a roof beam.

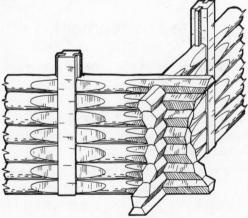

Figure 2–2. Shaping logs back from the joinery intersection.

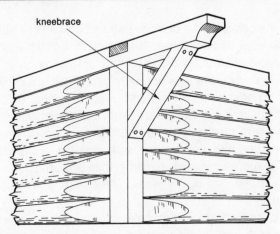

Figure 2–3. Kneebracing connects horizontal and vertical logs while adding strength to the roof beam.

The exterior finish of a wooden house should seek to reflect nature. In the forest the tree's roots grow from soil and rock; in the same way, a rock foundation can give the impression of a house as an integral part of nature. To pursue the theme of unity with nature, as well as because I am convinced of its superiority, I have included procedures for constructing a sod roof. (See Chapter 13, section **14.**) Inside the house, highlighting the wood with contrasting materials works well. Drywall (gyprock) plastered and painted white is inexpensive, yet serves to enhance the wood's natural tones while at the same time providing the necessary reflective light. The colors red, orange, blue, and green look well with the golden hues of wood, and especially brighten the kitchen and bathroom areas.

The Environment

No two building sites are the same, unless all vegetation and land contours have been bulldozed and flattened. In approaching a piece of land, sensitivity and respect are of great importance. We North Americans can learn much from the Japanese who are very sensitive to the blending of the tame with the wild.

The obvious first step is to survey the property line and establish natural and man-made borders. A schematic drawing or model of the landscape's features showing ground elevations, existing vegetation, streams, ponds, etc., will give you an objective view of your microenvironment. Once this is done you can maximize your use and integration of inside and outside space. The house's shape will start to take form, guided by the elements of view, privacy, and utility, and molded by the character of the landscape.

The orientation of your house and internal rooms is dictated by the cyclical climatic conditions. Imagine yourself naked on your property, exposed to both the benefits and assaults of the weather. In cold climates you would seek a location away from the wintry winds, presenting your back to the north and your face to the south. However, during the hot summer, cooling breezes often come from a new direction. Good house design takes all these factors into consideration. Certain rooms, depending on their function, will be oriented to receive morning light, while others are better suited to afternoon light. The best way to obtain a feeling of the climatic changes on your property, is to camp out and experience a taste of each season.

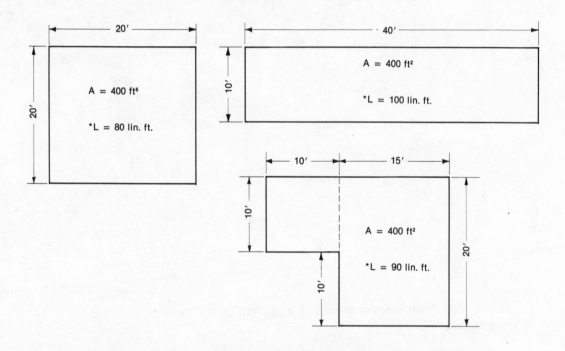

Figure 2–4. House layouts in relation to lengths of exterior wall.

The Inhabitants

What are your needs and wants, movements, tastes, lifestyle, future aspirations, and your budget? Good design will involve a self-analysis by all members of the family, and will evolve over time, examining and re-examining daily activities, entertainment, solitude, hobbies, likes, dislikes, and so on. From this analysis spatial requirements will

Figure 2–5. This country house combines a squared timber frame with log, rock, and glass infills.

Figure 2–6. A timber frame with squared timber infill and hip roof completes an early Canadian traditional post and beam house that would not look out of place in any suburban setting.

Figure 2–7. This ranch house uses the blockwork style of notched corner construction. Short log post and beam can include notched corners without the difficulty of acquiring long logs and a machine to lift them. The post and beam method also permits the inclusion of large floor to ceiling glass areas without structural problems.

Figure 2–8. Simplicity and harmony with the natural environment are the key to a successful rural or vacation home. In such areas tools, frame materials, and labor are scarce commodities. This log post and beam country cottage can be constructed by an owner-builder with materials gathered primarily from the land.

begin to unfold, starting with the number of rooms, their uses and sizes, colors, lighting and, along with this a careful pruning of duplicated or wasted space. Remember, that as size is directly related to cost, it is best to avoid building an inflated, "impressive" house unless you have the money to pay for it. Cost is also directly related to shape. Figure 2–4 shows a square, a rectangle, and a square combined with a rectangle. All the internal areas are the same, yet the amount of outside lineal wall varies with the shape. In constructing a house the cost increases with the amount of exterior lineal wall. Taking both cost and design factors into consideration, the combined square with rectangle becomes the most interesting design with less exterior lineal wall than the lone rectangle.

Figure 2–9. This half-timbered post and beam house can fit into both a country and city environment. Its non-structural stud framing with stucco exterior finish contrasts with the wood and the large glass areas placed for maximum solar gain. The two insets show a woodsiding finish with a 2 x 4 infill and a stackwall infill.

CHAPTER THREE

Wood

Wood is the flesh of a living tree. For many species of animal and bird the tree is shelter and protection, for others it provides nourishment. The tree's roots bind earth's precious film of topsoil and protect it from the ravages of erosion. Throughout history we have used wood for shelter and to fuel our fires. Once we gained knowledge of iron's cutting edge, we used wood to explore and master the world, for wood alone provided the vehicle with which to sail the oceans and build new civilizations. Since wood is the primary material for the post and beam building methods described in this book, it is important to gain a basic understanding of its structure and properties before applying a tool to the material.

The Cellular Structure of Wood

Woods are classified into two broad groups: softwoods and hardwoods. This classification is somewhat misleading, for some so-called softwoods are harder than some species of hardwoods. A more accurate and simpler classification groups together as softwoods those trees which bear needles and for the most part, retain them throughout the winter, and as hardwoods those which bear broad leaves and lose them over the winter months. Another feature which distinguishes the two groups is their overall size and shape. The needle bearing softwoods generally grow tall and straight, with little tapering of the trunk, while the broad leafed hardwoods tend to be shorter, with a more pronounced tapering of the trunk. For these reasons (size and taper), softwoods are frequently used in solid wood construction. Amongst the various species of softwoods some are stronger while others are less susceptible to rot and decay. Such characteristics help to determine where the various woods would best be placed in a building. (See Appendix II.)

Figure 3–1 shows the cross-section of a softwood tree. The outer bark protects the tree from injury and loss of vital fluids. Just under the bark is the thin cambium sheath of

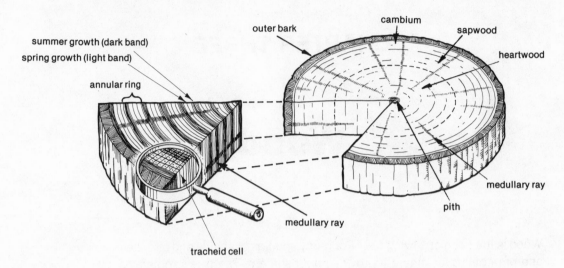

Figure 3-1. Cross-section of a softwood tree trunk.

active growth cells which creates the new growth. This "sapwood" transports water and nutrients from the roots to the leaves. (In conifers water moves upward almost entirely through the sapwood.)

The next layer is the heartwood, made up of dead sapwood cells which store resins and gums. This portion of the tree is sealed off from the growth process, and serves primarily as the structural backbone. In comparison to the living sapwood, the heartwood is less subject to decay and shrinkage. The medullary rays which run at right angles to the axis are an alignment of additional storage cells which provide nutrition for the sapwood during winter dormancy.

The last layer is the pith, the first year growth of the seedling tree which lies at the very center of the heartwood.

The enlarged section of a tree trunk shows the annular growth pattern of the tree. During the winter the tree stores most of its watery sap in the roots, which keeps it from freezing and then splitting the wood. At this time no growth occurs. The warmth of spring stimulates a hormone which causes the sap to run and brings about the rapid growth indicated by the wide band of lighter, thin-walled cells. The heat of summer slows down the growth rate, producing a narrow band of darker, thick-walled cells. These two bands of light and dark wood make up an annular ring or one year's tree growth. The magnifying lens in the same diagram shows how the wood cells are arranged in a side-by-side vertical alignment down the length of the tree. Called tracheid cells, they comprise ninety to ninety-five percent of the tree's volume of wood. The length of their column-like bodies is approximately one hundred times greater than the diameter. These facts explain why wood is stronger when it is vertical (i.e., in a post) rather than horizontal (i.e., in a beam).

Shrinkage: Cause, Effect and Remedies

A tree standing in the forest is said to be in the "green" state, meaning that the wood is saturated with water. The amount of water it contains varies with the seasons, the least being in the winter and the greatest in the spring. Consequently, the best time to fell a tree is during the winter. Once the tree is felled it will begin to lose its trapped water until its moisture content equals that of its environment. During this time the wood cells will undergo their greatest amount of shrinkage. Figure 3–2 shows an individual wood tracheid cell before and after water loss. The dry cell has collapsed, shrinking in width but with no significant reduction in its length. Multiply this effect by the millions of tracheid wood cells in a tree, and the result is that the log shrinks in diameter while the length remains the same. (Figure 3–3.) When a number of horizontally placed green logs or timbers are fitted between vertical posts, their cumulative shrinkage will lead to a reduced wall height, while the posts will stay the same height. (Figure 3–4.) The posts will shrink very little in width, even if the wood is green, because the removal of the water-saturated sapwood in cutting flat surfaces for joinery has removed the cells most prone to shrinkage.

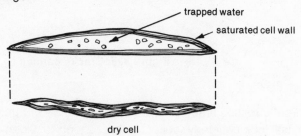

Figure 3–2. Tracheid cellular shrinkage.

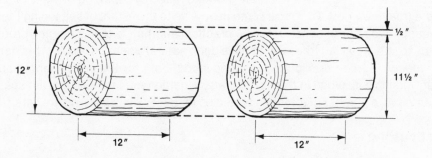

Figure 3–3. Log shrinkage.

The too rapid drying of green wood will cause excessive checking or cracking. Peeling a green log and leaving it in the hot sun will quickly dry the outer surface of the wood while the inner wood remains wet. The resulting cellular shrinkage around the outside

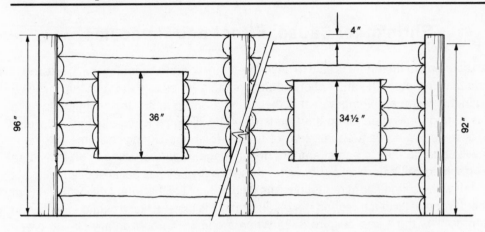

Figure 3-4. Shrinkage of a log wall—estimated at ½ " per vertical 12".

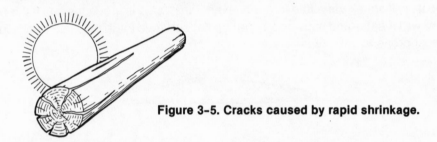

Figure 3-5. Cracks caused by rapid shrinkage.

will set up internal stresses leading to cracks. (Figure 3–5.) Such checks, especially the large ones, will look unsightly, collect dirt, and tend to widen over time due to the wedging action of freezing water. Extreme checking can cause structural weakening in load carrying beams.

Checking can be reduced and practically eliminated by retarding the loss of surface moisture from the wood. To do this some people go to the extent of seasoning the wood for a year or two prior to construction. A practical alternative to this lengthy procedure would be to use fire-killed trees which have been naturally seasoned. Most builders prefer to work with green or slightly seasoned wood, both for the convenience, and the ease of working with wood in this softer state. Whether you are building with seasoned or green wood, a number of effective remedies for excessive checking are listed below.

Winter cutting

Cutting the trees in the late fall or winter when the sap is in the roots is essential, whether the intension is to build with green wood or to season it first. A method for determining if the sap has stopped running is to peel a small patch of bark off the trunk and wait a while. If no sap oozes from the wound it is time to cut. Cutting, then skidding after the first snowfall has the advantage of not scarring the logs too badly. Logs should be decked on pole skids spaced a few feet apart so as to keep the logs off the ground. When stored, the logs should be spaced to provide ventilation, and turned every few days to prevent bowing.

Seasoning

Essentially the process involves leaving on the protective bark for a year or two, and waxing or painting the log ends. The sealed ends force the moisture to leave via the trunk's surface, thereby maintaining an equilibrium between the outer and inner wood. During the hot summer, decked logs should be either shaded or sprayed with water each morning and evening to prevent rapid evaporation.

Girdling

A Bavarian tradition involved climbing the standing tree and removing a strip of bark from around the trunk, just below the crown. With photosynthesis cut off from the rest of the tree, the roots cease absorbing nutrients while the leaves continue to draw the vital fluids. Slowly the portion of the tree below the girdle dries out, in effect seasoning the tree while it is still standing. The problem with this method is the labor involved in climbing and girdling each tree. A slight adaptation of this process is to cut a deep girdle at the base of the tree, well into the sapwood, so as to "choke" it.

Surface application

In building with green wood you run the risk of excessive checking unless some means of protection is applied to the log's surface right after peeling. This surface application can be thought of as an invisible bark. There are commerical sealers available to do the job, but a salt brine works just as well. The brine is made by dissolving as much salt as possible in water. (Heating the water increases saturation levels.) Salt retains water, and once the solution is brushed onto the surface, evaporation is inhibited.

An interesting, as yet experimental, alternative is the application of antifreeze to the surface of the wood. The sealing ingredient is ethylene glycol, which is the same as the P.E.G. (polyethylene glycol) solution which wood carvers use to prevent checking of their materials. It appears that this waxy, water soluble liquid penetrates into the wood, replacing the cell wall's moisture and preventing their collapse and shrinkage. How well various finishes will work with this surface application has not yet been thoroughly examined. In all cases they should be applied to the entire surface of the wood, including any hidden joinery and the ends as well.

Pre-stressing

Here the wood surface is pre-stressed by first making a kerf, or cut, parallel with the wood grain. Usually this is done with a simple axe cut. Next, a wedge of wood is hammered into the kerf, expanding and pre-stressing the surface. Such stressing will limit the checking which can be localized in such a way to be hidden from view, as in the lateral groove.

Properties of Wood

Longevity

Stripped of its bark and protected only from direct rain and damp ground, wood will weather away at the slow rate of one centimeter per century. Over 1,300 years ago the Buddhist Golden Hall (679 A.D.) and Pagoda (693 A.D.) were built in Japan and survive today as the oldest wooden structures in the world. These buildings were constructed with no metal fasteners. In fact, metal is the "Achilles heel" of wood. For metal is hard and unyielding where there is movement, causing excessive wear and eventual joint failure. Wood fiber, however, has an inherent resilience, enabling it to withstand repeated flexings and distortions—one reason why many of the finest ships' masts are still made of wood. But a true test of longevity is a material's ability to age with dignity. What other material carries the lines and tones of age as naturally as wood? It is easy to see how, with each passing year, a wooden house is that much more at home in its natural environment.

Strength

When compared by weight, wood is stronger than steel. But as a natural material, wood is not homogeneous in consistency, and its strength is relative to its species, grain direction, the presence of defects, and moisture content. For example, the softwood species, yellow cedar, does not have the fiber strength of Douglas fir for reasons of fiber length and density. Thus the fir would be better suited for structural loading applications, such as floor joists or roof rafters. Wood is stronger by far where loading is applied parallel to the grain (as with vertical posts) than it is at right angles to the grain (as with horizontal beams). For this reason, additional care must be exercised when selecting wood structural beams. Defects such as loose knots, or cracks, splits, and shakes break the grain continuity and weaki)en the beam, most dangerously at its midpoint where stress is greatest. Furthermore, moisture saturated wood will bend and become permanently deformed more readily than dry wood. Such deformities could, over time, cause sagging of load-bearing beams.

Thermal value

Thermal value is a collective term for the two factors considered in determining the insulative worth of a material—specifically heat conductivity and thermal mass potential. Heat conductivity refers to the material's ability to conduct heat. The less well it conducts heat, the better its resistivity (R factor). Dry wood's R factor is between 1.8 and 2.0 per inch, compared with common fiberglass insulation, which has an R factor of 3.3.[1] This R factor rating indicates that the fiberglass has better heat resistivity than wood.

Thermal mass potential refers to the material's ability to trap and store heat energy within its physical mass. This mass, in turn, creates a time lag in conducting heat which results in a balanced daily thermal condition. Consider what Victor Olgyay says of thermal mass. "The larger the heat storage value, the slower the temperature change that is propagated through the material. This delay is called the 'time lag' of the construction; it gives an opportunity to store peak heat loads and release them at low temperature periods."[2] Solar heated houses rely heavily on the heat storage potential which only materials of large mass can provide. For comparison purposes consider a house which is insulated with typical fiberglass insulation, having a high R factor but low thermal mass. While the internal heat source is functioning the house is warm, but should the fires go out on a cold, wintry night, the very short time lag due to a small thermal mass storage causes the house to cool very quickly. Just the opposite is true for a house with walls built of solid wood. The millions of air cells and physical mass of the wood trap and store heat, allowing the house to stay warm throughout the night. These facts also explain why log and timber houses remain cool inside on a hot day. Due to the controversy surrounding the thermal value of a scribe-fitted log wall I would like to state two points. First, according to the Timber Construction Manual of the American Institute of Timber Construction: "Thermal conductivity is approximately the same in radial and tangential directions but is generally about 2½ time greater along the grain." When examining a log wall, many building inspectors assess the thermal value of the wall based on its average thickness. For example, wall logs with a mean diameter of 12″ (300 mm) and lateral groove width of 4″ (100 mm) would be assessed on an average wall thickness of 8″ (200 mm). This is a false assessment, since the heat flows into and through the wood 2½ times faster along the cellular alignment, which comprises the grain. As described above, the tracheid cell alignment is arranged in such a way that the heat path is down the length of the log, in toward its heart, and along the annular rings. In each case the path is not the shortest distance through the log, but rather a considerably longer distance into, around, and down the length of the log. This roundabout heat flow augments the wood's thermal mass potential still further. Hence, a correct thermal assessment should, at the very least, be based on the 12″ (300 mm) wall thickness.

Equally important is the fact that a house's overall thermal effectiveness depends primarily on the amount of air exchange. Excessive drafts rob the average house of ap-

1. Nanassy and Szabo, "Thermal Resistivity of White Pine," Interim Report # EFPL-6-3-307 (Ottawa: Eastern Forest Products Laboratory, Canadian Forest Service, Department of Fisheries and Environment).
2. Olgyay, Victor, *Design With Climate,* (Princeton: Princeton University Press. 1963).

proximately forty percent of the heat. Proper weather sealing and a heating system which creates a positive pressure inside the house by drawing its air source from outside will do much to rectify a cold house. In a hierarchy of heat-loss situations the roof is next in importance, since as heat rises it tends to concentrate near the ceiling. As well, large windows, not placed to take advantage of solar radiation benefits, amount to a large B.t.u. loss, as do lightweight doors. Unheated crawl spaces below the floor will absorb the damp cold like a sponge. Solid wood buildings have often been slandered, as have other natural building forms, by proponents and beneficiaries of the mass-produced housing market.

Acoustical properties

One simple way of appreciating wood's acoustical properties is to compare sounds in the interior of a contemporary stud framed and drywalled house with that of a solid wood walled house. Without furniture to absorb reflective sound waves your voice will bounce off the flat drywall and cause an echo, but not where there are wood walls. Wood has the ability to absorb and dampen sound vibrations. At the turn of the century the streets of London were inlaid with wood blocks to mute the noise made by the iron-shod hooves of horses. Because of wood's cellular structure and its porous surface, sound energy is converted into heat energy by frictional and viscous resistance within the pores, and by vibration of their fibers. Because of this high internal friction wood has a greater dampening capacity than most other structural materials. This dampening reduces both the tendency of a surface to transmit vibrations over long distances, and the magnitude of resonant vibrations. When wood's microphysical properties are combined with the curved surfaces of a log wall, sounds are both deadened on impact and redirected, though not towards their source to cause echo as with flat-surfaced walls. Musical amphitheaters are constructed with curved surfaces for just this reason.

Psychological properties

Although today we live in a technical, automated world, we are not automatons. Though we tend to calibrate and analyze things scientifically, we are still motivated by our feelings. This is quite natural, and to deny that nature is a part of us and we of it, leads to profound confusion. It is quite possible that there are so many confused individuals in the world today because of our attempts to ignore nature and to worship technology. Bruce Hoadly, author of *Understanding Wood,* exactly articulates my sentiments when he writes, "I suggest that the psychological appeal of wooden objects develops through the interaction of two vital elements working together: nature and mankind. That wood is a direct and unchanged product of nature undeniably attracts us. . . . Wood has values or powers that cannot be quantified in scientific terms. These aspects of wood, without being well understood or even explainable, may well be among the most important and powerful."

CHAPTER FOUR

Material and Tools

A common fault which plagues many owner building projects is lack of preparation in assembling all the materials and tools needed to complete the job. Poor preparation leads to disruptions of the construction flow. Think of the construction site as your stage and your helpers as your critics. As disruptions lead to work slow-down the builder's enthusiasm begins to erode, and this in turn affects the attitude of the helpers. Persistent disorganization very quickly shows itself in overall deterioration of the level of workmanship, and the whole problem begins to feed upon itself. In such circumstances I have seen production decline to the point of actual work stoppage. This is why it is important to have all the preparatory work completed, and a clear idea of each day's activities before you begin construction.

Log Materials: Selection and Harvesting

Selection

Since the majority of logs or timbers used in post and beam solid wood construction will be under 10′ (3 m) long material acquisition is usually not a problem. Common methods of obtaining log materials include salvaging from concluded logging operations, harvesting trees privately, or with a timber sales permit from the local Forestry Department, or by direct purchase from a logging contractor or mill. Although historically hardwoods have been used extensively for solid wood construction the majority of buildings today are built of softwoods for reasons mentioned earlier. This, however, will depend entirely on the material's abundance in the area.

Generally, fir, spruce, larch, pine, and cedar are the softwoods most often used in log and timber construction. (See Appendix II.) Intermixing various softwood species in wall construction poses no problems, but strive to divide the mix equally amongst all the walls so as to avoid possible settling discrepancies. Logs ideally should have tops no smaller than 10″ (250 mm). Squared timbers used as posts or sill and top plate beams will be of larger size to offset wastage and minimize wane (rounded corners).

When scouting for trees it is better to avoid trees growing on river banks or near lake and sea shores. These trees serve to protect the area from wind and water erosion, and their removal can bring about adverse effects. Moreover, such trees have been exposed to high winds and, over a period of time, take on twisted growth patterns. This spiral wood growth goes unnoticed until the tree has been stripped of bark and dried. Building with such wood can cause beams and posts to twist out of shape after drying.

Instead, seek out a thick growth stand on a northfacing hill or gently sloping mountainside. It is in such a location that, due to the competition for sunlight, the trees grow straighter with least taper and least branches. On a south slope, however, sparsely populated stands will tend to have greater taper and more branches. The tree stand should have road access for a skidder or horse team, and an area or landing to accommodate the stock-piled logs and a truck.

Once an area has been found with a suitable tree stand and accessible landing, individual tree selection can begin. To identify the trees for later harvesting you will need a tape measure and orange spray paint or surveyor's ribbon. As you scout through the forest, assess the individual trees of your preferred species, their girth, height, and their lack or abundance of limbs. Next "plumb" each tree for its straightness and direction of lean. Do this by sighting the tree from a distance of about 50′ (15 m) or so. Take note of the following:

The presence of excessive bows or dog-legs (S curves).

The direction and amount of lean, and how these will affect its later removal.

Any possible snags or problems resulting from its direction of fall.

If the tree passes the test, mark it for later falling and move on to the next.

Harvesting

Selective harvesting is good forest management. The resulting increase in space created by removing a few mature trees gives the surrounding smaller trees the additional sunlight needed for growth. Harvesting a tree requires falling, limbing, and removal. The amount of debris clean-up required is determined by the local Forestry Department, but at the very least the limbs should lie flat on the forest floor to facilitate quick decay.

It is important to remember that falling a tree involves a great deal more than merely bringing it to the ground. It requires a knowledge of chainsaw use and falling procedures. The following information should not be considered either all-inclusive or a substitute for actual field experience. Tree falling is *dangerous* and should only be undertaken with the assistance of a seasoned faller.

Chainsaw safety considerations

- Using the tip of the chainsaw bar, especially the top of the tip, can lead to severe kickback (see Figure 4–1).

Figure 4-1. Kickback due to operating the chainsaw too close to the bar tip.

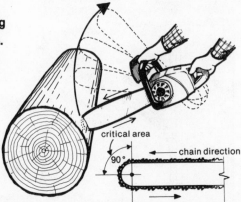

critical area

chain direction

90°

- Most accidents are caused by unstable footing, so before you begin, make sure you are in a stable position and that there is no debris to trip on.
- Let the saw cool off before refueling.
- Never let the chain become too loose on the bar.
- Always wear the appropriate safety protection when operating a chainsaw.
- Figures 4–2A, B and C show felling, limbing, and bucking techniques. A few basic safety considerations for felling trees are described below.

Safety considerations for felling

- Ensure all workers are clear of the hazardous area before felling a tree.
- Remove brush and debris from around the base of the tree, and establish a clear path to safety (to one side and behind the stump in relation to the direction of fall).
- Fell the tree in the general direction of its prevailing lean. Felling against the lean can be done to facilitate easier bucking or removal, providing the degree of lean is not considerable. Too much lean exists for this purpose when the weight of the tree forces it to fall in a particular direction.
- Ensure the undercut is complete and cleaned out.
- Start a wedge in the backcut as soon as room allows.
- Observe the tree as it falls to the ground and guard against flying limbs and debris.

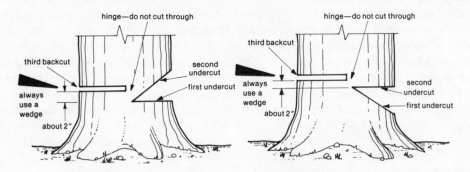

Figure 4-2A. Cutting procedures for felling trees.

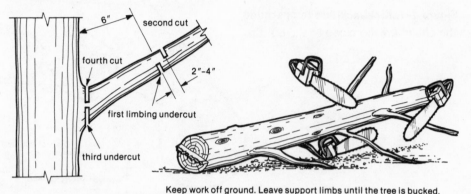

Keep work off ground. Leave support limbs until the tree is bucked.

Figure 4-2B. Procedure for limbing.

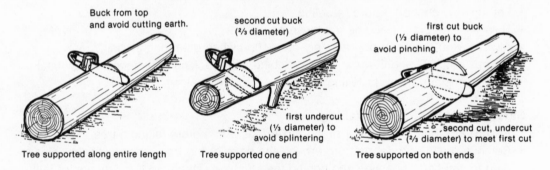

Buck from top and avoid cutting earth.

second cut buck (⅔ diameter)

first cut buck (⅓ diameter) to avoid pinching

first undercut (⅓ diameter) to avoid splintering

second cut, undercut (⅔ diameter) to meet first cut

Tree supported along entire length   Tree supported one end   Tree supported on both ends

Figure 4-2C. Procedure for bucking.

Tools

A. The chainsaw

On the whole, this is probably the most expensive, most used, and least understood of building tools. To begin with, the chainsaw should suit its function; trying to do serious log construction using a saw that is underpowered is a waste of time, while an over-powered, overweight saw is unnecessarily fatiguing. But just buying any medium-weight, powered saw can be a waste of money if it's not a good one with the right options. Before describing what makes a good saw, let me drop a few names. During my years in log building, I've noticed that the majority of professional log builders use either the Stihl, Husqvarna, or Jonsered chainsaws for their dependability and quality. Whether or not you choose one of these brands or opt for another may also depend on the available sales and servicing in your area. Whatever chainsaw you do finally decide on, make sure it is reasonably quiet and has antivibration rubber mounts protecting the operator from engine vibrations. Below is a checklist of things to look for in a log-building chainsaw:

a) Medium size, between 3.0–5.0 cubic inches (50–80 cubic centimeters), capable of maintaining a high cutting speed for planing cuts.

b) Weight range of 15–20 lbs (7–10 kgs).

c) Good antivibration system.

d) Front mount exhaust to blow the sawdust away as you cut.

e) Adjustable automatic chain oiler.

f) Chainbrake.

g) 16–21″ (400–540 mm) sprocket nose bar. This bar length is ideal for log construction as it will handle the majority of log sizes. The sprocket nose has a roller bearing which prevents excess heat buildup by reducing the amount of friction.

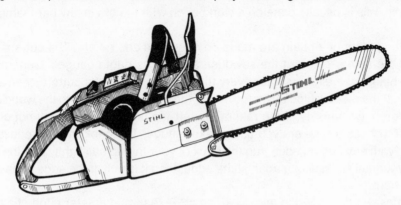

Figure 4-3. The chainsaw.

Chainsaw maintenance

a) Read owners manual.

b) Dislodge any packed sawdust and clean daily.

c) Clean air filter daily with unmixed gas.

d) Clean bar grooves and grease roller bearing daily.

e) Check for fuel leaks or broken castings daily.

f) Periodically remove carbon from muffler.

g) Mixed gas requires 16 parts regular gas to 1 part lube oil. (This ratio may change with synthetic oils.) Always mix gas and oil thoroughly.

For the safe operation of a chainsaw, the operator should always wear the appropriate safety equipment especially eye and ear protection. As with any cutting tool, a dull cutting chain has a greater chance of injuring the operator than a properly filed, sharp one. The operator must trust the tool to "bite" the wood at the intended point of contact. Should the tool slip, as a dull one will, control is lost and accidents can result. The following describes the correct procedure for sharpening the cutting teeth of a chainsaw.

Sharpening the chainsaw's cutting teeth

The best advice for filing the cutting teeth of a chainsaw is to follow the basic instructions and always "pay attention." The cutting teeth on a chainsaw are like a multitude of miniature chisels. If they are not all filed correctly and evenly, some will cut more than others and some will not cut at all. There are filing guides available, but it is impractical and unnecessary to take the time and effort to set up a guide on the job site for only a light touch-up. If there is not too much dirt or sand embedded in the wood, you need only touch up the cutting teeth by hand with a file right at the job site at the end of the day. After five or six such touch-ups it will be necessary to use a mechanical guide, which holds the file in a fixed position in relation to the cutting teeth, in order to realign all the teeth. This is usually done on a workbench with the chainsaw bar clamped in a vice.

The cutting teeth of a chain are made up of cutters and rakers. The cutters cut the wood and the rakers rake out the sawdust, and act as depth gauges. Generally, you check the height of the rakers after every third sharpening of the cutters, then adjust if necessary. If the raker is filed down too much, the cutters will bite into the wood and the chain will grab. Conversely, if the rakers are left too high, the chain will not cut to its capacity. To check the rakers you use a raker gauge. To check the sharpness of the cutters, as with any cutting edge, run the back of your thumb nail lightly into the cutting edge—if your nail slides along against the edge, then it is dull; if the edge bites into the nail, it is sharp.

The chainsaws described in this book use a $3/8''$ (9 mm) diameter pitch chain and a $7/32''$ (5 mm) diameter round file. Once the cutters have been filed back more than half their length, I suggest you use the next smaller file.

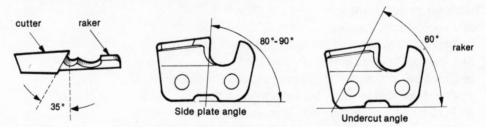

Figure 4-4. A correctly filed cutter tooth.

Filing the cutters

Figure 4–4 shows the general specifications of a correctly filed cutter tooth.
1) Secure the chainsaw bar in a vise and tighten the chain tension. Position the file in the cutter opposite your side as shown in the diagram and insets of Figure 4–5.
2) Apply three or four steady file strokes to each cutter, filing enough to remove any damage to the cutting edge. Keep all cutters at approximately the same length. (Check this visually.)

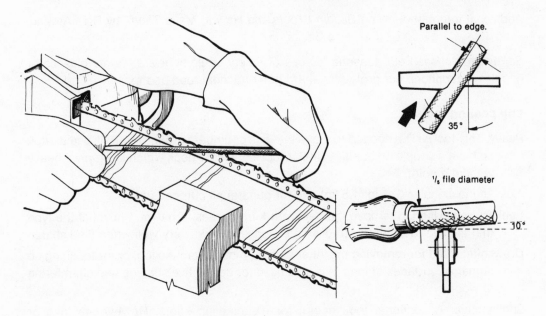

Figure 4–5. Filing the cutter.

Filing the rakers

Check the raker height with the raker gauge. Any projection should be filed level and rounded as shown in Figure 4–6.

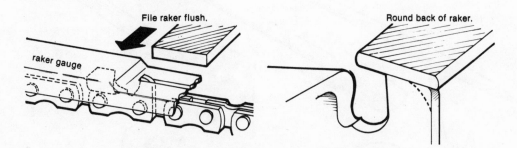

Figure 4–6. Filing down and rounding the rakers.

B. Hand, power, and lifting tools

Quality tools are expensive initially, but when amortized over the period of their lifetime they work out to be less expensive than cheap tools which have had to be replaced. With tools, more than anything else, you get what you pay for. I have included a list, with diagrams, of the major tools you will need during the construction of your house.

Additional Information: *Log Building Tools and How to Make Them,* by R. D. Arcand. (See also Bibliography.)

Safety protection: Four essential pieces of safety equipment are: safety glasses or goggles, headphone ear protection, hard hat, and steel toed boots.

Log peeling tools

Peavy: This tool will be needed to move the logs or timbers around; you will use it often so have a couple on hand. A similar tool is the cant hook which is simply a peavy without a point.

Axe: An inexpensive 3½ lb (1.6 kg) axe for general all purpose use.

Peeling spud: Used to remove the heavy bark from trees. A narrow shovel of the type that is used to clean the tracks on bulldozers works very well when filed sharp.

Drawknife: Used for removing the inner cambium bark from the log, or for touching up damaged surfaces of logs. It is also used for decorative shaping and chamfering of wood.

Spokeshave: An optional tool, useful for cleaning up knots. However an axe or drawknife will do as well.

Tape measure: A good tape, of 50′–100′ (15–30 m) length will be needed.

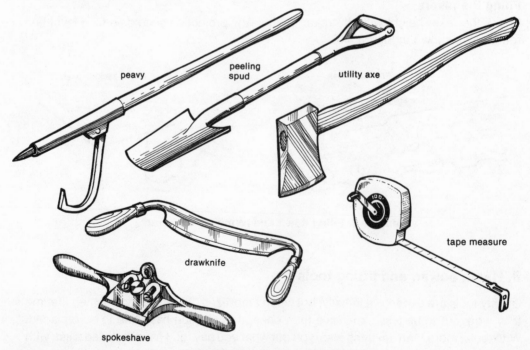

Figure 4-7. Log peeling tools.

Mortar tools

Shovel

Wheelbarrow

Mortar hoe: This hoe is like any other hoe, with the addition of two holes in the blade.

Mortar mixer: A power driven mixer is easier to use, and does a better job of mixing than working by hand.

Trowel: Used for applying and smoothing the mortar.

Jointer: Used for finishing the mortar. A spoon can be used instead.

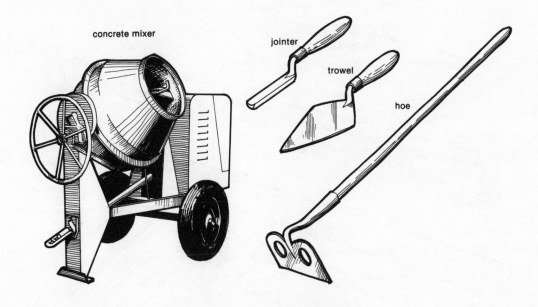

concrete mixer

jointer

trowel

hoe

Figure 4–8. Concrete or mortar tools.

Layout tools

Scribers: These tools are used for transcribing from one surface onto another. You can go all the way and purchase the Starret #85 – 9″ (230 mm) dividers with a bubble attachment like the one shown in Figure 4–9 from a good machine tool store. I prefer the #85 over the #92 because it is sturdier and can accommodate two indelible pencils instead of just one—useful in some circumstances. The alternative, and probably more accurate tool for solid wood construction, is the rigid, scratch-type scriber made from ⅛″ (3 mm) strap iron. This scriber is affordable and several sizes can be homemade from various widths of strap iron.

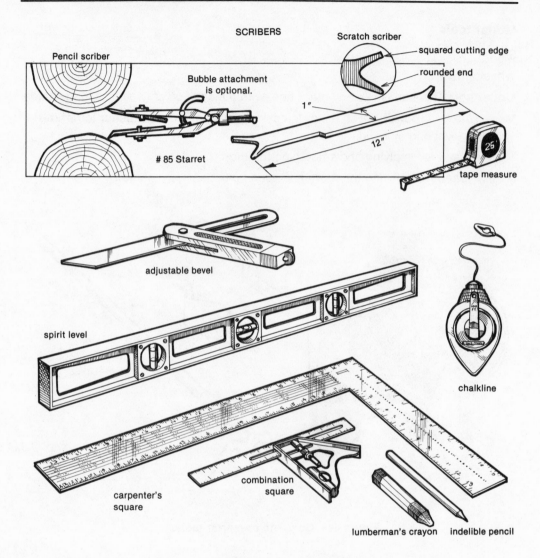

Figure 4–9. Layout tools.

Tape measure: A 25′ (8 m) one is ideal for general construction purposes.

Spirit level: Used to indicate plumb (vertical) and level (horizontal) planes. A 24″ (610 mm) and 48″ (1220 mm) one are recommended.

Adjustable bevel: Used for copying and transferring angles and bevels.

Carpenter's square: Used for timber layout, and a basic necessity.

Combination square: Used for 90° and 45° layouts, most frequently in timber construction.

Chalkline: A string wound in a case containing colored chalk dust. When it is unwound, pulled tight and snapped against boards or logs, it leaves a straight guide line of chalk dust along its stretched position.

Crayons and pencils: Lumberman's crayons and indelible pencils are used to mark the logs; the latter can be used for marking on wet surfaces.

Building tools

Axe: A 4 lb (2 kg) Arvika or its equivalent, will be in constant use. The grain of any axe handle should extend its full length.

Broad-axe: An 8–10 lb (3.6–4.5 kg) broad-axe with a 12″ (300 mm) cutting edge is used for hewing a log square. Its outstanding characteristic, aside from size and weight, is its flat face. This face initiates a chisel cutting action which produces a broad, flat surface. The handle is offset to provide clearance and prevent hitting the log as you hew.

Chisels: A 1″ (25 mm) and a 2″ (50 mm) firmer chisel and mallet are all you really need, although a corner or mortising chisel would be useful.

Slick: Just an overgrown chisel, the large 3″ (75 mm) wide × 12″ (300 mm) long blade works well for preparing and planing tenons or similar joints. If the blade has a very slight concave arc to its length, it will plane without lifting up on the handle. The socket handle should be angled upward slightly so knuckles will not get scraped when planing long timbers.

Log dogs: To prevent the log from moving while you are working on it, the dog is embedded into the log and the skid it is resting on. One or two log dogs are all that will be needed. Note the chisel points are at right angles to each other to facilitate easier entry into the wood grain.

Hand plane: Another useful tool used in timber work to reduce the size of a tight fitting tenon. For truing up long timbers consider a longer, jointer plane.

Jointer plane: This is simply another hand plane with a longer base, which allows for squaring up uneven surfaces on timbers.

Handsaws: A 6–8 point crosscut saw is recommended.

Circular saw: If you have power, a circular saw is a necessity, for timber frame work joinery cuts.

Electric drill: A ½″ (12 mm) reversing drill strong enough to bore through logs or timbers is almost a necessity. It should have ½″, ¾″, and 1″ (1.25, 2.0 and 2.5 cm) ships auger bits. The alternative is the hand auger.

Hand auger: A hand operated drill bit used when no electric power is available.

Hammers: A framing and a 4 lb (2 kg) sledge hammer will be needed.

Utility knife: Also called razor knife, handy for sharpening pencils, etc.

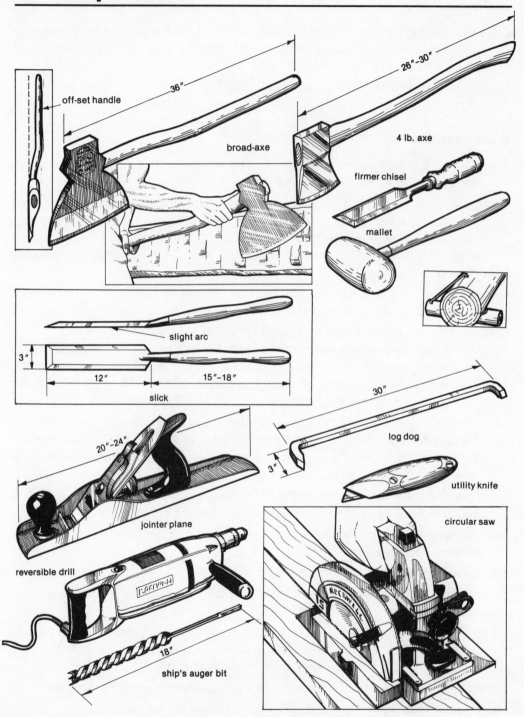

off-set handle

36"

broad-axe

26"–30"

4 lb. axe

firmer chisel

mallet

slight arc

3"

12"

15"–18"

slick

30"

log dog

3"

utility knife

20"–24"

jointer plane

circular saw

reversible drill

18"

ship's auger bit

Figure 4–10. Building tools.

Accessory tools

Router: A heavy duty commercial power router with a ¾ " (19 mm) or 1 " (25 mm) carbide "straight" bit can be considered a necessity for solid wood post and beam work. It is invaluable for post, wall, and window spline grooves, as well as for stair treads and other finishing jobs.

Adze: This is a tool especially suited for wood removal on wall channels where a frame partition joins a horizontal log wall. It is also used, though less frequently, for flattening log surfaces.

*Angle grinder: Very useful for dressing up the ragged edges of logs, timbers, archways, and other embellishments.

*Builder's level: As the name implies, this tool is used for testing levelness, transferring points, and locating angles on a horizontal plane. It is extremely useful during foundation excavation when the foundation levels are to be determined and transferred.

*Note: This tool can be rented for the period of time when it is needed.

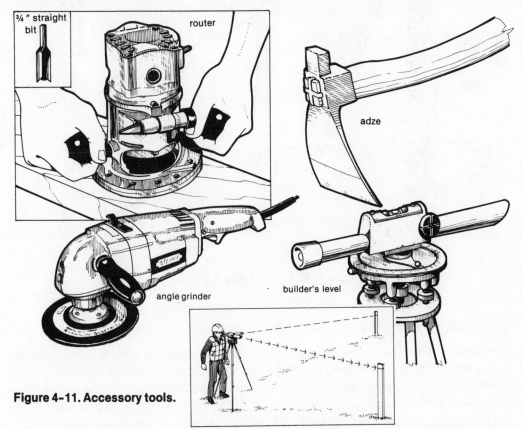

Figure 4–11. Accessory tools.

Lifting equipment

There are two ways to lift heavy objects, brute force and mechanical advantage. Building with the shorter length materials used in log post and beam construction does not require the same expensive lifting devices as does long log construction. But to save your back I do recommend obtaining the help of a few able bodies or else resorting to some form of mechanical advantage. Mechanical advantage usually involves the use of pulleys, or a gear systems which is either manually operated or powered. The "advantage" referred to is the reduction of effort needed to lift the heavy object.

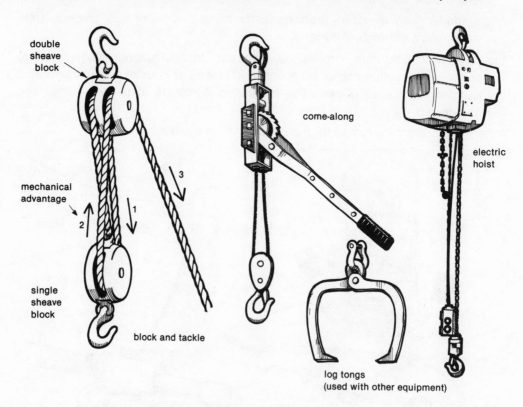

Figure 4–12. Lifting equipment.

Sharpening handtools

Working with a dull tool is both dangerous and frustrating, for the tool cannot be trusted to bite into the wood; it will tend to glance off instead. It is essential to work only with sharp tools. There are no absolute rules for tool sharpening, only preferred ways. The novice who is confused by a deluge of advice and a multitude of gadgets, should follow the basic steps outlined below, and find the style which suits him or her best.

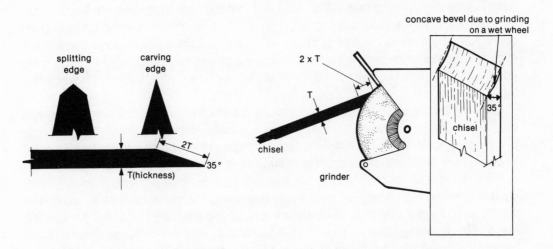

Figure 4–13. Cutting angles.   **Figure 4–14. Wet grinding.**

The cutting edge

A new tool comes with a nearly useless factory edge, and it will be necessary to condition the edge for the type of cutting the tool will do. If an axe is filed to a steep bevel it will function best for splitting, as the abrupt angle causes a wedging action. Conversely, a long bevelled cutting edge is better for carving, but it will also lose its sharp edge more quickly. For most tools the best cutting bevel angle falls between 30° and 40°, or from 2 to 2½ times the thickness of the blade iron. This general cutting bevel angle falls between the two extremes. You will find your own preference, depending on the type of wood and desired cutting action. (See Figure 4–13 for examples of the cutting angles.)

On heavier tools which take a bigger bite into the wood, such as large chisels, or slicks and axes, a slight curvature of the edge will produce better results than a straight right angled edge. Tools such as the broad-axe and drawknife, are sharpened only on one side. This allows for the other, flat side to rest up against the wood and initiate a flat, planing type of action similar to a chisel's. Sharpening both sides of such a tool will render it useless, so note the pre-sharpened surfaces when you purchase the tool. Despite the various cutting-edge bevels and curves, the procedures for attaining a sharp edge are the same: wet grinding, rough honing, and lastly, fine honing.

Wet grinding Grinding on a grindstone or emery belt is the first step in conditioning the edge of the cutting tool. During this procedure the edge is first ground straight. Then, if a slight curvature is wanted, the corners are sloped in a gradual arc which crowns at the center, with the same curve as an axe blade. Next, the desired bevel is ground. A pencil line for reference to show the length of the bevel from the edge works well. During this grinding stage it is important that the tool edge does not become too hot, for it will draw the hardness and ruin it. The safest method, therefore, is to wet grind or frequently immerse the tool in cool water as it becomes hot. If done correctly, a slightly concave bevel with a faint wire-edge will result. (See Figure 4–14.) The wire-edge is the thin metal burr which forms on the back of the cutting bevel after wet grinding.

Grinding can be replaced by filing, first using a double cut file, followed by a single cut file. This is a more laborious method but will suffice when a grindstone or emergy belt is not handy. Filing is usually done for touch-ups at the worksite, followed by a quick honing—then back to work without too much time lost.

When filing, the procedure is to file into the cutting edge working from the bevel shoulder toward the edge itself. In this way you can follow the abrasive line created by the file as it nears the edge. Ordinary chalk rubbed into the file grooves will prevent the metal chips clogging the file. Note that the tool should be firmly secured against movement. Also, never run your fingers along the filed surface of a fine tempered tool during sharpening, for the oily residue from your fingers will make it very difficult for the file to bite into the metal again.

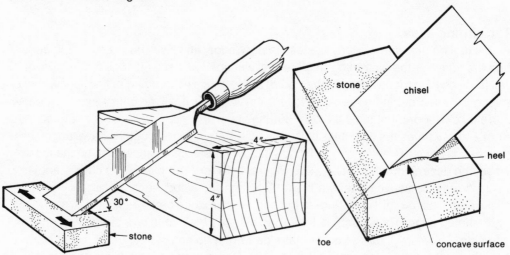

Figure 4–16. Honing large chisels and slicks.   **Figure 4–15. Rough honing.**

Rough honing   Honing the tool with a soft, coarse oilstone is the next step after wet grinding. Oilstones come with a variety of grits and hardness—the harder the stone the finer the grit. During the honing process the idea is to remove more metal with a soft, coarse grit stone. Then, as the edge becomes keener, change to a harder, denser grit stone that will not remove as much of the metal. On a microscopic level, the large scratches produced by grinding are being worn down and replaced by smaller scratches. Clearly, it would be fruitless to go directly from grinding, which removes a lot of metal and produces quite deep scratches, to a hard, fine grit stone, for it would take forever to wear these scratches down to produce a fine edge.

Oilstones can be natural or manmade, but the manmade ones do not last as long, because the bonding agents which hold the stone particles together break down. Unlike a grindstone which uses water as a flushing lubricant, oilstones are made to be used with oil. A refined oil thinned with solvent or ordinary car brake fluid should be used for all honing, as common oil is too thick to remove the clogged metal particles from the stone surface. After use, a stone should be washed with soapy water, rinsed and dried.

You will notice after wet grinding that a wire-edged burr has formed along the cutting edge; it will be necessary to remove this. The rough honing procedure begins by placing the blade bevel flat on the stone with the heel and toe touching. The slightly concave bevel surface created by grinding eliminates the need to raise the heel. (See Figure 4–15.) Once this angle is attained, hold it constant and hone the tool using either reciprocating strokes or a figure eight motion. Check periodically to see if the concave surface has been ground flat from heel to toe, and add more honing oil. Continue rough honing, using the entire surface of the stone. To remove the wire-edge burr completely will require turning the tool on its back so it lies flat against the stone, then sliding it back and forth across the surface a few times.

Honing large chisels or slicks can be difficult; try using a 4″ × 4″ (100 × 100 mm) block as a guide. (See Figure 4–16.) Axes, because of their weight, are best honed by moving the stone into the tool's cutting edge in clockwise, circular motions, while the axe is held motionless.

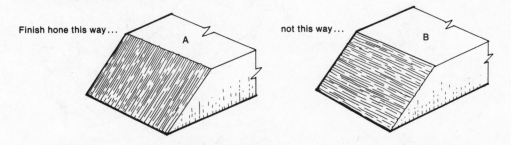

Finish hone this way...   not this way...

Figure 4–17. Finish honing.

Fine honing   Basically this is the same metal removing procedure as rough honing only a harder, finer grit oilstone is used. The following tips may be useful for obtaining a "shaving" edge. When finishing up, the last few strokes should be made so as to align the minute scratches as shown in Figure 4–17. This alignment produces less surface drag as the tool enters the wood. For the perfectionist with access to a buffing wheel, buffing the entire bevel and sides will practically remove all surface scratches and abrasions. The difference made by buffing is amazing. You can see this in the axes used by professionals at competitons, for their axes look chromed. But a buffed blade does not only look good, it cuts well too.

How to sharpen auger bits

Auger bits are very important in solid wood post and beam construction. Their main uses are for drilling holes to pin or join wood members together, and for electrical wiring access holes. When drilling through solid wood the auger bit must be straight and sharp; a dull or bent bit can lead to undue stress on the electric drill. Figure 4–18 shows how to maintain an auger bit.

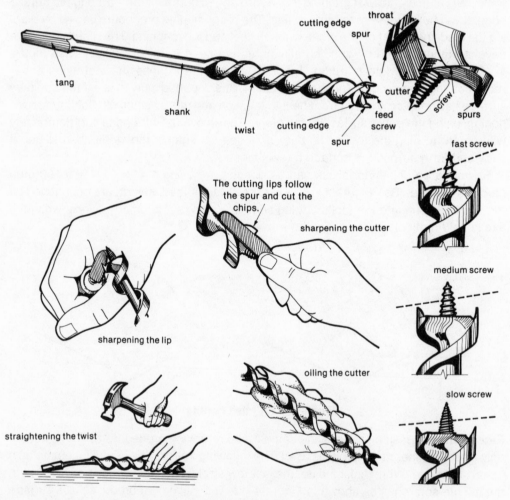

Figure 4–18. Sharpening and adjusting auger bits.

CHAPTER FIVE

Foundations

By definition a foundation is a supportive body which serves to raise the house structure above the decay-causing earth, at the same time transferring and equally distributing the weight of the building to the ground. A foundation can be as primitive as a rock wedged under each corner of the building. More often, it is a continuous or intermittent supportive body composed of either concrete, rock and mortar, or preserved wood. The foundation of a log post and beam house is the same as that in any conventional frame house.

The installation of any foundation involves the same basic procedures:
• Soil testing
• Foundation layout
• Grade levels and excavation
• Foundation construction

Soil Testing

The optimum building site will have a slight grade or slope to allow for good drainage. A stable, sandy gravel is the best substrate. Stay away from low land with wet clay soil and a high water table. Many building authorities require a perculation test of the soil substrate to determine its drainage ability, and may recommend the inclusion of perimeter drainage tile and gravel around the foundation footing. Another factor which must be considered is the frost level, which is the depth that the winter frost penetrates into the ground. This level can be ascertained from the local building authority or your neighbors. The foot (called footing) of the foundation must be below this level of frost penetration to prevent frost heave damage to the foundation which will throw the building off level.

Foundation Layout

1. How to lay out foundation lines.

The outside perimeter of a building's foundation will be the same as the outside dimensions of the building itself. Therefore the foundation will be the same shape as the building you want to construct. Consider a simple 30′ × 40′ (9 m × 12 m) rectangular building. In order to make all the corners 90° angles you must first start with a right angle triangle. This can be done easily on site by using multiples of 3-4-5 as described below. Once this first right angle triangle is determined it is a simple matter to locate the fourth corner of the rectangle and check for its overall squareness. The procedures are as follows:

Tools: tape measure, 3 lb (1.5 kg) hammer.

Materials: 6 – 2″ × 2″ × 18″ (38 mm × 38 mm × 450 mm) stakes, string which will not stretch, nails.

Procedure:
1) Clear the vegetation from the proposed site.
2) Establish corner A by sinking a nial-topped stake into the ground. Refer to Figure 5-1.
3) Beginning from corner A lay out a right angle triangle by measuring out a distance of 3 and 4 units (feet/meters) or multiples thereof. (See inset in Figure 5-1.) When the hypotenuse equals 5 (or multiples thereof) the corner will be 90°.
4) To find corners B and C simply extend the legs of the triangle the length and width of the foundation.
5) From corners B and C locate corner D. Corner D will be at the intersection of the foundation length and width measurements.
6) All corner angles should be 90°. Check for squareness by measuring the diagonals. AD should equal BC. (See Figure 5-2.) Any adjustment can be done by moving corner D slightly. Connect the string to the nail-topped stakes to form the foundation outline.
7) Diagonals can be obtained mathematically by using the Pythagorean theorem:

$$a^2 + b^2 = c^2$$
$$30^2 + 40^2 = c^2$$
$$900 + 1600 = c^2$$
$$2500 = c^2$$
$$\sqrt{2500} = c$$
$$50 = c$$

8) Variations to a square or rectangular building (i.e., L-shaped) simply require additional right angles and can be laid out accordingly.

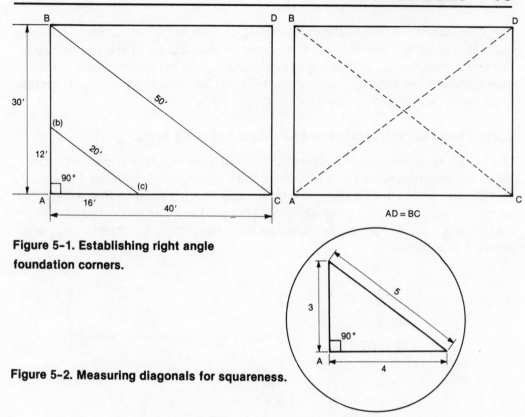

Figure 5-1. Establishing right angle foundation corners.

Figure 5-2. Measuring diagonals for squareness.

Grade Levels and Excavation

Since the earth's surface or grade is not perfectly flat it is necessary to establish marks at each of the foundation corners which are level to one another so the house will not sit at an angle. A grade level can be determined by using a "builder's level" like the one described in the tool section of this book or by using a "water hose level." Procedures on the use of both these levels are explained below.

Once a level grade mark is determined the next step is to excavate or remove the required amount of earth down to an equal depth below the grade mark. In areas where there is no frost penetration, the ground need only be scraped level to remove the top soil down to undisturbed substrate. In areas of frost penetration it is necessary to excavate a minimum of 1' (300 mm) below the frost line.

Before establishing grade levels, decide whether you want a continuous or pier foundation. If a continuous foundation is desired it will be necessary to extend the foundation lines 3' (1 m) beyond the corners to allow working room around the building foundation. A building whose dimensions are 30' × 40' (9 m × 12 m) would be extended to 36' × 46' (11 m × 14 m) in this case.

In order to preserve the foundation lines and grade level for continuous foundations after the ground has been excavated, the common procedure is to erect batterboards. The builder has the option of doing this or repeating the foundation layout in the excavated cavity. The process of extending the foundation lines or erecting batterboards is not necessary for pier foundation.

2. How to establish grade levels using a builder's level.

This instrument is merely a telescope mounted on a tripod which can rotate 360°. Once set up and placed level it will give a level horizontal reading in any direction it is pointed. As the instrument is more comfortable for the operator if it is set up at eye level, it is necessary to transfer the reading closer to the ground so it can be marked directly on the foundation corner stakes. The procedure for establishing grade levels using this instrument is as follows.

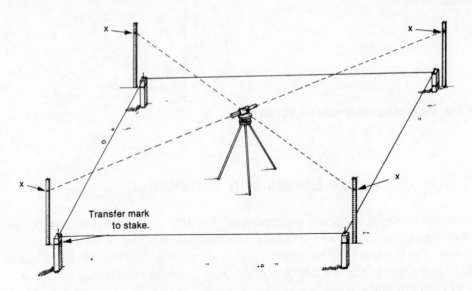

Transfer mark to stake.

Figure 5-3. Establishing equal grade levels with a builder's level.

Tools: Builder's level, rod marked in feet and inches or meters and centimeters, pencil.

Procedure:
1) Rent a builder's level and rod. (The rod can be substituted for a stick.)
2) Set up and level instrument (according to instructions) in the center of the building location.
3) Establish a grade level mark that is common to all corner points. (See Figure 5-3.) Transfer this mark onto the stake.

3. How to establish grade levels using a water hose level.

As water finds its own level, a level can be fabricated using a common garden hose and water. Because of its flexibility this type of level can accurately set grade levels even around blind corners. Outlined below is the procedure for constructing a water level and using it to establish equal grade levels. I will take this opportunity to illustrate setting equal grade levels onto batterboards which will be used where a continuous foundation is desired:

Tools: Hammer, level, pencil.

Materials: 50' (15 m) semi-clear garden hose, water, 2 corks, nails.

Procedure:
1) Lay the hose on the ground with the ends turned up. Then cork one end of the garden hose and fill with water to within 6 ″ (150 mm) or so from the other end and cork that end also. Remove the corks, cut a groove in each one and replace them in each end. This is to prevent the water from spilling out while at the same time preventing a vacuum being created inside the hose which will give a false reading. Make sure there are no trapped air bubbles in the hose.
2) Set and level the batterboards at the high ground corner of the extended building foundation line. Use a common level for this procedure and refer to the next section (**4**) for information concerning batterboard construction.
3) Have someone hold one end of the hose so the water line is level with the set batterboard. Mark on the batterboard stakes where the corresponding water level shows at the opposite end of the hose. (See Figure 5–4.)
4) Continue this procedure and mark equal grade levels on all the batterboard stakes.

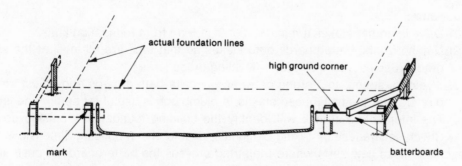

Figure 5-4. Establishing equal grade levels with a water level.

4. How to erect batterboards (for use with continuous foundations).

After the corners of the house have been located the next step is to erect batterboards. The batterboards preserve the outline of the house and the grade level during the excavation.

It is important that the batterboards are solidly placed to resist movement and are of equal elevation. Error here can greatly affect the building's dimensions.

Tools: 3 lb (1.5 kg) hammer, tape measure, handsaw, plumb bob, level.

Materials: 2″ × 4″ × 30″ (38 × 89 × 750 mm) stakes, 1″ × 6″ (19 × 140 mm) batterboards, strong string, nails.

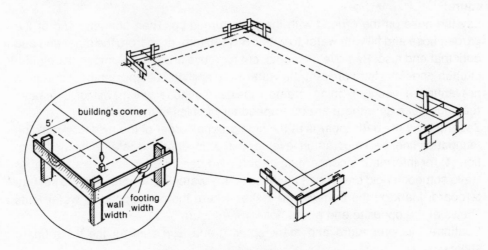

Figure 5–5. Batterboard placement.

Procedure:
1) Drive in corner stakes a minimum of 5′ (1.5 m) from foundation lines.
2) Nail horizontal batterboards onto stakes so that tops are all level at the same grade. (See section **3** above for leveling procedures.)
3) Stretch a strong, taut string between opposite batterboards and adjust so it is directly over the nail-topped stakes. A plumb bob is useful for setting the lines.
4) The intersecting strings will identify the building foundation's outside corner. Check squareness by taking diagonals, double check building dimensions now also. Make saw kerfs where the string crosses the batterboards in case string breaks later.
5) Excavate 3′ (1 m) outside the building foundation's line.

5. How to establish excavation depths.

Besides serving the function of outlining the building's perimeter, batterboards establish a level plane over uneven ground. By measuring down an equal distance from these batterboard string lines in all four corners, a level plane below the frost line is quickly established.

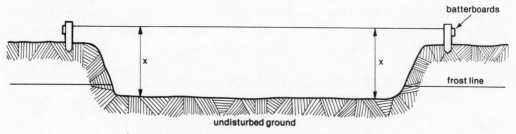

Figure 5-6. Checking excavation depth.

Tools: Tape measure, shovel, pick.

Equipment: Backhoe or tractor with front end loader.

Procedure:
1) Determine the frost line depth from the local building authorities.
2) Excavate 1'–2' (300 mm–600 mm) below frost line and 3' (1 m) outside the building's foundation lines. It is important to place the footings on *undisturbed* ground.
3) Check excavation depth by measuring down from the batterboard string lines. (See Figure 5-6.)

Foundation Construction

Within the realm of continuous and intermittent supportive foundations there are many types. For example, continuous foundations would include poured concrete, concrete block and mortar, rock and mortar, preserved wood, steel, and rigid foam block. Intermittent or pier foundations would include the same supportive mediums with the exception of rigid foam block. There are less materials and labor associated with pier foundations. However, you may choose a continuous foundation if basement space is wanted, or in order to meet local building requirements. Due to the numbers of good books about foundation construction I will touch only briefly on the actual assembly procedures of the formwork and will emphasize such neglected areas as foundation construction in permafrost and marshy locations.

6. Building pier foundations.

Pier foundations lend themselves to post and beam buildings, for it is not essential to provide continuous support under a wall sill log or timber that is strong enough to need only periodic support. Besides the saving on labor and materials, there is an added advantage. This is the possibility of an earlier start, since the structural support piers can be placed and the work begun, leaving the spaces between the piers to be filled in at a later time. It must be noted that pier foundations are not usually used where there is a basement. For information on the types of anchor fasteners to use for the various sill types refer to section **1,** Chapter 7, on floor systems.

Tools: Eye and ear protection, chainsaw (if using wood posts), chalkline, tape measure, handsaw, hacksaw, level, hammer, pencil, cement mixing tools if applicable. (See Concrete and mortar, section **8,** below.)

Materials: Cement forms or wood posts, anchor fasteners, cement ingredients (if applicable, nails.

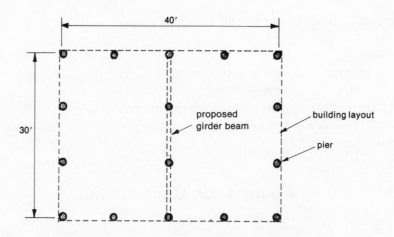

Figure 5–7. Pier location around building perimeter.

Procedure:
   1) Lay out foundation lines and take diagonals. Batterboards are not necessary.
   2) Locate Piers: under corners, at intersecting walls, at 8′–10′ (2.5 m–3 m) spacings around the building's perimeters. The piers are to be placed to the inside of the foundation lines. (See Figure 5–7.)

3) Dig holes below the frost line and place a 4″ (100 mm) thick concrete footing so it fills the base of the hole, and then the forms or treated posts.
4) Using a water or builder's level, establish equal elevation levels on all pier form-work.
5) Construct the piers in the following manner. (See Figure 5–8.)

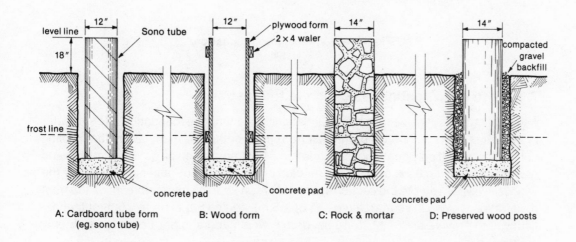

Figure 5–8. Pier formwork types.

Place reinforcing bar into forms and pour concrete to level line. (See Figure 5–8A and B.) Refer to section **8,** below, for information on concrete. Insert anchor fasteners while the concrete is still wet.

Or, using the excavated hole as the form, construct piers from rock and mortar. (See Figure 5–8C.) Refer to section **8** for information on mortar. Insert anchor fasteners while the mortar is still wet.

Or, place the preserved posts into the excavated holes and backfill with gravel. (See Figure 5–8D.) Transfer the level line to the posts and cut off waste with a chainsaw.

6) Place a moisture barrier grout, such as tar, between the piers and floor sills. Alternatively tar paper, fiberboard, or rigid foam will suffice as a moisture barrier.
7) Skirt or fill between the piers with rock and mortar to protect against weather and prevent creatures from entering the crawl space. (See Figure 5–9.)
8) Apply metal flashing to prevent moisture from accumulating between foundation and sills.

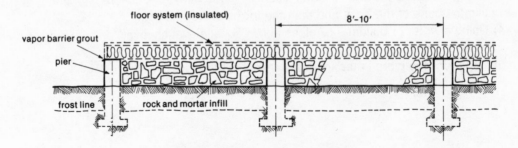

Figure 5-9. View of pier foundation.

7. How to build continuous concrete foundations.

Although more expensive than pier foundations, a continuous foundation affords better structural support and better protection from the weather. In many areas the building authorities permit only continuous foundations. For information on concrete mixing and pouring see section **8,** below. For information on which anchor fasteners to use for the various sill types refer to the section **1,** Chapter 7, on floor systems. Note that if the frost penetration is deep in your area (i.e., 5′, or 1.5 m), adding the extra few feet of foundation wall to provide a 7′6″ (2.25 m) headroom would add another floor area with only marginal costs:

Tools: 4′ (1220 mm) level, tape measure, hammer, handsaw, sledge hammer.

Materials: Plywood forms, 2″ × 4″ (38 × 89 mm) (studding, walers, stakes, bracing), 2″ × 10″ (38 × 235 mm) footing forms, ½″ (12 mm) reinforcing rod, tie wire, nails, cement ingredients.

Procedure:
1) Construct footing forms and place reinforcing rod. Refer to a good carpentry book for more details. (See bibliography.)
2) Pour concrete footings and insert a beveled strip of oiled wood to form a keyway (to be removed after drying). This keyway will serve to lock the foundation wall to the footing.
3) Construct wall forms according to Figure 5-10. If a dropped floor system (i.e., where the top of the floor is level with the concrete foundation wall) is desired then add a flooring ledge as shown in the diagram. Use additional reinforcing rod if the wall is tall, as in a full basement.
4) Brace wall forms securely.
5) Pour concrete walls to level line and insert anchor fasteners while the concrete is still wet.

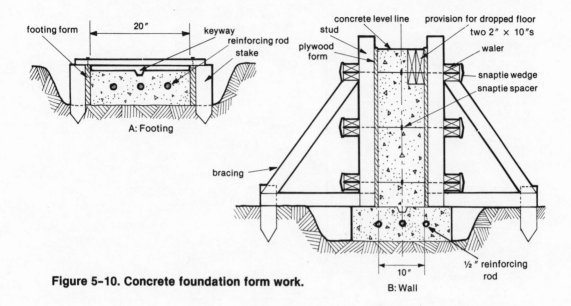

Figure 5–10. Concrete foundation form work.

6) Strip forms in 5 days but keep concrete moist for an additional 7 days.
7) Place moisture barrier and flashing to prevent moisture accumulation between foundation and sills. Standing moisture will rot unpreserved wood.
8) If properly proportioned and mixed, a concrete wall is waterproof. However the usual procedure is to coat the exterior wall with a bituminous (waterproof) layer.
9) A basement or crawl space will be warmer if the outside of the wall is insulated. (See Figure 5–11.)

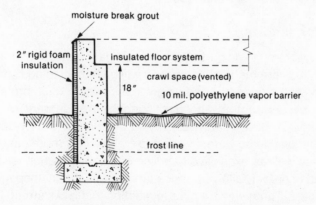

Figure 5–11. Continuous concrete foundation with crawl space.

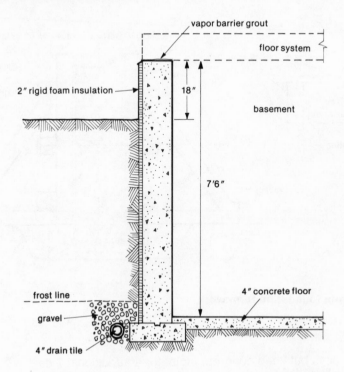

Figure 5–12. Continuous concrete foundation with basement.

10) Drain tile and gravel should ring the perimeter of the foundation unless the substrate has good drainage. (See Figure 5–12.)

8. Concrete and mortar.

A house is only as strong and durable as the foundation that supports it. Since the majority of foundations are made of concrete it will be helpful to add some practical hints on how to work with it. Indeed, observing various construction projects has made me aware that many contractors and tradespeople are ignorant of concrete and its material properties. I have seen ready-mixed batches of quality controlled concrete delivered on site, only to be watered down to make it flow more easily and further with less paddling, as well as excessive handling and over-vibration leading to aggregate separation, and improper follow-up procedures leading to a stoppage of the hydration ("curing") process. The result is a poor foundation that lacks strength, watertightness, and durability—all of which could have been prevented. Listed below are a few tips to making good concrete.

Procedure:

1) Select the proper ingredients and rent or borrow the necessary tools.
2) Correct proportioning: Formula 1–2–3 mix is one part cement, two parts sand (moist), and three parts gravel by volume.
3) Thorough mixing: Every particle of sand and gravel must be completely covered with cement paste. The strength, durability, and watertightness of concrete are controlled by the amount of water used per sack of cement. The less water the better the quality of concrete—as long as the mixture is plastic and workable. It is best to mix a small trial batch according to the table formula. If this batch is not satisfactory—DO NOT ADD WATER—instead add or reduce the quantity of aggregate or change the proportion of fine and coarse aggregate.

How to mix concrete

a) Set mixer in motion.
b) Add specified amount of water.
c) Add a small quantity of both fine and coarse aggregate.
d) Add the amount of cement necessary.
e) Add the rest of the aggregate a little at a time, alternating between small amounts of sand, then gravel.
f) After all the ingredients are in the mixer, continue mixing for at least three minutes, or until all the materials are thoroughly coated and the concrete has a uniform color.

  Placing the concrete into the forms should be done within 45 minutes. Transport the concrete carefully to avoid excess agitation which can cause separation of the fine and coarse aggregate.

How to place concrete

a) Place as near as possible to final resting position in the wall.
b) Begin at a corner and deposit concrete uniformly in even layers around the forms, not more than 12″ (300 mm) at one time.
c) Spade or vibrate the concrete to compact it and eliminate air pockets and honeycombing. Overworking the mix causes an excess of water and fine material to be brought to the surface.
d) Further care is required to see that the concrete is worked into the corners and angles of the forms, and around reinforcing work.
e) If the mixture becomes sloppy as forms are filled, make a stiffer mix by varying the proportions of sand and gravel.
f) Trowel off to the level line indicated on forms.

How to cure concrete
Proper curing increases the strength and durability of the concrete. Hydration (hardening) of the concrete continues only in the presence of water and a suitable temperature. Loss of water stops hydration and

causes concrete to shrink, creating surface stresses which may result in surface cracking. Correct curing and hardening occurs if concrete is kept moist and warm. Concrete gains strength rapidly within seven days, while near maximum strength is achieved in 28 days.

- Leave forms in place to reduce surface moisture loss.
- In hot weather, sprinkle or apply wet coverings.
- Seal the surface with plastic sheets or a liquid membrane compound.
- Cure for a period of five days in warm weather and seven days in cool weather.

Mortar   Mortar is a bonding agent designed to join elements such as rock, brick, or concrete blocks together. A mortar mix contains water, masonry cement, and sand but no coarse aggregate. A proper workable mixture is recognized when it will readily adhere to vertical surfaces and to the underside of horizontal surfaces. It should spread easily yet not be so fluid that it runs out of mortar joints.

Apply mortar only to DRY rocks, bricks, or blocks.

9. Constructing foundations for permafrost areas.

When moisture in the ground freezes it expands in volume causing a buckling of the ground, known as frost heaving. When thawing occurs during the summer air spaces are left which collapse once weight is applied. This ground movement is disastrous for building foundations and structures, causing distortion and breakage. In areas with minimal frost depth, placing the foundation footings below this unstable frost penetration (called the "frost line") is the answer. In areas of very deep frost penetration, or where the earth stays permanently frozen below the surface, a concrete wall foundation is not the answer.

Experiences in the Arctic have shown me three proven methods of constructing foundations in permafrost locations. The first, and most expensive, is to simply drill down to stable frozen earth, insert piers, and build the structure on these supports. A less expensive method is to lay a compacted gravel pad down and build on this stable surface. The third, and cheapest method is to excavate a trench down to permafrost if possible, insulate and fill with compacted gravel, and use this stable surface to build on. These last two methods require that the crawl space under the house be left cold in order to minimize ground movement caused by freeze-thaw cycles. A cold crawl space necessitates an insulated floor as well as heat-taped plumbing and waterlines where they may be exposed to freezing. Illustrated below are the two methods involving the gravel pad and trench construction. The footing and piers can be of either concrete or preserved wood for both types.

Procedure:
Gravel pad   Ideally the gravel pad should be placed during the winter when the ground is still frozen, however, the winter working conditions often prevent this.

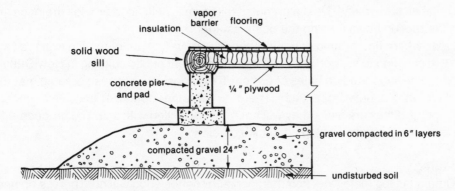

Figure 5-13. Section of a compacted gravel pad for permafrost areas.

Lay the coarse gravel down in 6″ (150 mm) layers, compacting each layer. Do not try to remove any of the top soil, as, once removed, the undersurface is like jello. Construct the foundation on top of the pad as shown in Figure 5–13.

Gravel trench The trench sould be excavated during the summer, when the ground surface is not frozen. Dig a 3′ (1 m) wide trench down to frozen ground along the building's perimeter line. The styrofoam and compacted gravel should be placed as the excavation proceeds, so as to avoid additional thawing of the frozen ground. Once this ground is thawed, annual freeze-thaw cycles will continue to create unstable ground. Construct the foundation on top of the gravel berm, as shown in Figure 5–14.

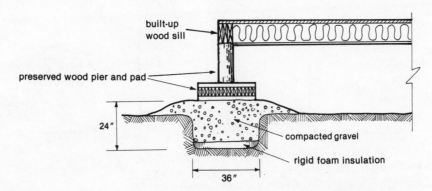

Figure 5-14. Section of a compacted gravel trench for permafrost areas.

10. How to construct foundations for marshy areas.

A building foundation must rest on firm ground. The common procedure when building in marshy or loose soil conditions is to drive posts down through the loose substrate until they rest on firm ground. Next a granular soil berm is built up to provide drainage and then construction begins, using the posts as a foundation.

In areas where firm ground cannot be reached a "raft" type of footing is placed in a shallow excavation to support the building. A prominent public building in New Orleans is known to be supported on bales of cotton. This is possible because organic material will not rot when deprived of oxygen. Therefore, whether cotton, straw bales, or a corduroy footing of logs are used, they will not rot if back filled with soil. The procedure for a raft footing constructed of logs is outlined below.

Procedure:
1) Obtain the log material—common poplar or cottonwood will do. There is no need to preserve these logs. It is best if the log lengths span the entire length and width of the excavated hole.
2) Excavate the building location to a depth of at least 3'–4' (1–1.2 m) below the ground surface. It may be necessary to pump the hole dry during excavation.
3) When the excavation is deep enough, set the first layer of logs down, side by side. Alternate butts and tops to compensate for the taper and to obtain a tighter course.
4) When the first layer is completed, lay the second layer in the same manner.
5) Apply a thick layer of gravel or sawdust over this cribbing.
6) Backfill the remainder of the cavity and berm slightly to permit runoff.
7) Sink preserved posts down to the sawdust/gravel layer and build on these piers.

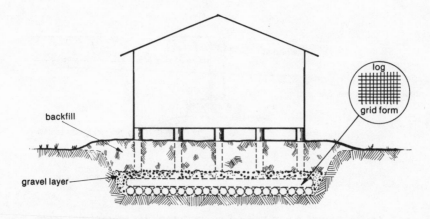

Figure 5-15. Section of a raft footing for marshy areas.

CHAPTER SIX

Preparing the Log Material

Joinery

Log preparation marks the beginning of the wood joinery phase of construction. The first concern is to expose enough flat or squared log surface to facilitate joinery of one log or timber to another. It is at this early stage that good attitudes and habits towards working with wood must be formulated. Holderlin's words that "the spirit of the forest still lives in it" (wood) expresses exactly the type of approach to be taken when working with it. Sometimes, because of the nature of the particular species, the wood's moisture content and internal stresses—both embodiments of the forest's spirit—can cause a perfectly laid out and executed joint to simply not fit. Strive to understand why, and with this understanding will come the patience so needed when working with wood.

The tool which cuts the wood must be of good quality and sharp. But the tool alone will not cut a tenon or construct a house—it must be commanded by the body and mind of the person using it. The body and mind must develop a sense of the tool, to feel comfortable with its grip, the way it cuts, to adjust to its eccentricities, to develop rhythm and balance, to sense which muscles are involved—the whole complex psychophysical coordination needed to operate the tool. Knowing this, if at first you feel a little awkward, you will realize the degree of education required and have patience.

All joinery requires a layout and cutting procedure. When using log materials there are no rectangular edges or flat surfaces from which to begin or end a measurement, therefore all layout work must originate from a centerline and progress outwards.

A centerline forms the line of reference and keeps joints in alignment even if the log takes a sweeping bend. It is good practice, therefore, to chalk a centerline on all log materials which will require flat surfaces or joinery, even if this seems like an unnecessary step.

Joinery follows nature in its divisions of male and female. In most instances, the male portion is laid out and cut first, and then its dimensions are traced or scribed to produce its female counterpart. Where tracing is not possible, measure the male's dimensions and transpose these to produce the female. Repetitive work will be simplified and accuracy increased by employing a template of the male, which is then used to trace its shape to produce the female. To save time, try to initiate all the layout before cutting. And to avoid mistakes, double-check the layout and visualize a logical assembly before beginning to cut. Remember, once removed, the wood cannot be put back.

When you cut, leave the layout lines. (Ideally they will be split in half.) If these layout lines are removed all reference to the shape and dimensions of the joint will be lost. Bisecting the layout line itself with a utility razor knife will sever the wood fibers, thereby defining the parameters of the joint as you cut while at the same time preventing splintering of the edges. Develop the practice of cutting only once in cross-grain situations; cutting close to the line and then trying to recut will only make a mess. As a general rule you shave the male to fit the female if a joint is too tight upon assembly. However to be more accurate, the mating surfaces of the joint have both parallel grain and cross-grain respectively, and if the joint is too tight, it is easier to shave the parallel grain of the members to fit, as shown in Figure 6–1.

The joinery diagrams throughout most of this book unveil just enough of the squared timber in the log to accomplish the joints. The person contemplating timber construction can use exactly the same layout procedures but will expose all of the hidden timber.

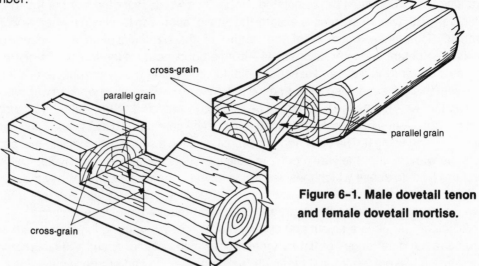

Figure 6–1. Male dovetail tenon and female dovetail mortise.

1. Square-cutting the end of a round log.

If the ends of a post are not square it will sit on an angle, when standing vertically. Outlined below is a simple method for squaring the end of a log.

Tools: Heavy tar paper (or similar material) cut square, pencil, chainsaw, eye and ear protection.

Procedure:

1) Secure the log on notched skids so it cannot roll.
2) Wrap the flexible square edge tar paper (or other material) around the peeled log 1½ turns and match the edges together.
3) Scribe a pencil line using the material edge as a guide.
4) Remove material and cut the end square with a chainsaw.

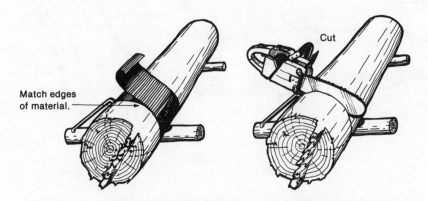

Figure 6-2. Square-cutting the end of a round log.

2. How to lay out a log for squaring or flat-surfacing.

Unlike regular frame dimensional materials, a log has no flat surfaces. In order to create flat, squared surfaces a layout procedure must be done on the log ends, after which these points can be matched together with chalked lines. The wise builder will group the same layout and cutting procedures and apply them to all the members he is working with so as to avoid duplication of steps. Note that when chalklining a log surface you *always snap the chalkline in the same direction as the cutting plane.* (See Figure 6-3D.) This is very important, for a log has an uneven surface and a line chalked from a horizontal angle will show differently than a line chalked from a vertical angle—or for that matter any other angle inbetween. This will become clearer as you progress.

Tools: Tape measure, chalkline, level, pencil, log dog.

Procedure:

1) Cut the log to the desired length.
2) Place notched skids under either end of the peeled log and secure with a log dog so that it will not move.
3) Working from the smaller end of the log, use a tape measure, level and pencil to find the radius of the log end, and pencil a vertical plumb line. (See Figure 6-3A.)

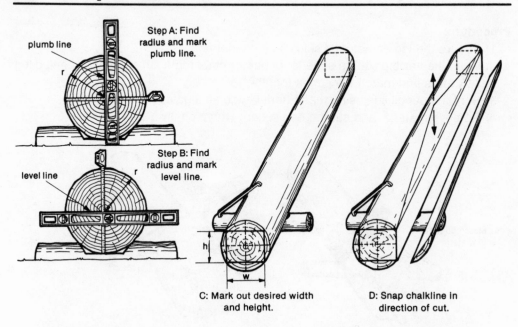

plumb line

r

Step A: Find radius and mark plumb line.

level line

r

Step B: Find radius and mark level line.

h

w

C: Mark out desired width and height.

D: Snap chalkline in direction of cut.

Figure 6–3. Layout and cutting procedures for flat-surfacing or squaring logs.

4) Repeat this procedure to find and mark the horizontal level line. (See Figure 6–3B.)

5) Using these center dividing lines as references, mark out the width and height dimensions desired. (See Figure 6–3C.)

6) Repeat this procedure on opposite end of log.

7) Join these two ends with chalked lines. See section **3,** below, for cutting procedures.

   Note: Always snap the chalkline in the direction of the cutting plane. Any other direction will result in inaccuracy. (See Figure 6–3D.)

   On longer logs a chalkline will droop due to gravity. Cut the span of the line in half by pressing it to the log surface at its midpoint, and then snap each length separately.

3. Wood removal: Two methods showing how to flat-side a log freehand.

Quick jobs not needing an extremely accurate flat-side can be done freehand with the chainsaw. When only one flat surface is required it is sufficient to keep the log stable, marking off the desired waste wood from each end using a level, and then joining these with chalked lines.

Tools: Eye and ear protection, level, pencil, chalkline, chainsaw, axe.

Procedure:

1) Secure the peeled log on a set of skids or on the ground so it will not move.
2) Determine amount of flat surface needed, then mark a level line on either end of log. (See Layout, Figure 6–4A.)
3) Join the level lines on either end of log with a taut chalkline and snap a line. *Always snap the line on the same plane as that marked on the ends of the log.* (See Figure 6–4B.)
4) Wood removal can be done using one of the two methods outlined below. Turn the chainsaw bar flat and enter the log at the plane shown in Figure 6–4, Cutting method A. While cutting use a pivoting action, digging the saw ''dogs'' (metal teeth at the base of the chainsaw bar) into the wood, then leaning over the log to observe the opposite cutting line. A chisel tooth chain works best for this ripping action.

    An alternative method is shown in Figure 6–4, Cutting method B, where successive cuts are made down to the line on both sides of the log. The waste wood can then be split off. Knots must be cut through, as they act like spikes holding the waste wood fast.

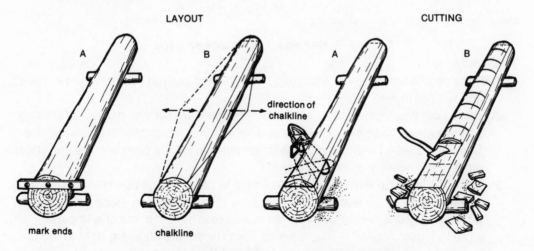

LAYOUT

CUTTING

direction of chalkline

mark ends   chalkline

Figure 6–4. Procedure for quick flat-surfacing jobs.

4. How to hew with a broad-axe.

For the most part, hewing a log with a broad-axe is reserved for more decorative jobs such as overhead beams in a dining room, or for elaborate truss work. For quick accurate flat-surfacing it is best to stay with the chainsaw. But speed and efficiency are not always the axiom. The axe is deeply embedded in our heritage and I experience a meditative state of mind when watching the wood pare off to reveal the inner grain patterns and when hearing the crisp, clean bite of a sharp axe, rather than the high pitched scream of a chainsaw.

Tools: 8–10 lb (3.5–4.5 kg) broad-axe, 4½–7 lb (2–3 kg) scoring axe, steel-toe boots, chalkline, level, log dog.

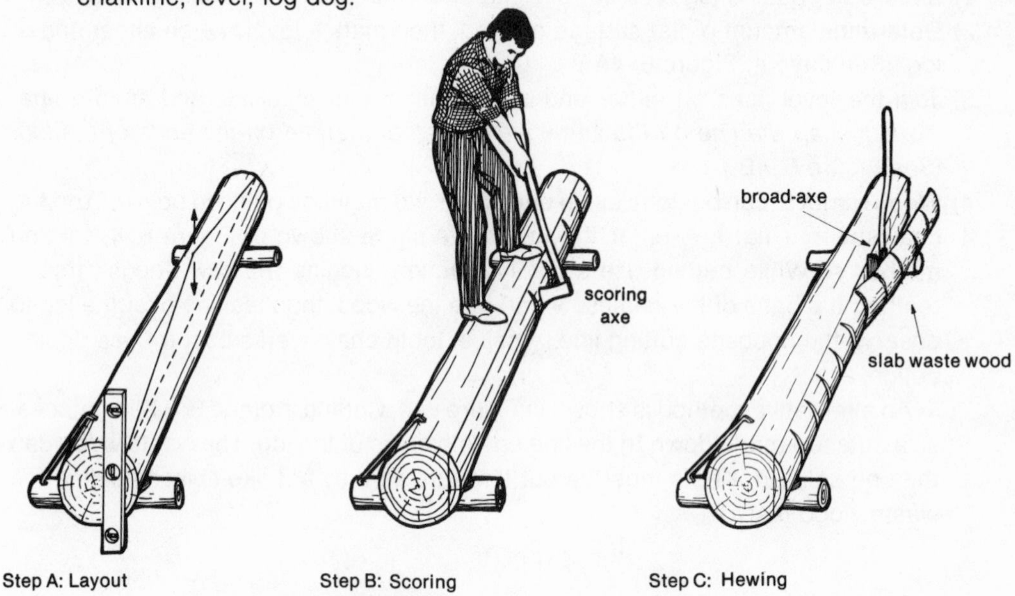

Step A: Layout   Step B: Scoring   Step C: Hewing

Figure 6–5. Hewing a flat surface on a log.

Procedure:

1) Place notched skids under each end of the peeled log and secure with a log dog so it will not move.

2) Chalk a cut line. Using a level, mark the amount of flat surface desired by placing a plumb line at each end of the log and joining the two ends with a chalked line. (See Figure 6–5A.) Remember to snap the chalkline in the direction of the cutting plane. In this case it is straight down.

3) Score the log as in Figure 6–5B. The aim is to create hinge-points that will allow the heavy slab waste wood to be hewn off with the broad-axe. Because a portion of holding wood is needed to hold the broad-axe in its kerf or cut, it is important to score to a depth of ½″–1″(12–25 mm) from the cut line. Scoring right to the cut line would necessitate continual restarting of the broad-axe kerf, for the slab of waste wood would simply chip off as each score cut is reached. This would cause the loss of rhythm and swinging force so necessary with hewing.

   Scoring is usually accomplished with a special axe that has little blade curvature, however a regular heavy, sharp axe works well, too. The scoring is done perpendicular to the chalked cut line, with the feet spread apart as shown in Figure 6–5B. Make a series of these relief cuts down the length of the log at 8″–10″ (200–250 mm) intervals, and wherever there is a large knot (acting like a spike). In cases where a large amount of slab wood is to be hewn off, a chainsaw may be substituted for the scoring axe, or else it will be necessary to repeat the scoring and hewing procedure a second time.

4) Figure 6–5C shows how to hew a vertical, flat surface using a broad-axe. Start from one end and step backward along the top of the log surface while hewing. This is a dangerous operation, and care should be taken. (Wear steel toe boots.) Generally, a full swing is used for medium and heavy slab wood removal. Light sized slabs need more axe control and a "choked up" grip on the handle facilitates easier handling.

As discussed earlier, buffing a cutting tool's surface so it is shiny removes a good percentage of the surface resistance, thus requiring less cutting effort. This technique works well on broad-axes with their large blades and (resistant) surfaces.

5. How to flat-surface a log using guide rails.

This portable method does an accurate job of milling shorter lengths of logs. It involves attaching a set of pads on the chainsaw bar which will slide along on parallel guide rails.

Tools: Eye and ear protection, level, tape measure, hammer, chainsaw, ½ " (12 mm) socket wrench.

Materials: ¾ " (19 mm) plywood pads, ½ " (12 mm) carriage bolts with nuts, 2 " × 6 " (38 × 140 mm) rails, nails, 2 " × 4 " (38 × 89 mm) stakes.

Procedure:
1) Secure and set up the log as shown in Figure 6–6, making sure the two side rails are an equal distance apart, down the length of the log.
2) Drill chainsaw bar and install plywood pads as shown in the diagram inset. For infinite adjustment mill two slots in the chainsaw bar.
3) Proceed to flat-side the log, having someone else apply a slight pressure on the pads (using two sticks) to keep them in contact with the rails.

Figure 6-6. Milling a log using guide rails and chainsaw pads.

6. How to flat-surface a log using a post and rail mill.

This mill is an expanded, more permanent version of the guide rails; it can accommodate longer log lengths.

Tools: Eye and ear protection, chainsaw, bar with pads, level, tape measure, hammer, shovel.

Materials: 2″ × 10″ (38 × 235 mm) straight lumber, posts, spikes, string line.

Procedure:
1) Determine length of material to be milled. This measurement will become the length of your mill.
2) Dig two parallel lines of holes and place 5′ (1.5 m) log posts in each. The distance between the lines should be wider than the thickest log to be milled.
3) Inset the top rails and bases as shown in Figure 6–7. It is important to have the top rails parallel and at equal height. The bases which the log rests on must be an equal distance below the top rails. This distance between the guide rails must be greater than the thickest log to be milled.
4) Place the log into the mill, blocking where necessary to obtain a continuous flat surface down its length.
5) Proceed to flatside the log, using a chainsaw with pads, with someone else to apply slight pressure on the pads to keep them in contact with the rails.

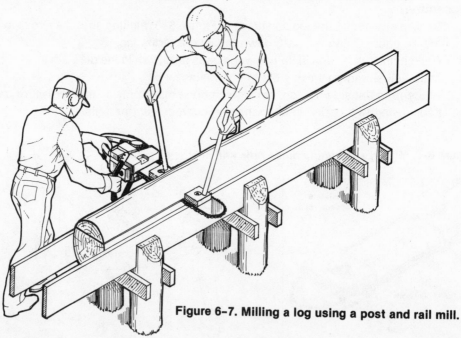

Figure 6–7. Milling a log using a post and rail mill.

7. How to flat-surface a log using a frame and track mill.

For the professional builder a mill such as the one described below is a necessity. This mill works quickly to produce accurate, flat surfaces on short and long logs. With a variable vertical adjustment, planks can easily be milled by someone inexperienced with a chainsaw. This mill is less portable than the others described here.

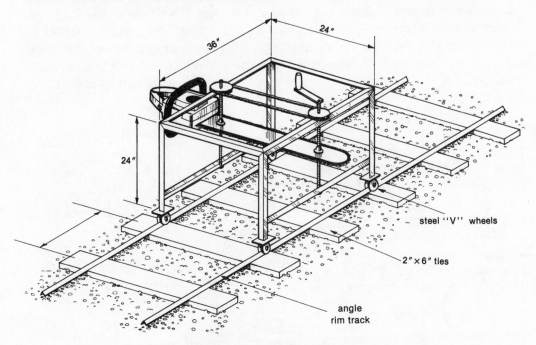

Figure 6–8. A frame and track mill.

Tools: Large chainsaw, 36″ (1 m) bar with chisel tooth chain, builder's level, level, shovel, hammer, tape measure, eye and ear protection.

Materials: Angle iron, ¾ ″ (19 mm) threaded rod, connectors, steel "V" wheels for the angle iron track, bicycle chain and two sprockets, handle, 2″ × 6″ × 36″ (38 × 140 mm × 1 m) plank-ties, gravel.

Procedure:
1) Construct the mill frame as shown in Figure 6–8.
2) Using a builder's level, level the ground and lay the track as indicated. Make sure the tracks are level and parallel to each other.
3) Roll the log into position, and secure it so it will not move. Adjust the chainsaw bar for depth of cut, and level it by placing a spirit level on the bar.
4) Milling can be done in both directions by simply pushing the carriage frame.

8. The mini chainsaw mill.

There are several portable mini mills available on the market. I have included this particular one because of its adaptability when used for plumb-cutting prefabricated log/timber wall infill panels. (See Chapter 8.) Its method of operation includes a mechanical clamp which holds the chainsaw bar in a fixed position. The clamp then slides along a V-shaped metal rail which is nailed to a straight 2″ × 8″ (38 × 184 mm) plank. This apparatus can be used in a horizontal or vertical position. Figure 6–9 illustrates its operation in flat-surfacing a log and in plumb-cutting the ends of a log wall. Since the end of the chainsaw bar is not held firmly in place, there is a chance the cut could "wander" if the cutting chain is improperly filed. (See chain-filing instructions in Chapter 4.)

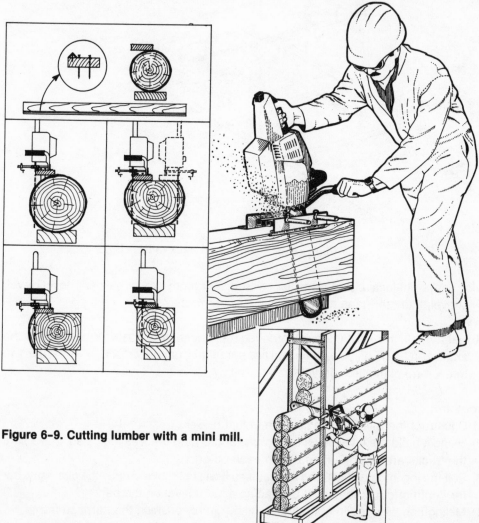

Figure 6–9. Cutting lumber with a mini mill.

CHAPTER SEVEN

The Floor System

Whether the foundation will be continuous or piers the most important point is that it be strong and level. Any large deviations of the floor's level surface will impair wall tightness between the posts and wood infill panels, especially if the panels are prefabricated.

The structural support components of a floor consist of sills, girders, and floor joists. Figures 7–1 to 7–5 show examples of floor types. The log floor components shown in these figures can also be applied to entirely squared timbers. The subsequent drawings show log joinery details with just enough flat surface and dimensional squaring to illustrate the work. However, the layout and cutting procedures for squared timber are identical.

1. The various floor systems, with sill anchorage.

Procedures:

Figure 7–1 shows two types of frame subflooring constructed on a continuous concrete foundation. The anchorage of the sill is either a bolt type, or none at all, as in the stepped foundation. The advantages of a frame lumber floor are its relative ease and speed of construction, and the level surface obtained. This type of floor does not make an attractive exposed ceiling in the basement or second storey homes. Note the additional support blocking under the posts, which is necessary because the weight of the roof is transmitted to the foundation via the posts.

Figure 7–2 shows a frame floor placed on a pier foundation. Here the built-up sill and girder are anchored to the piers with anchor bars. A built-up sill of this type will not need additional blocking under the posts.

Figure 7–3 shows a log or timber floor placed on a continuous preserved wood foundation. Here the midspan support girder is positioned below the floor joists with the joists spiked or lag bolted into it. This type of floor, when deaked with $2'' \times 6''$ (38×140 mm) tongue and groove flooring, makes an attractive exposed ceiling for a basement or

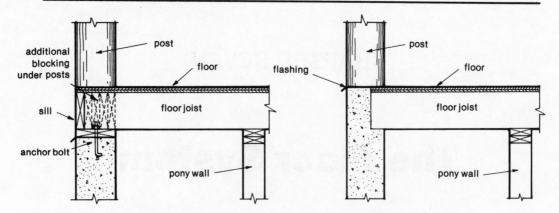

Figure 7-1. Frame floor system on continuous foundation.

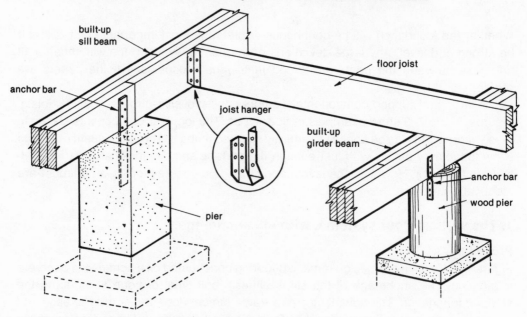

Figure 7-2. Frame floor system on a pier foundation.

second storey. Note that headroom is lost under the support girder so the ceiling should be planned high enough to allow for this.

Figure 7-4 shows a log or timber sill anchored to the foundation by upturned spikes embedded in the concrete. Here the girder and floor joists are at the same level as the sills, and no headroom is lost as in the previous method. In this case, however, strength is taken from the girder, and intermittent support posts should be placed. Further in-

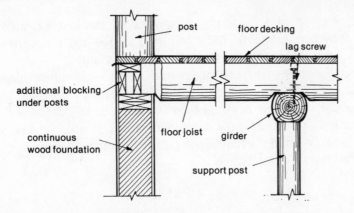

Figure 7-3. Log or timber floor system on continuous preserved wood foundation.

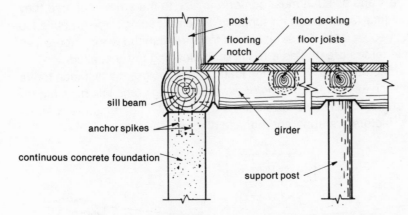

Figure 7-4. Log or timber floor system on a continous concrete foundation.

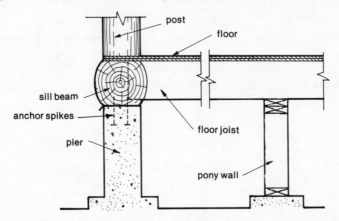

Figure 7-5. Combination log or timber and frame floor system on a pier foundation.

structions for this type of sill, girder, and joist joinery follow later in this chapter, sections **4–11.** When decked with 2″×6″ (38×140 mm) tongue and groove this floor makes an attractive open ceiling for a basement or second storey.

Figure 7–5 shows a floor system for use on a pier foundation when an insulated floor is necessary. It is a method quite similar to the one in Figure 7–2, except that the laminated sill and girder have now been replaced by a log or timber sill and frame ponywall. A pony wall is a short structurally supportive frame wall which, in this case, is substituted for the girder beam. If the foundation piers were made of preserved wood, the sill could be either spiked or lag bolted.

2. Stress forces.

A floor system is comprised of horizontal beams called sills, girders, and joists. These are structural members and as such must conform in size to the amount of load they will carry over the distance (span) between supports. When a loading force is applied to a beam (by furniture, people, etc.) it creates stress forces within the wood. Figure 7–6 illustrates the internal forces created as a result of the loading force applied.

When a beam is expected to carry too much load or span too great a distance for its size, limiting factors such as fiber failure and/or excess bending come into play. Figure 7–7 illustrates how proportionally less load can be carried by a beam as the span increases. The limiting factors are apparent in these diagrams as well.

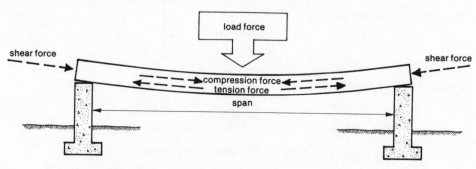

Figure 7–6. Forces at play on a horizontal beam.

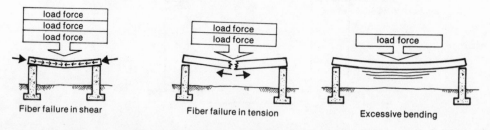

Figure 7–7. Limiting factors created by variable loading and span.

In the majority of cases excessive bending will be the main limiting factor in relation to the floor beam size and span. Excessive bending of the beams creates a "springy" floor—not in itself unsafe but bothersome nevertheless. The National Building Codes specify that main floors bend or deflect no more than 1″ in 360″ (1 mm in 360 mm) of span. Roofs are to deflect no more than 1″ in 240″ (1 mm in 240 mm) of span.

See Appendix III, for determining structural beam sizes for a given load and span.

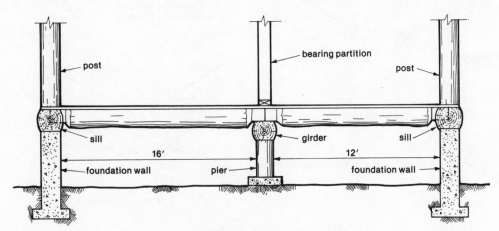

Figure 7–8. Girder spacing.

3. Determining girder sizes and spacing.

Girders are considered the "backbone" of a floor system, since they carry most of the floor weight. To determine the size of the girder beam needed for a given span refer to Appendix III.

Girder spacing between supports is usually no more than 16′ (5 m). Thus, a building with a span of 30′ (9 m) between foundation walls would have one mid-support girder, while a 40′ (12 m) span would have two. Girders should be placed directly below bearing partitions. This may call for a slight adjustment in the girder spacing (see Figure 7–8). Note that in a pier foundation there must be a pier located directly below the sill to provide extra support wherever there is a joinery intersection.

4. Sill corner joinery: How to lay out and cut a half-lap corner joint.

Once the foundation is in place the next job is to flat-side the sill logs to sit on the foundation, and to join these together at the corners of the building. One way to produce a level sill plate is to join the logs together at the corners with a half-lap joint.

Tools: Eye and ear protection, chainsaw, tape measure, chalkline, carpenter's square, slick, level, pencil.

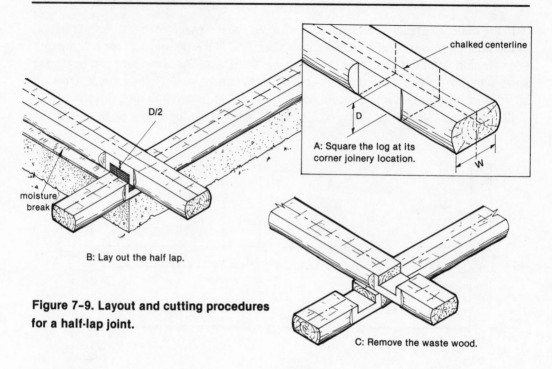

chalked centerline

A: Square the log at its corner joinery location.

D/2

moisture break

B: Lay out the half lap.

Figure 7-9. Layout and cutting procedures for a half-lap joint.

C: Remove the waste wood.

Procedure:

1) Flat-surface the sill logs to a uniform thickness (8"–10", or 200–250 mm).
2) Place the first two opposing sill logs on the building. If flashing is not being used place them slightly overhanging the foundation edge to provide a dripcap.
3) Square the sides of these sill logs where they cross the corner of the foundation. (See Figure 7-9A.) Always work from a chalked centerline.
4) Place the next two sill logs in position on the foundation so the ends rest on the sill logs below.
5) Trace the sides of each timber at the joints and lay out the depth of each half-lap by extending vertical lines at the corners. (See Figure 7-9B.) The depth of the notches are to equal half the sill depth (D/2).
6) Roll the sidewall sill logs back and remove the waste wood in all notches. (See Figure 7-9C.)
7) Join the sill logs together, providing the necessary moisture break between the sills and foundation. The moisture break can be either tar paper or a bituminous (waterproof) coating. It prevents moisture siphoning from the concrete foundation into the sill members—a process which can eventually lead to rot.

5. Sill corner joinery: How to lay out and cut a dovetail corner joint.

Another way of joining sill logs at the corners is by using a dovetail mortise and tenon joint. This method, like the last, produces a level sill plate. Mating the timbers and trac-

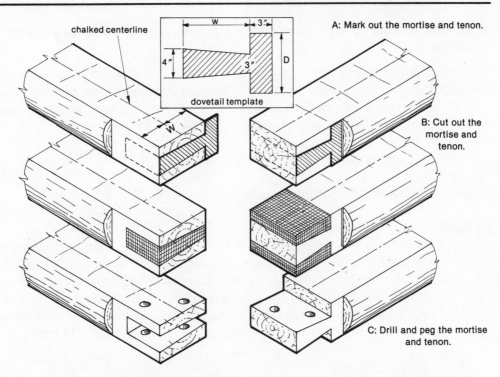

A: Mark out the mortise and tenon.

B: Cut out the mortise and tenon.

C: Drill and peg the mortise and tenon.

Figure 7–10. Layout and cutting procedures for a dovetail corner joint.

ing the joint is not possible here, so a dovetail template is employed to save time and simplify the layout for this and other occasions:

Tools: Eye and ear protection, chainsaw, pencil, tape measure, level, hand crosscut and ripsaw, electric drill with ¾ ″ (19 mm) bit.

Materials: ⅛″ (3 mm) hardboard template, ¾ ″ (19 mm) hardwood pegs.

Procedure:
1) Flat-side the sills to a uniform thickness (8″–10″, or 200–250 mm).
2) Cut the sill logs to the exact length of the foundation. Allow for a drip cap overhang if flashing is not used.
3) Square the side of the sills back from each end so that all sills are of equal width. (See Figure 7–10A.) Always work from a chalked centerline.
4) Make a template, such as the one shown in Figure 7–10 inset out of ⅛″ (3 mm) hardboard.
5) Trace out the mortise and tenon as shown in Figure 7–10A.
6) Cut out the mortise and tenon as shown in Figure 7–10B. Test the mortise with the template, and if the joint is too tight shave the tenon slightly.
7) Repeat for all corners, then drill and peg, as shown in Figure 7–10C.

6. Joining girders to sills: How to lay out a housed dovetail tenon and mortise.

The housed dovetail accomplishes the job of locking a girder between two support sills. (See Figure 7–11.) The dovetail portion locks the joint while the housed portion retains the timber's strength. To simplify and duplicate layout procedures a template is used for the joint. For cutting procedures see sections **7A** and **7B,** below.

Tools: Pencil, tape measure, chalkline, level.

Materials: 1/8″ (3 mm) hardboard template.

Procedure:

1) Cut the girder to final length. Squaring the two ends makes tenon layout and cutting easier but is not necessary. The final girder length is measured from between the sill plate centerlines. Refer to section **4,** above, for squaring procedures.

2) Make a template, such as the one shown, out of 1/8″ (3 mm) hardboard. The width and length dimensions may vary according to the size of the logs used. It is wise to have several different sized templates on hand. (See Figure 7–11 inset.)

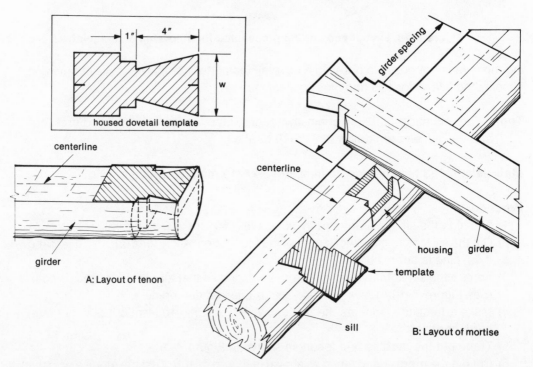

Figure 7–11. Layout procedures for a housed dovetail joint.

3) Mark out the housed dovetail tenon as shown in Figure 7–11A, aligning the template with the chalked centerline on the beam. If all tenons can be of equal dimensions joining procedure will be simplified.

4) Cut the tenons. (See section **7A,** below.)

5) Mark out the girder spacing by measuring down the sill centerline.

6) Using the template lay out the housed mortises. For the housed portion drop the lines down using a level. (See section **7B,** below.)

7) Cut the mortises. (See section **7B,** below.)

8) Position the girder between the sills.

7A. Joining girders to sills: How to cut a housed dovetail tenon.

This procedure for wood removal of a housed dovetail tenon is applicable to various other joints. Try to visualize the completed tenon before cutting.

Tools: Eye and ear protection, chainsaw, slick, handsaw, pencil, carpenter's square.

Procedure:

1) Drop layout lines down vertically, using a carpenter's square. (See Figure 7–11A.)

2) Make vertical cuts and remove waste wood sections 1, 2, and 3. Remember to barely leave the layout line. (See Figure 7–12A.)

3) Roll timber upside down and remove waste wood sections 4, 5, and 6. Clean up with a slick. (See Figure 7–12B.)

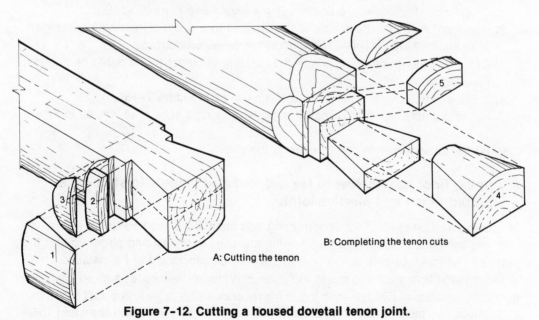

B: Completing the tenon cuts

A: Cutting the tenon

Figure 7–12. Cutting a housed dovetail tenon joint.

Note: Horizontal cuts are difficult to execute with a chainsaw. An alternative method is to make a series of vertical kerfs to the line and remove the waste wood with a slick or a handsaw.

4) Repeat procedures for the opposite end of the timber.

7B. Joining girders to sills: How to cut a housed dovetail mortise.

This procedure for the wood removal of a housed dovetail mortise is applicable to various other joints. Again, try to visualize the completed mortise before cutting.

Tools: Eye and ear protection, chainsaw with safety chain, 1″ (25 mm) auger bit and electric drill or hand brace, tape measure, slick, 1″ (25 mm) chisel, level.

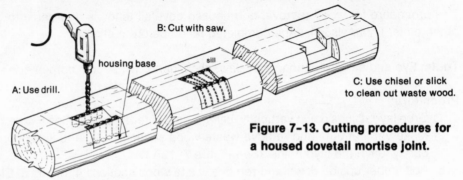

Figure 7–13. Cutting procedures for a housed dovetail mortise joint.

Procedure:
1) Drop layout lines down vertically using a level. (See Figure 7–11B.)
2) Drill holes along the back side of the dovetail to a depth of its male counterpart. (See Figure 7–13A.) These holes allow for easier wood removal.
3) Drill holes along the back side of the housing shoulder to the depth of its base. (See Figure 7–13A.)
4) Make a series of kerf cuts using a chainsaw as in Figure 7–13B.
5) Remove waste wood and clean the mortise, using a slick or chisel, as in Figure 7–13C.
6) Fit the girder beam in place between the sills.

8. Joining floor joists: How to lay out, cut and place a joist using a squared tenon and mortise joint.

This is the easiest method for constructing and installing a log floor joist. It requires squaring the ends of the joists, then cutting mortises in the sill and girder so that the joists can sit level. Once this has been done the floor decking can be installed.

Refer to the floor joist size tables in Appendix VI for joist sizes for a given span. Appendix VI consists of two tables, a log to frame conversion table and a joist size table. From these two tables one can obtain the correct joist size for a given span and spacing, whether for log, timber, or common lumber.

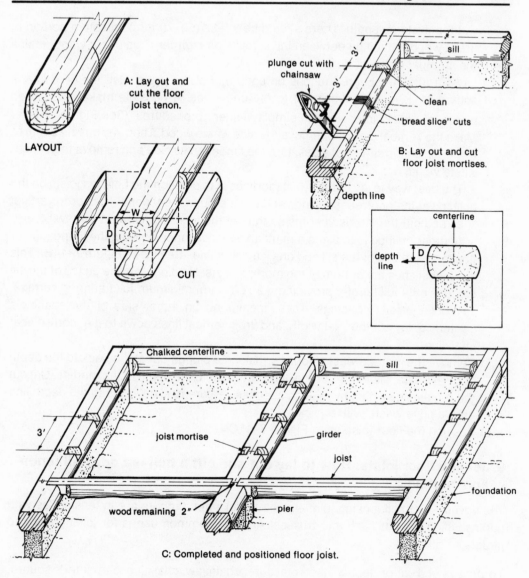

Figure 7-14. Constructing and placing a floor joist.

Tools: Eye and ear protection, chainsaw, chalkline, tape measure, carpenter's square, slick, pencil.

Procedure:

1) Flat-surface a 2"–4" (50–100 mm) nailing surface on all the floor joists.
2) Chalk a centerline onto the flat surface. This will ensure that the squared tenons will be in alignment during layout.

3) Cut the joists to length. There should be 2″–3″ (50–75 mm) minimum portion of uncut wood remaining between inline joists on a girder. This uncut wood retains the strength of the girder.

4) Lay out and cut squared tenons on each end of the joists. Use the carpenter's square for layout by aligning it to the centerline. If possible make all squared tenons of equal dimensions to simplify joinery procedures. (See Figure 7–14A.) Make the vertical cuts and remove the side waste wood. Then, lay out the depth of the tenon on the sawn flat sides, turn the timber on its side and remove the bottom waste wood.

   The best way to lay out the joist mortises is to position the finished joists on the building at their correct spacings and trace around the tenons. Then drop vertical lines and cut the mortise depths so that all the joist top surfaces sit level.

   Another method is to place a mark an equal distance up from the foundation or floor on each end of the sill and chalk a depth line. (See inset, Figure 7–14B.) This line establishes the bottom of the mortise seats. Next chalk a line on top of the sill log, down its full length, providing a 3″ (75 mm) minimum joist bearing surface. Lay out the joist spacings. Then, measuring on either side of the spacing's centerline, lay out the joist width, and drop vertical lines down to the mortise seat chalkline.

5) Remove the mortise waste wood by making a plunge cut at the back to the depth of the mortise. Make the vertical side cuts next to the depth of the mortise. Cut out the remaining portion by making successive "bread slice" cuts to the depth line and remove waste with a slick.

6) Position the floor joist, as in Figure 7–15C.

9. Joining floor joists: How to lay out and cut a half-lap dovetail tenon and mortise.

The dovetail is a self-locking joint—most useful when timbers are in tension, as with purlins which are set flush into trusses. Another common use is for joining joists to girders or sills.

Tools: Eye and ear protection, tape measure, chainsaw, chalkline, carpenter's square, pencil.

Materials: ⅛″ (3 mm) hardboard template.

Procedure:

1) Cut the joist or purlin to final length. Squaring the two ends makes tenon layout and cutting easier, but is not necessary.

2) Out of ⅛″ (3 mm) hardboard make a template like the one shown in the inset to Figure 7–15. The width and length dimensions may vary according to the size of

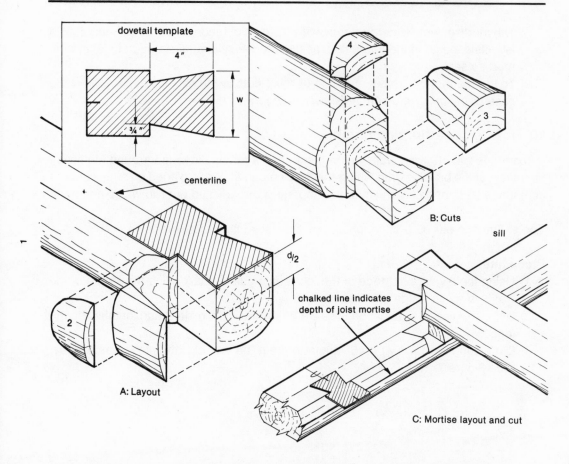

Figure 7-15. Layout and cutting procedures for a half-lap dovetail joint.

logs used. Again, it is wise to have a couple of different size templates on hand.

3) Mark out the dovetail tenons as shown in Figure 7–15A, aligning template center marks with the chalked centerline on the timber. If it is possible to make all tenons of equal dimensions this will simplify joinery procedure.

4) Make vertical cuts and remove waste wood sections 1 and 2.

5) Roll timber upside down and remove waste wood sections 3 and 4, as in Figure 7–15B. Clean with a slick.

6) For joist spacing, chalk a centerline down the girder and sill and mark out spacings. There should be a minimum of 2″–3″ (50–75 mm) uncut wood remaining between inline joists on the girder.

7) It is best to lay joists in place and trace around the tenon, especially with severely bowed timber. Or use the template to cut the mortises if manual help is not on hand to assist in lifting the joists.

8) The mortise depth is determined by the amount of tenon wood remaining. Chalk a level line, equal to the tenon thickness, onto the sill and girder face to locate the mortise seat.

9) To cut the mortise, make a couple of relief cuts to the mortise depth. Chisel the base of the mortise clean, as shown in Figure 7–15C.

10. How to cut a flooring notch.

If flooring is laid after the walls are in place then a notch is needed around the inside perimeter of the building onto which the flooring can fit. Walls placed on a full subfloor do not need a flooring notch since the flooring is already laid prior to wall placement.

Tools: Eye and ear protection, chalkline, chainsaw, tape measure.

Procedure:
1) Using the level top surface of the joists as a guide, chalk a line the length of the wall. Do so on inside of all walls.
2) Using this line as a guide, chainsaw a 2″–3″ (50–75 mm) kerf horizontally into the logs.
3) Cut diagonally down at a 45° angle to meet the first cut and clear waste away. (See Figure 7–16.)

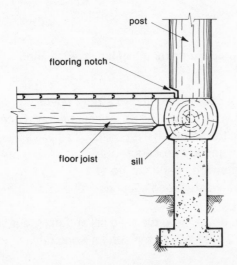

Figure 7-16. Cutting a flooring notch.

CHAPTER EIGHT

Log Post & Beam Walls

The log post and beam method requires a minimum of material preparation and purchase. For this reason it is the most favored technique for both professional and owner-builders. The outlined construction procedures entail scribe-fitted wall log joinery prefabricated on a remote jig. Such a jig can be either on the building site or separate from it entirely. A practical method of wall storage and shipment is described, so that a builder may transport the disassembled component parts across the country, if desired. Also included in this chapter are instructions for a post and beam walk-in basement wall. Many builders of long-log notched corner buildings will choose to use a post and beam basement access wall to avoid settling problems while still maintaining the log theme. For those building with either timber or an alternative infill (stackwall, etc.), it will still be necessary to refer to this chapter from time to time, as many aspects of the construction procedures are identical for all these types of walls.

1. Parts of a log post and beam building.

Figure 8–1 shows a post and beam log house together with all its parts, so the reader may become familiar with these terms.

2. Constructing a wall panel jig.

A jig is a device used to hold work during manufacture or assembly; in this case it will enable prefabrication of log infill wall panels as separate from the building foundation. Such a jig allows one to pre-build all the wall parts for later shipment, as well as assembly onto a foundation which has limited worksite room. It allows construction and storage of the building components inside a barn or large shed over the course of a winter. Above all it is a more accurate method of wall construction. With this jig an entire wall can be pre-built and the ends plumb-cut to a specific width. With the wall still in place on the jig the ends can now be grooved to receive the spline which keys it to the

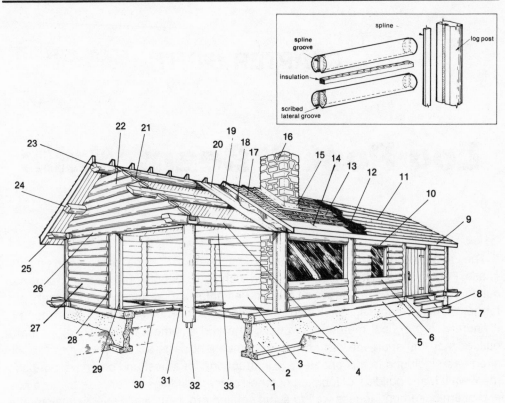

1. Footing
2. Foundation wall
3. Finished floor
4. Side wall top plate
5. Sill
6. Window sill
7. Stair stringer
8. Stair tread
9. Facia
10. Window header
11. Wood shakes
12. Building paper
13. Furring strips
14. Eave protection
15. Chimney flashing
16. Chimney
17. Insulation

18. Polyethylene vapor barrier
19. Rafter
20. Roof decking
21. Log gable end spline groove
22. Log gable end
23. Ridge pole
24. Purlin
25. Roof eave
26. Gable end top plate
27. Scribed log wall panel
28. Midpost
29. Post spline groove
30. Girder
31. Floor joist
32. Post anchor pins
33. Corner post
34. Tie beam

Figure 8-1. The parts of a post and beam building (with log infill).

post. The alternative is to individually fit each log between stationary posts—no easy feat, for a log is a tapered cylinder and inevitably a gap results between the post and in-fill log.

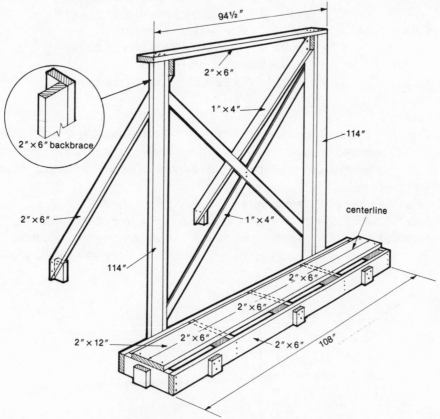

94½"

2"×6"

1"×4"

114"

2"×6" backbrace

2"×6"

1"×4"

centerline

2"×6"

114"

2"×6"

2"×12"

2"×6"

2"×6"

108"

Figure 8–2. Wall fabrication jig.

The wall panel jig is comprised of two pieces: a base and a back-brace. The base represents the building's subfloor; it must be level and securely staked to prevent any movement. It is wise to check its position with a builder's level from time to time. The back-brace serves to stabilize the wall as it is being built and also forms part of the plumb-cutting jib outlined in section **6,** below. If a "mini" mill such as the one described in Chapter 6, section **8** is used to plumb-cut the wall sections then the positioning of the back-brace is not as important. The jig described below is dimensioned for 8' (2440 mm) long wall panels, using logs with approximate 12" (300 mm) mid-diameter. It can be scaled for longer or shorter panels, or to suit your own log sizes.

Tools: Builder's level or water level, hammer, handsaw, tape measure, carpenter's square, chalkline, sledge hammer, axe, chain hoist (optional), pencil.

Materials:

Base: 2″ × 6″ × 13″ (38 × 140 × 330 mm) (5 pieces)
2″ × 6″ × 108″ (38 × 140 × 2743 mm) (2 pieces)
2″ × 12″ × 108″ (38 × 286 × 2743 mm) (1 piece)

Back-braces: 2″ × 6″ × 114″ (38 × 140 × 2895 mm) (6 pieces)
2″ × 6″ × 94½″ (38 × 140 × 2400 mm) (1 piece)
1″ × 4″ (19 × 89 mm) crossbracing

Stakes: 2″ × 4″ × 15″ (38 × 89 × 380 mm) (10 pieces)

Procedure:

1) Construct the base as shown in Figure 8–2. Ensure that the 2″ × 12″ (38 × 286 mm) is centered on the base frame and the chalked centerline is also centered. Accuracy here will pay off, especially if you plan to use a mini mill to plumb-cut the wall panel ends.
2) Level the base and stake securely.
3) Nail the back-braces to the base as shown in Figure 8–2. Accuracy can be disregarded if you plan to use a mini mill. Cross-brace and stake securely.
4) Build any number of these jigs, depending on how many wall panels you want to build simultaneously.

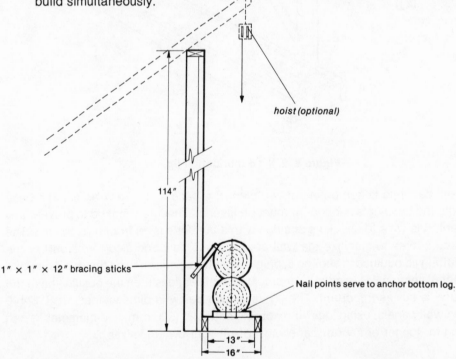

Figure 8–3. Side view of a jig with first and second wall log in place.

3. How to place and scribe a wall log.

Before the scribing and fitting of wall logs can begin, the first bottom log must be placed. Since this bottom log will sit on the subfloor it should have a 6″ (150 mm) ± flat surface. Make a chalked centerline on the underside of this log to align with the centerline on the jig base. This bottom log should be quite large so that it will slightly overhang the subfloor edge to provide a drip cap. (Where metal flashing is used this will not be necessary.) If an 8′ (2440 mm) finished wall panel is desired, the logs should be 9′ (2743 mm) long to allow for wastage.

After the bottom log is placed, additional logs will be scribed, one upon the other, to build the wall. The scribing procedure transfers the contours of the top surface of the log below onto the under surface of the log placed above it. The resulting two scribe lines will appear on the under surface of the top log in the form of a scratched line if using a scratch-type scriber, or a pencil line where a pencilled type scriber is used. The wood between these two lines is then removed to make the lateral groove, taking care not to cut away the scribe line. If the scriber is held level and the lateral groove has been cut properly, a tight fit joins the two logs together, entirely eliminating the need for exposed chinking material. It is always best to keep the scriber setting to a minimum, as accuracy is lost when the scriber setting is widened.

The wall logs will look much better if they are on the same parallel plane along the entire length of the building's wall. That is, if the second, fourth, sixth, and eighth log up from the bottom is set at the same height in all of the wall panels, this uniformity is more attractive than if these logs were at different heights on the various walls. To accomplish this, simply place reference marks on the back vertical braces of each jig at equal heights to correspond to each even numbered wall log. (See Figure 8–6.) Build up one wall panel and use it as an example for the height measurements.

As you build up the wall make sure that it does not become bowed. This can be done by marking a vertical plumb line on the log ends.

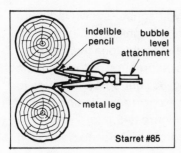

Pencil scriber

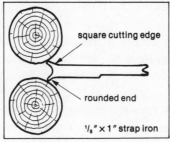

Scratch scriber

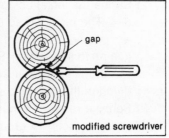

Finishing scriber, used to rescribe if any small gaps

Figure 8-4. Types of scribers.

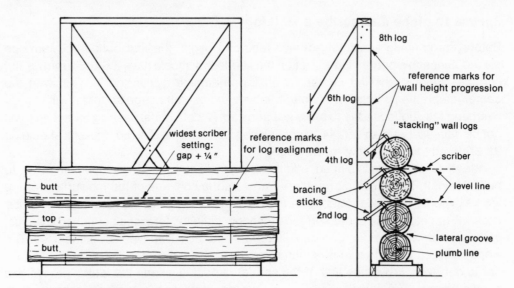

Figure 8-5. Constructing a log wall panel on a jig (front view).

Figure 8-6. Constructing a log wall panel on a jig (side view).

Tools: Scriber, tape measure, level, hammer, pencil.

Materials: Wall logs, nails.

Procedure:

1) Place the second log directly over the first so that it is aligned along the center of the wall, and brace-nail into the vertical back-brace supports. (See Figure 8–6.) Alternate butts and tops.

   Note: It is possible to "stack" up to two or three logs and then scribe them all at the same time.

2) Scribe the log(s) using either the pencil or scratch-type scriber shown in Figure 8–4. The modified screwdriver is only used to rescribe troublesome logs which are poorly fitted. Set the scriber to the widest gap between the logs then add ¼ " (6 mm) to this setting (Figure 8–5). Remove any knots beforehand so the log rests close to the log below. Scribe *both* sides of the log. A light spray of water to dampen the path of the indelible pencil produces an easily readable line.

3) Pencil a reference mark for easy realignment. (See Figure 8–5.)

4) Remove log(s) to ground skids and cut the lateral groove. Refer to section **4,** below.

5) Reposition the log(s) and check for fit. Adjust if necessary.

6) Brace-nail the log(s) to the back-brace and extend a plumb line up the log ends. (Figure 8–6.)

4. Cutting a lateral groove to fit the wall logs.

The lateral groove, when properly scribed and cut, allows for moisture to drain away, and provides a chinkless fit between wall log members to prevent wind and weather from entering and heat from escaping the building.

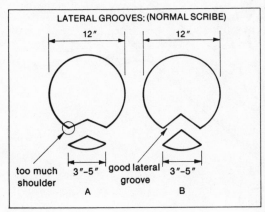 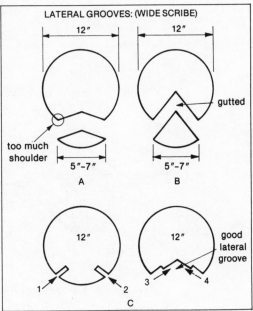

Figure 8-7. Lateral grooves for normal and wide scribes.

Tools: Eye and ear protection, chainsaw, indelible pencil, axe.

Procedure:
1) Turn the log upright and pencil clearly over any lightly scribed lines. Also pencil the desired angle of cut (whether a normal or wide scribe) on the log end. (See Figure 8-7.)
2) Position and wedge or dog the log so the saw blade enters at the proper angle and depth.
3) Keeping the blade $\frac{1}{8}$″ – $\frac{1}{4}$″ (3–6 mm) inside the line, cut down the length of the log. Repeat for the opposite scribe line and remove the waste wood.
4) Using an axe, pare with the grain down to the scribe line. *Do not remove scribe line.* The finished lateral groove cut should resemble the "good" grooves shown in Figure 8-7.

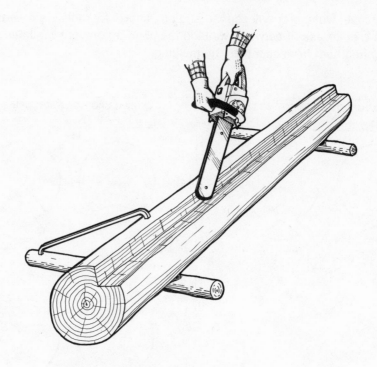

Figure 8-8. Finished lateral groove on a wall log.

Lateral cut: Normal Scribe
- Shouldered: The log will not fit properly. Too much inner shoulder rather than edge is riding on the lower log.
- Good scribe width and depth. Strong edges with good bearing.

Lateral cut: Wide Scribe
- Shouldered: same as above.
- Gutted: Too much wood removed causing excessive checking and weak edges.
- Good procedure for a wide scribe, with sharp, strong edges yet not gutted.

Hints for cutting the lateral groove.
1. When you cut the lateral groove walk backwards pulling the saw as you go. It is wise to clean your pathway of debris.
2. Dry logs splinter a lot. Cut further from the line if this happens.
3. On a curvy scribe line, lifting the bar and working more with the nose does a better job.

5. Leveling the walls.

A log is a tapered cylinder. By alternating butts and tops on each course much of the leveling problem will be taken care of. However, it will be necessary to take accurate readings and make appropriate adjustments, so that the wall comes up level, especially when approaching the top. Level readings can only be taken on even numbered courses, there being equal numbers of tops and butts at each wall end.

Wall construction progresses rapidly up to about the sixth course, after which it becomes increasingly difficult to lift the logs. To overcome this problem, included in this procedure is a simple method for separating the wall into two sections, using the sixth log as the starter log for the top section.

Tools: Tape measure, level, scriber, pencil, wooden wedges, hammer.

Procedure:
1) Position and align the sixth log on the wall, and brace it securely to the vertical supports. Note that you can only check for level when there is an ''even'' number of logs in the wall.
2) Place a level on each end of the wall (Figure 8–9A) and measure the distance down to the jig base. Then note the difference between the two ends of the wall.
3) If there is only 1″–2″ (25–50 mm) difference, block the low end up so the log sits level and scribe the log. Then remove the log to cut the lateral groove.
4) If there is more than 2″ (50 mm) difference, replace this log with one that is more suitable, bringing the wall near level. Then block the low end and scribe the log in place. *Do not readjust or move the log while scribing.*
5) Once the sixth log has been fitted into place on the wall, remove it and position it on a second jig, as shown in Figure 8–9B. Match the center plumb-lines on the ends of this sixth log with the centerline on the jig base.
6) Since the entire length of the top surface of this sixth log was an equal distance from the jig base prior to its removal, it should be blocked so that its top surface is again on a level plane with that of the base. (See Figure 8–9B.) Using a level, plumb the log ends so they are vertical and in alignment with the jig base centerline.
7) Nail-brace this sixth log securely to the back-brace supports and complete the wall. The wall height will be 1″ (25 mm) lower than the post length. In the examples used here, the posts are 8′ (2438 mm) long, thus the wall panel will be 7′11″ (2413 mm). The top log of this wall will require flat-surfacing and minor preparation. It is easier to accomplish this at this stage rather than when the walls are in place. Refer to section **17** or **18,** below, for details, depending on the type of top plate chosen.
8) Replace this top wall section to its lower portion in preparation for plumb-cutting the ends.

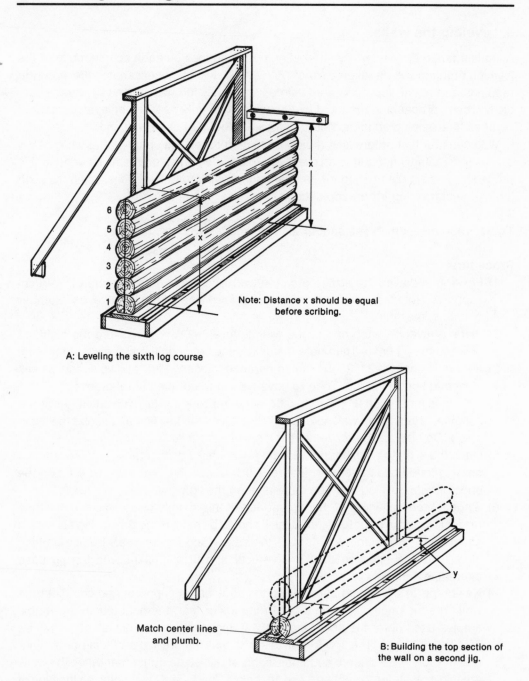

Note: Distance x should be equal before scribing.

A: Leveling the sixth log course

Match center lines and plumb.

B: Building the top section of the wall on a second jig.

Figure 8-9. Leveling the log wall and constructing it in two sections.

6. How to plumb-cut a wall panel using a jig.

This procedure outlines how to use a jig to cut the ends of the wall panel so they are perfectly straight and vertical. This jig is simply an upright version of the post and rail mill shown in Chapter 6. Should the builder wish, the mini mill illustrated in section **8** of the same chapter also works well for plumb-cutting, and has the advantage of being more portable. Whichever device is chosen, a guide of some sort is necessary to make an accurate vertical cut. It is also equally important to have the cutting chain of the chainsaw filed correctly to avoid a "wandering" cut.

Tools: Eye and ear protection, chainsaw with 26″ (660 mm) bar and chisel chain, bar pads, hammer, 4′ (1220 mm) level, tape measure.

Materials: *Jig.*
2″ × 6″ × 114″ (38 × 140 × 2895 mm) (2 pieces)
2″ × 6″ × 94½″ (38 × 140 × 2400 mm) (1 piece)
2″ × 4″ × 19″ (38 × 89 × 482 mm) (2 pieces)
1″ × 4″ (19 × 89 mm) bracing
nails

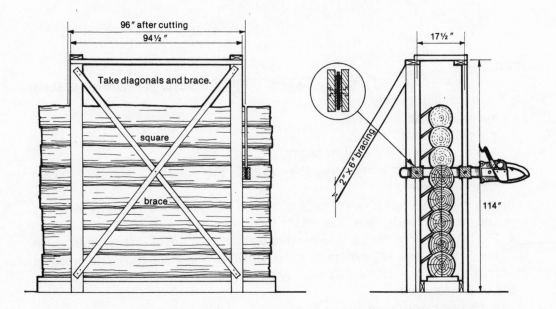

Figure 8–10. Plumb-cutting a wall panel.

Figure 8–11. Plumb-cutting a wall panel. (side view.)

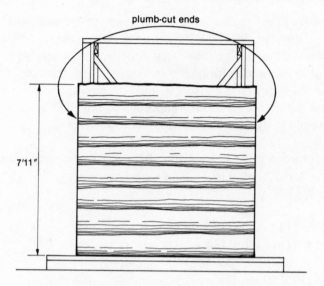

Figure 8–12. Log wall infill panel with plumb-cut ends, ready for spline-grooving.

Procedure:

1) Erect the 2″ × 6″ (38 × 140 mm) plumb-cut jig according to Figure 8–10. Make sure that the uprights are:
   - parallel to each other
   - exactly plumb
   - braced securely to prevent flexing.
2) Fit a sharp, properly filed chisel chain to a 26″ (660 mm) bar. Improper filing will cause a curved cut.
3) Attach ¾″ (19 mm) plywood pads to the bar. Carriage bolts should be recessed into the wood pads. (See Figure 8–11 for correct pad placement.)
4) Start the cut from the top, making sure that the pads are always in contact with the 2″ × 6″ (38 × 140 mm) rails. Have someone else place moderate pressure holding pads against the rails by using two sticks.
5) Complete the cut.
   If the saw starts to cut crookedly STOP!
   Turn the saw upside down, cutting with the back of the bar, and the cut will correct itself. If the cut does not correct itself, move the guide rails back 3″ (75 mm) and cut again. Add 3″ (75 mm) to the opposite end.

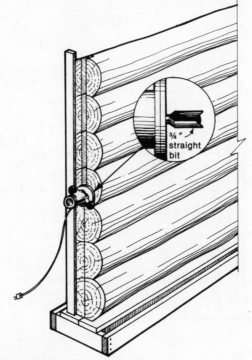

Figure 8-13. Routing a spline groove in the log wall panel.

7. How to spline-groove a wall section.

The aim is to produce a straight, uniform groove in the wall panel to match a similar groove in the post, so that a spline can be used to key the wall panel to the vertical post. This method replaces the laborious tenon and groove method. The directions for this task describe the groove being made with a router. Less strain is placed on the router if relief cuts are made with a circular saw or chainsaw.

Tools: Router, eye and ear protection, ¾ ″ (19 mm) straight bit, level, hammer, circular saw or chainsaw.

Materials: 1 ″ × 4 ″ (19 × 89 mm) straightedge, nails.

Procedure:
1) Fasten a ¾ ″ (19 mm) straight bit to a router.
2) Nail a straight length of 1 ″ × 4 ″ (19 × 89 mm) against the outer edge of the log ends. *Make sure it's plumb.* This will serve as a guide to rout a groove down the center of the log ends.
3) Make relief cut(s) with a chainsaw or circular saw.
4) Make two passes with the router, extending the bit each time to get the 1 ⁵/₈ ″ (41 mm) maximum depth. (See Figure 8-13.)

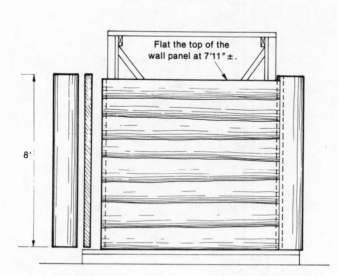

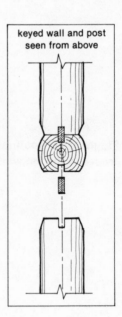

keyed wall and post
seen from above

Flat the top of the
wall panel at 7'11" ±.

8'

Figure 8–14. Wall panel and posts, grooved and keyed together with a spline.

5) Repeat for the opposite end of the wall. Figure 8–14 and its inset shows a keyed wall and post.

   Note: This groove will accommodate a ¾ " × 3 " (19 × 75 mm) marine plywood key strip which has a great deal of shear strength. Due to the tight fit against the post no other materials are necessary. However, if a 2 " × 2 " (38 × 38 mm) spline is desired, simply move the guide over to accommodate the extra width. As any other replacement spline material must be resistant to shear stress, use such woods as a clear grain Douglas fir or a laminate material.

6) Number the individual logs in each panel before disassembly. The post need not be connected to the wall panel at this time.

   Note: Placing the top plate onto the walls requires a certain amount of advance preparation on the wall panels. It is easier to do this work while the wall is still in its construction jig by making the necessary measurements, removing the top log, and then making the necessary cuts. Refer to section **17** or **18,** below, for the type of top plate provisional work.

8. Two ways to store and ship intact log wall panels.

The metal clamping devices described below allow the removal of the entire wall from its construction jig in one complete unit. This permits the walls to be stored indefinitely, ready for shipment, without danger of the individual logs twisting. Such a procedure would be very advantageous for the person wishing to build in stages, as he or she can afford it, for those wishing to get a head start for the spring by constructing the walls during the winter, and for the contractor needing to ship to a distant client.

Included here are two slightly different options for this metal clamping device. The first requires disassembly of the wall logs for insulating, then predrilling for wiring and pinning. This option is sufficient if there will be no lifting device available at the foundation site and the logs will have to be individually placed piece by piece.

The second option involves some minor changes to the hardward and the wall panel itself, but the time saved in wall erection is tremendous. With these alterations it is possible to completely finish the wall panel to include insulation and predrilled holes for wiring and pinning, then to ship, and finally place each of these panels on the building's subfloor.

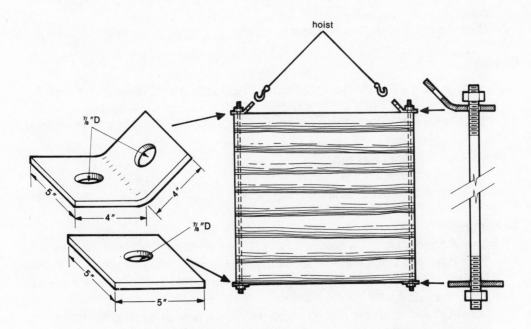

Figure 8-15. Metal clamping devices to facilitate storage and shipping of completed wall panels.

Option A:

Materials: ³/₈″ × 5″ × 5″ (9 × 125 × 125 mm) HRMS plate iron (2 pieces)

³/₈″ × 5″ × 8″ (9 × 125 × 200 mm) HRMS plate iron (2 pieces)

¾″ × 8′6″ (19 × 2590 mm) CRMS bar (2 pieces) threaded 8″ (200 mm) at each end

¾″ (19 mm) washers (4)

¾″ (19 mm) nuts (4)

Procedure:

1) Fit the threaded rod into the routered groove at each end of the log wall.

2) Slip the two 5″ (125 mm) square pieces of plate iron under each end of the wall so that the threaded rod passes through a hole in the plate iron. Then attach a washer and nut. (See Figure 8–15.) Alterations will have to be made to the jig base in order to fit the metal plate iron in position.

3) Slip the remaining pieces of plate iron over the threaded rod at the top of the wall. Place a washer, and cinch down with a nut.

4) To remove, slip a hook into each eye at the top and winch clear of ground. A trolley, overhead crane, or derrick truck will be required to move the wall unit for storage.

Note: As the wall shrinks, cinch nuts down.

Option B:

Materials: ³/₈″ × 5 × 5″ (9 × 125 × 125 mm) HRMS plate iron (2 pieces)

³/₈″ × 5″ × 8″ (9 × 125 × 200 mm) HRMS plate iron (2 pieces)

½″ × 8′6″ (12 × 2590 mm) CRMS bar (2 pieces) threaded 8″ (200 mm) at each end

½″ (12 mm) washers (4)

½″ (12 mm) nuts (4)

Rented metal banding maching (optional)

Procedure:

1) On the bottom log cut a groove 1½″ (38 mm) deep by 5½″ (140 mm) wide by 5½″ (140 mm) long on the under side. (See Figure 8–16.) This groove is necessary to recess the plate and nut of the bar clamp, so that it will not prevent the wall panel from sitting flat on the subfloor.

2) Construct and finish the wall on its jig, insulating, predrilling for electrical wiring, and pinning each log as you work. (Refer to sections **14** and **15,** below, for insulation and pinning.)

3) Plumb-cut the wall ends as previously mentioned and rout the spline groove. Though it is possible to use this groove for the threaded bar, it is better to deepen

the groove another ¾ " (19 mm) and recess the ½ " (12 mm) bar into this further groove. In this manner the wall can be firmly joined to the post before the bar is removed.

4) To remove the wall from the jig insert the bar clamps and, as an additional precaution, band the wall at its midsection. Use the same metal bands as those used for banding lifts of lumber or cedar shingles together. The entire machine can be rented or purchased from a tool distributor.

5) Refer to section **16,** below, for assembly instructions for the finished wall panels onto a subfloor.

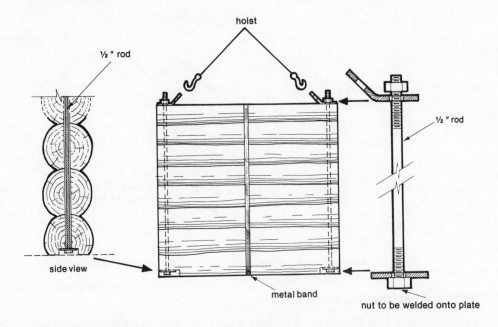

hoist

½ " rod

½ " rod

side view

metal band

nut to be welded onto plate

Figure 8-16. Finished wall panel ready for storage, shipping, and assembly on building's subfloor.

9. Constructing mid and corner posts.

The posts, like the wall panels, can be milled and stored ahead of the actual building assembly. They should however, be stored in a manner which will minimize twisting or warpage. For this reason it is best to use dry, straight grained log material. The posts for a building will all be the same length, unless they are to include tenons. (See tenon layout and cutting, Chapter 10, section **1.**)

Tools: Tape measure, level, square, pencil, hammer, and nails.

Procedure:

1) Select straight grained, sound logs, and dry, if possible.
2) Flat-side the logs using one of the mills described above, and remove equal waste from each side of the log. *All posts must be milled to the same thickness* (i.e., 9", or 228 mm). Accuracy is essential. Posts with uneven flat surfaces will lead to gaps between the posts and log infill panels.
3) To obtain a corner post, mill a flat side, then rotate 90° and mill this surface. (See Figure 8–17.) Check the right angle with a carpenter's square.
4) If a mortise and tenon joint is intended at the sill and top plate, allow for the increase in post length.

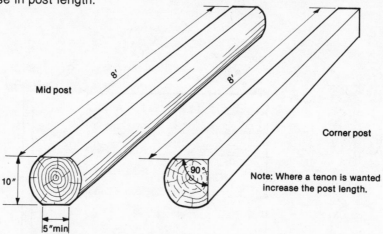

Figure 8–17. Mid and corner posts ready for spline grooving.

10. How to spline-groove a post.

To spline-groove a post is to rout a groove down the midline of the post. When matched to the wall panel's groove a spline can be inserted to key the two together. This method replaces the tenon and slot method. An alternative method for cutting a groove is shown in Chapter 10, section **1,** above.

Tools: Eye protection, router, ¾" (19 mm) straight bit, chalkline, tape measure, hammer, chainsaw or circular saw.

Materials: 1" × 4" (19 × 89 mm) straightedge, nails.

Procedure:

1) Measure the log diameter and find the center at each end of the log. (See Figure 8–18.)
2) Chalk a line joining these points.

3) Offset a 1″ × 4″ (19 × 89 mm) straightedge to one side of this line, the distance of the router base radius. Be sure it is parallel to the centerline. This will act as a guide to rout a groove down the center of the log.
4) Make relief cut(s) using a chainsaw or circular saw.
5) Make two passes with the router, extending the bit the second time to the 1 5/8″ (41 mm) maximum depth.
6) Repeat this procedure for all posts. See Figure 8–18 for a top view of a corner post with the log wall panels keyed in place.

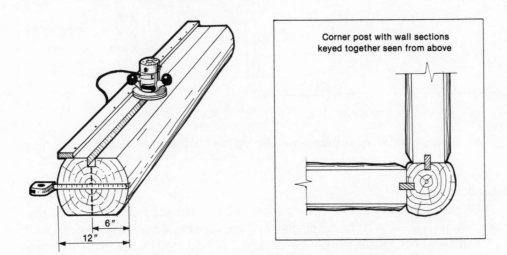

Figure 8–18. Routing a spline groove in a post.

11. How to place the prefabricated log wall on the subfloor.

It is very important that the log sill, or subfloor, on which the log wall will sit is level and even. Distortions in the subfloor can cause imprecisions in the joinery between posts and wall panels. A frame subfloor is recommended for this reason, and also because of the simplicity of joining the posts to this floor system. Where a frame subfloor is used, remember to provide additional support blocking under the posts.

The information given here and in sections **12** and **13** describes assembly of individual wall pieces. For information on placing the completely finished wall panels onto a subfloor refer to section **16,** below.

Tools: Tape measure, chalkline, 4′ (1220 mm) level, come-along, hammer, 3 lb (1.5 kg) sledge and drift pin.

Materials: Posts and wall logs, 2″ × 6″ (38 × 140 mm) bracing, nails, spikes, rope.

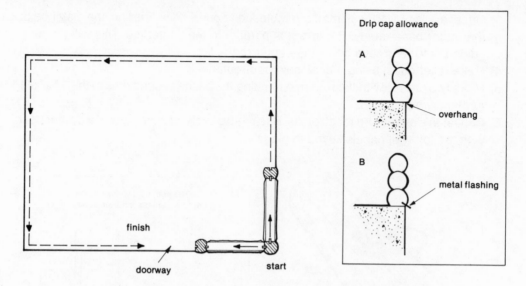

Figure 8-19. Work sequence for placing the fabricated walls and posts.

Procedure:

1) Chalk a centerline at the building's perimeter to correspond with the wall panel midline. Square off by taking diagonals. If the log work is planned to provide a drip-cap allowance, offset this centerline 1″–2″ (25–50 mm) closer to the foundation edge. (See Figure 8–19.)

2) Erect and firmly brace a corner post that is nearest a doorway. (Refer to section **12** for methods of attaching a corner post to a log sill.) Work simultaneously toward the door and around the building, aligning the routered grooves on the centerline. A post is followed by a panel of horizontal filler logs, another post, then another panel, and so on around the building, until the door is reached again. The wall logs will be drilled for electrical wiring, insulated, and pinned during this assembly procedure.
Note: Until the final top plate is in place, it is important to firmly brace the walls. (See Figure 8–20.)

3) Large windows, like doors, are usually placed between posts. Consult the procedures for top plate placement, section **17,** below, and openings, in Chapter 12, before actual assembly of the walls.

4) The last log wall panel before reaching the door should be left with only one end plumb cut. Then, before placing the last door post, the panel can be custom cut to the correct length to adjust for any discrepancies that have arisen. Alternatively, the door opening can purposely be left wider than the required width, allowing the doorway to be framed in later.

5) When assembling a wall panel to sit tight against a post, be careful not to knock the post out of plumb.

6) Mid-posts should be tight against the wall panel, then two holes can be drilled into the base of the post with spikes embedded through the post and into the sill. This works well to snug the post base to the log infill panel.

7) To keep the assembled walls from spreading apart at the top, a temporary 2″ × 6″ (38 × 140 mm) tie should span and nail to each post, as shown in Figure 8–20.

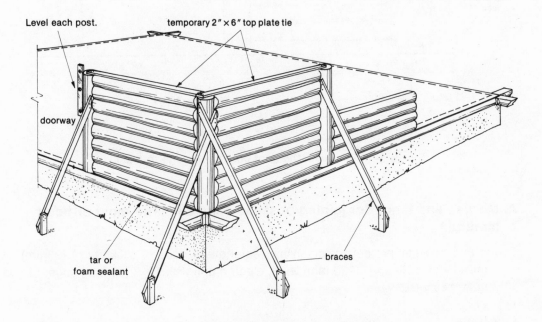

Figure 8-20. Wall assembly.

12. Three methods for joining posts to a log sill.

Joining posts to a frame subfloor is simply a matter of drilling up from under the floor into the post base and firmly screwing in lag screws. The posts can be joined to the log sill in a number of ways. A few methods with varying degrees of difficulty are described below. If the bottom horizontal infill log in each wall panel is drilled and lag screwed or spiked to the sill log or subfloor, there is no need to fasten mid-posts as well, as they will be secured from any sideways slippage by the keyed splines. While each of these methods will adequately anchor the posts to the floor, the first is for the builder who wishes to use only traditional methods, and the third is especially suited to those who prefer the simplest approach.

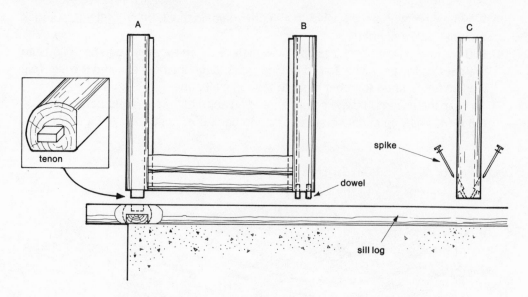

Figure 8–21. Three methods of post anchorage to a sill.

A. Mortise and tenon for joining posts to a log sill. (The most difficult method.)

Tools: Eye and ear protection, chainsaw, carpenter's square, slick, 1½ ″ (38mm) chisel and mallet, 4′ (1220 mm) level, electric drill with 1¾ ″ (45 mm) auger bit, tape measure.

Procedure:

1) Cut all the posts to length, measuring from sill log to plate log plus a 4 ″ (100 mm) tenon. If a similar joint is intended for the top plate include the additional tenon length as well. (See Chapter 10, section **1.**)
2) Lay out all tenons using the 2 ″ (50 mm) wide body of a crapenter's square as a template and the centerline of the post. (See Chapter 10, section **1.**)
3) Cut the tenon and chamfer all edges and corners.
4) Lay out only the first corner mortise. The other mortises will be laid out as the wall panels and posts are positioned on the building.
5) Cut the mortise to fit the dimensions of the tenon, using the drill and bit and cleaning with the chisel. Alternatively, construct a modified electrical box cavity jig as described in Chapter 14.
6) Apply a waterproof tar coat to tenon and mortise to prevent any air leaks and possible dry rot conditions caused by condensation.
7) Position, plumb, and brace the post securely.

B. Doweling for joining posts to a log sill. (Easier than method A.)

Tools: Electric drill with ⅝″ (16 mm) bit, tape measure, hacksaw, file, 3 lb (1.5 kg) hammer, 4′ (1220 mm) level.

Materials: ⅝″ (16 mm) CRMS round bar.

Procedure:
1) Cut all posts to length, measuring from sill to plate.
2) Bore two ⅝″ (16 mm) holes 3″ (75 mm) into the bottom of the posts.
3) Insert two pointed ⅝″ × 3½″ (16 × 89 mm) steel pins into the holes, so the points protrude.
4) Place post in final position and hammer down on the top of it. The pins will indicate the drilling spots on the sill log.
5) Drill two ⅝″ × 3″ (16 × 75 mm) holes into the sill log, using the indicated marks as guides.
6) Insert two 5½″ (140 mm) lengths of CRMS round bar into the post holes.
7) Apply a tar coat to underside of post.
8) Position, plumb, and brace the post securely.

C. Joining posts to a log sill with spikes. (The easiest method.)

Tools: Electric drill with ½″ (12 mm) and ¾″ (19 mm) bits, 3 lb (1.5. kg) hammer, drift pin, tape measure, 4′ (1220 mm) level.

Materials: 12″ (300 mm) spikes, ½″ (12 mm) washers, waterproof glue, ¾″ (19 mm) wood dowel.

Procedure:
1) Apply a coat of tar to underside of the post.
2) Position, plumb, and brace post securely.
3) Drill two ¾″ (19 mm) countersink holes two inches (50 mm) diagonally into the post base.
4) Change bits and bore a ½″ (12 mm) hole into each of the countersunk holes diagonally through the post base, *but not into the sill log.*
5) Secure the post to the sill by driving a spike with a washer into each hole, embedding it into the sill log. Countersink the head, using the drift pin.
6) Plug the hole, using a wooden dowel and glue.

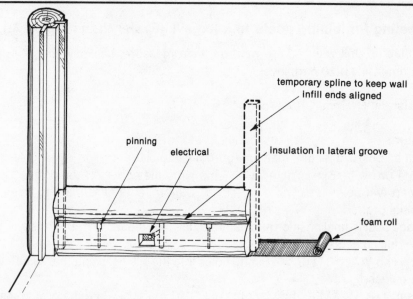

Figure 8-22. Placement of prefabricated walls on the building's subfloor.

13. How to join infill logs to posts.

With the first corner post nearest to a door positioned, plumbed, and braced, the assembly of plumb-cut infill pieces can proceed. Insulating the lateral grooves of the infill logs, pinning the logs, pre-drilling for electrical wiring, and cutting of window headers will all be done as the numbered wall logs are placed. Detailed instructions for these steps will follow below. (See Chapter 8, sections **14** and **15;** Chapter 14, sections **1** and **2;** and Chapter 12, section **3.**

Tools: Electric drill with ⅝″ (16 mm) extended auger bit, hammer, 4′ (1220 mm) level, sledge hammer, drift pin, come-along, lumberman's crayon.

Materials: ¾″ × 3″ × 8′ (19 × 75 × 2440 mm) plywood key strips cut from standard 4′ × 8′ (1200 × 2400 mm) plywood, 12″ (300 mm) spikes with washers, ½″ (12 mm) nylon rope, lag screws, tar or foam roll. Foam roll serves as an air and moisture seal in the same way as tar, and can be purchased at any lumber store.

Procedure:
1) Fit the plywood key strips into the groove of the posts. Infill logs are then free to slide down the keyed spline strips during settling.
2) Apply a coat of tar or a layer of foam roll to the underside of the first flat-surfaced infill log, and snug up against post. The spline will fit into the spline groove of the infill log.

3) Drill a ⅝″ (16 mm) hole through the bottom log, then lag screw this first log to the subfloor. The holes will be covered by the lateral groove of the following log. It may be easier to lag screw from under the subfloor. (See Figure 8–22.)

4) Predrill for electrical wiring where appropriate. (See Chapter 14, sections **1** to **2.**)

5) Place the next filler log, and snug it up against the post, and then check for fit. The ends should be flush. To keep these ends in alignment fit a temporary spline into the grooves of the infill panel. (See Figure 8–22.)

6) Lift the free end of the infill log and insulate the lateral groove. (See section **14,** below.)

7) Reposition the log and pin it securely (see section **15,** below), mark lightly with a crayon to indicate where pins are. *Do not pin where a window will be placed.* Most large windows, however, will be flanked by posts. (See Chapter 12.)

8) Continue placing the infill logs. Check periodically to make sure the post is not knocked out-of-plumb. See Figure 8–22.

9) Continue to construct the wall to top plate height. Place another post, then another wall infill panel and so on until the building walls are erected. Remember to number all the infill logs. This is done so that they do not get misplaced in the wall, since once the wall logs are dismantled from the construction jig they can easily be mixed up.

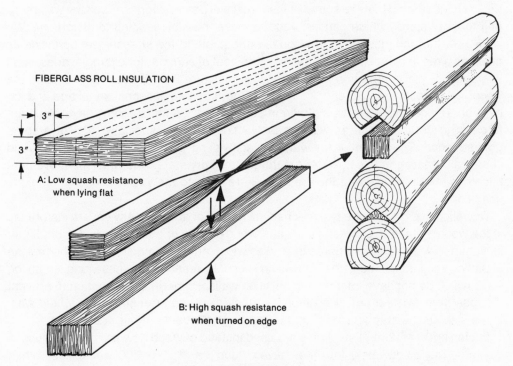

Figure 8-23. Insulating the lateral groove.

14. Insulating the lateral groove.

Although the insulation in the lateral groove is not visible, it plays an important thermal role and care must be taken to ensure that it fills the entire groove. Substances as complex as polyurethane foam (injected), and as basic as moss have been used for insulation. However, as the most commonly used material is fiberglass, this is the material that is discussed below.

Tools: Sharp, long-bladed knife.

Materials: 3″ (75 mm) thick fiberglass batts.

Procedure:
1) Cut the batts into 3″ (75 mm) ± strips (depending on the average depth of the lateral grooves).
2) Check the fit of the log and then raise it a couple of inches, using a block of wood.
3) Place the insulation into the groove by hand. As shown in Figure 8–23B, in order to fill the groove completely turn the batt on edge.

15. How to dowel or pin a wall log.

When Hölderlin said that the spirits of the forest were still at work in wood, he was referring to that "spirit" which causes wood to move, possibly leading to distortions. We know now that the movement in wood is attributable to the stresses set up inside its fibers as a result of moisture fluctuations. The heat of summer for example, dries wood fibers, causing a contraction in tension while moisture from the fall rains expand the wood fibers, relieving this tension. We view the result as seasonal shrinkage and expansion. Depending upon the log's grain pattern, tension can become severe enough to cause distortions such as warping or twisting. This is especially true for a spiral grained wood. The potential for warpage or twisting is at its greatest as the wood changes from its green (i.e., water saturated) to its dry state. After this, the movement becomes less intensive and then minimal in relation to the yearly seasonal humidity conditions.

Doweling and pinning are two mechanical means of arresting any severe distortions in the wood members. Doweling uses hardwood dowels or pegs (usually 1″, or 25 mm in diameter) which are hammered into holes which have been drilled down the midline of the log and into the log below. Doweling is usually reserved for those long length log walls which do not have intersecting partition walls. Primarily they function to prevent the logs from twisting out of position, but they also add strength to the whole wall. Dowels should be staggered (i.e., not aligned one above the other in the wall).

In pinning ½″ (12 mm) steel pins are used instead of wood dowels. They function in the same way as dowels unless they have a head (i.e., 12″, or 300 mm spikes). When enlarged with a washer, the head of the spike serves to create downward pressure, effectively pressing the pinned log into the log below. This is advantageous for log infill as

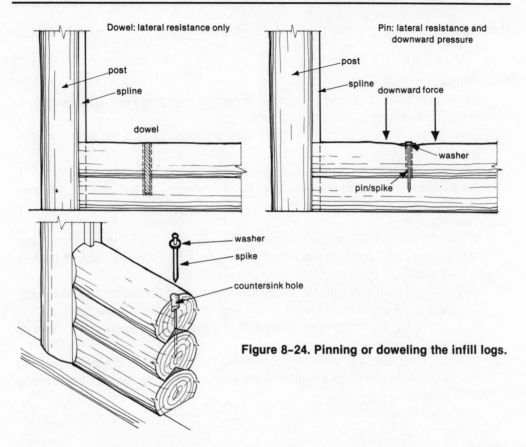

Figure 8-24. Pinning or doweling the infill logs.

the shorter, lighter logs often "float" due to the fiberglass insulation within the lateral groove. Thus spike pins, while preventing any twisting, will also produce a tighter fit between log wall members than will dowels.

The builder should be warned, however, that unless spike pins are correctly installed, disastrous problems can result. Merely spiking one log to another without careful pre-drilling will eventually cause gaps to appear between the logs when they have completed their drying process. It is essential, therefore, to drill a slightly oversize hole completely through a log which is to be pinned. After this is done, insert the spike and washer, then sledge hammer the spike firmly into the log below. The spike head and washer will compress the wood of the top log (see Figure 8-24) which will produce the downward pressure. In this manner the pinned log is not rigidly bound by the spike shaft, but is free to undergo its seasonal expansion and contraction while still being firmly pinned. A similar procedure is used in cabinetmaking, when two pieces of wood are fastened together with screws rather than spikes.

Tools: Electric drill with 5/8" (16 mm) ships auger bit (for pins), 1" (25 mm) hand auger (for dowels), tape measure, 3 lb (1.5 kg) sledge hammer, drift pin.

Materials: 12″–14″ (300–350 mm) spikes with washers *or* 1″ (25 mm) hardwood doweling.

Procedures:

1) Identify all the logs where openings will be situated, and keep well away from these spots when positioning steel pins.
2) Pinning/doweling is to be done as each log is insulated and placed in its final position in the wall.
3) Pins/dowels should be placed on the midline of the log spaced approximately 5′ (1.5 m) apart so that the lateral groove of the following log will conceal the hole. (See Figure 8–24.)
4) *Doweling a log*
   Drill a 1″ (25 mm) hole completely through the log and half way into the lower log. Then hammer the dowel in place and cut it flush with the top surface of the log.
5) *Pinning a log*
   Drill a ⅝″ (16 mm) hole completely through the top log *but not into the lower log.* Countersink the spike head, where necessary. Then drop the spike (with washer) through the top log and sledge hammer it into the log below, pressing the head into the log surface.
6) Continue the process of insulating, predrilling, and pinning or doweling each log until all the walls and posts are up. When this has been done the top plate is ready to be placed.

16. Erecting finished wall panels on the subfloor.

When the wall panels are constructed and finished on the building site, there is not much more work involved in placing them onto a foundation subfloor. But as there is crane and truck time involved here it is most important to be as thoroughly prepared as possible. You will need at least five people: one to handle the wall sections on the truck and four to handle the wall sections on the subfloor. With all the tools and materials on hand, a 1200 sq. foot (112 sq. meter) house—including walls and roof members—can be easily erected within a day. The clamping mechanism for such a unit assembly is described in section **8,** above. (See Figures 8–15 and 8–16.)

Tools: Sledge hammer, crescent wrench, hammer, 4′ (1220 mm) level, tape measure, chalkline, electric drill with ½″ (12 mm), ¾″ (19 mm), 1″ (25 mm) auger bits, come-along, rope.

Materials: Roofing tar or foam roll, 2″ × 6″ (38 × 140 mm) bracing, nails, 12″ (300 mm) spikes with washers, 6″ (150 mm) lag screws, lumberman's crayon.

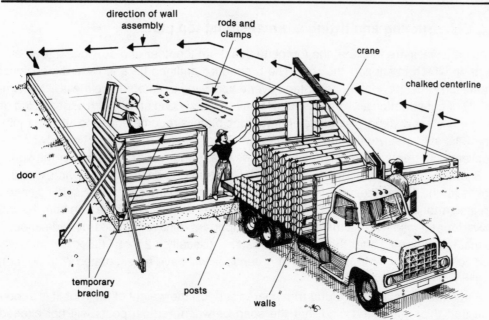

direction of wall assembly

rods and clamps

crane

chalked centerline

door

temporary bracing

posts

walls

Figure 8-25. Transporting and assembling finished wall panels onto a subfloor.

Procedure:

1) Label all the wall panel and post pieces and keep a written record of their assembly sequence on the foundation subfloor.

2) Start by positioning and bracing the corner post closest to a doorway. Apply a tar layer to its bottom and fasten it to the subfloor using one of the methods previously prescribed.

3) Chalk a centerline around the perimeter of the subfloor.

4) Place the wall panel so its spline groove mates with the spline of the post. Make sure that there is a tar barrier between the wall and the subfloor; that any electrical access hole on the wall panel has been marked on the subfloor; and that the wall is aligned on the chalked centerline, and is plumb and well braced.

5) Fasten the wall panel to the subfloor by lag screwing it to the floor from underneath. Another alternative is to fasten only the post to the subfloor. It makes no difference which of these methods is used as long as there is some anchorage of the walls to the floor.

6) Remove the bar clamps. (See Figure 8-16, above.)

7) Position, plumb, and secure the next post so that its spline mates with the panel groove.

8) Attach a temporary brace across the tops of the posts, as shown in Figure 8-25.

9) Repeat this procedure until all the walls are up.

10) When this has been done, place the top plate and roof members. (See sections **17** and **18,** below.)

17. Constructing and fitting a dimensional top plate.

Once the walls are in place, the top plate ties them together and provides a level surface on which to support the roof. The procedure outlined here is for a dimensional frame top plate. Its primary advantage over a heavy log or timber top plate is in the simplicity of construction and placement. However, if a second storey with exposed log or timber joists is desired, a solid log or timber top plate is recommended to allow for joinery while still retaining the top plate strength. This type of top plate particularly suits a conventional frame roof system as it provides flat surfaces for truss and soffit work.

Basically, this top plate uses structural frame trim boards which sandwich, and are bolted to, the posts. The top infill wall log is recessed into the cavity. The settling space created after shrinkage of the horizontal filler logs is concealed by the trim boards, and a weather-tight seal is still maintained. It is important to have trim boards wide enough to maintain this seal after the walls have settled. (Usually a 2″ × 8″ (38 × 184 mm) will suffice.) An 8′ (2440 mm) wall built of green logs will have an estimated 4″ (100 mm) settling.

Since the posts and structural trim boards support the weight of the roof, it is important that they are sound, and that the span between vertical posts will not exceed building code specifications. A span of 8′ (2440 mm) between posts is recommended.

Tools: Eye and ear protection, chainsaw, chalkline, tape measure, hammer, handsaw, drill with ⅝″ (16 mm) auger bit.

Materials: 2″ × 8″ (38 × 184 mm) and 2″ × 12″ (38 × 286 mm) rough fir, ⅝″ (16 mm) lag bolts, glue, insulation, nails.

Procedure:

1) All the posts should be at a level height from the floor (e.g., 8′, or 2440 mm).
2) The height of all the wall panels should be 1″ (25 mm) lower than the top of the posts, with the top log pinned to the log below.
3) Square off and chalk a line along the center top of the log walls. It should strike the top center of each post as well. (See Figure 8–26A.)
4) Chalk a parallel line 4″ (100 mm) on either side of this center line, leaving a space of 8″ (200 mm) between the inner and outer lines. If your logs are not very large, 6″ (150 mm) will suffice, however make similar adjustments to the top plate in that case.
5) Using the inside and outside lines as guides, cut a ledge equal to the trim board depth around the inside and outside walls of the building.
   Note: These lines can be marked out and the ledge cut while the wall panel is still in its construction jig.

6) Lag screw the structural trim boards to the posts on both inside and outside of the building. *Do not attach the trim boards to the filler logs,* as this will prevent their settling.

7) Run a bead of glue along the top surface of the filler logs, then place an 8″ (200 mm) strip of insulation in the space, then run a bead of glue on the underside of 2″ × 12″ (38 × 286 mm) top plate and nail this plate to the trim boards. As the filler logs settle, the insulation will be pulled down to fill the void.

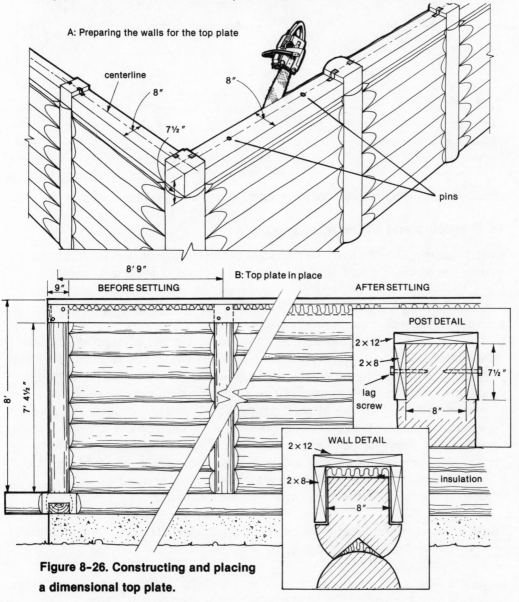

Figure 8-26. Constructing and placing a dimensional top plate.

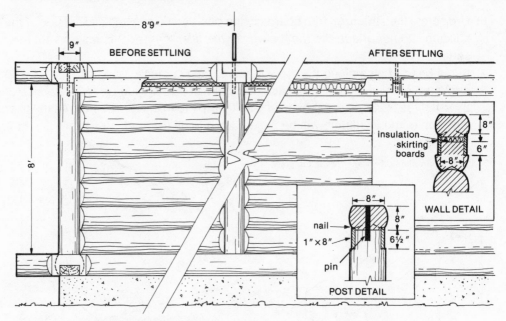

Figure 8-27. Constructing a log or timber top plate.

18. Preparing and fitting a log top plate.

A log top plate is used for houses which have second storey log floor joists, and where cantilevered strength is needed. The integration of notched corners in Chapter 9, section **9,** requires a log top plate for just this reason. The problems associated with handling a long, heavy log can be overcome by splicing shorter lengths together. However, such splices must be made over a post.

The log top plate will bear directly on the vertical posts and will support a portion of the weight of the roof between the post span. The infill wall logs do not support any roof weight but are free to settle on their own. Because this top plate is a structural beam it must conform in size to the amount of roof weight it supports over a given span.

Consider a 32' × 40' (9.75 × 12 m) building, and with a 4/12 roof pitch, with only one ridge pole roof support, built in an area subject to 40 lbs per sq. foot snow load. According to the information for calculating beam sizes in Appendix III, the minimum size of the top plate needed for an 8' (2440 mm) span between posts would be 6" × 6" (150 × 150 mm) or a 4" × 8" (100 × 200 mm). We would, however, be using a large log so as to match the infill logs and post sizes. (See Figure 8–27.)

Tools: Eye and ear protection, chainsaw, tape measure, chalkline, electric drill with ⁵/₈" (16 mm) auger bit, handsaw, hammer.

Materials: Plate logs flat-surfaced on two sides to 8" (200 mm) thickness, ⁵/₈" (16 mm) steel pins, insulation, 1" × 8" (19 × 184 mm) skirting boards, nails.

Procedure:

1) All the posts should be at a level height from the floor, (e.g., 8′, or 2440 mm).
2) All the wall panels should be at a level height of 1″ (25 mm) lower than the top of the posts with the top logs pinned to the log below.
3) Square off and chalk a line along the center top of the log walls. It should strike the top center of each post as well.
4) Chalk a parallel line 4″ (100 mm) on either side of this centerline, leaving a space 8″ (200 mm) between the inner and outer lines. If the logs are not very large, 6″ (150 mm) will suffice.
5) Using the inside and outside lines as guides, cut a ledge equal to the skirting board depth around the inside and outside walls of the building (see Figure 8–26A).
   Note: These steps can be marked out and the ledge cut while the wall panel is still in its construction jig.
6) Prepare the flat-surfaced top plate logs by cutting a 1″ (25 mm) deep rabbet groove down each side as shown in the inset diagrams of Figure 8–27. There should be 8″ (200 mm) between the rabbet grooves and remember to always work from a centerline.
7) Place the sidewall top plate logs on the building first, making half-lap splices over every second or third post or where necessary. Allow projection at both front and back of building for roof overhang support.
8) Place the gable wall top plate logs on the building and half-lap join these at the corners, splicing where necessary. (See Chapter 7, section **4** for half-lap joinery instructions.)
9) Pin the top plate securely to each post with ⁵/₈″ (16 mm) pins.
10) Insulate the space between the top plate and infill logs, and nail the skirting boards to the top plate— never to the infill logs.
    Note: Walls exceeding 16′ (5 m) in length and without interior partitions for bracing should include tie beams to tie the walls together. Tie beams also provide support for second storey floor joists. They are placed before the roof system, in the same manner as girder beams, as described in Chapter 7, section **6**.

19. Log post and beam method for a basement wall.

Basements do not have to be dark, damp holes, rarely used except as storage areas or laundry rooms. Building a house into a gentle hillside, or grading to provide one, allows a basement to be constructed so that one wall—usually facing south for maximum solar benefit—has a fully exposed ground access. Such a ground access wall provides a separate entrance into the basement, as well as good ventilation and illumination.

A long-standing problem for log homes with notched corner construction has been how to build this basement wall while keeping within the natural log theme. The notched corner construction method could not be employed because of settling problems, and the difficulty of joining the log work to the concrete walls. A conventional frame wall was out of the questions, as it would destroy the appearance of the house.

The answer, not only for a post and beam house, but for notched corner construction as well, is to build this wall using the post and beam method. It serves the purpose of providing aesthetic continuity without the worry of settling problems. Described below are the steps for constructing a log post and beam basement wall with an open timber ceiling.

Tools: Electric drill with ¾ ″ (19 mm) and 1 ″ (25 mm) auger bits, crescent wrench.

Materials: Roofing tar or foam roll, ⅝ ″ (16 mm) threaded anchor bolts (for posts), 1 ″ (25 mm) wood dowels, glue.

Procedure:
1) Construct the concrete foundation walls to a height of 8′ (2440 mm). While the concrete is still wet embed two ⅝ ″ (16 mm) threaded bolts in each wall, as shown in Figure 8–28. In this diagram, where the corner posts are 10 ″ (250 mm) thick, the anchor bolts project 9 ″ (225 mm) from the concrete face.
2) Apply a coat of tar or a layer of foam roll to the wall face and bolt the corner posts as shown.
3) Assemble the wall panels as previously described.
4) Place the top plate as previously described. Here a log top plate is shown supporting a log girder and floor joists.

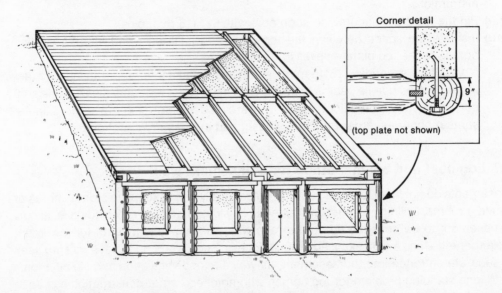

Figure 8-28. Basement post and beam.

CHAPTER NINE

Log Post and Beam with Round Notch Corners

A very attractive option in post and beam building is the addition of round notch corners. In this chapter are described procedures for constructing and integrating these graceful corners, using the log wall infill method described in the last chapter. It is important to be aware of the wood's shrinkage factor here, since ignorance of this factor can lead to failure in combining the notched corners with the vertical posts.

If the log materials used for these notched corners are green (with a high moisture content), the roof must be cantilevered and its weight supported by the strength of the top plate. For if the roof weight were to rest directly on the corners, the roof would sag at its corners after settling. To prevent this, every effort should be made to obtain dry log materials for the corners. However, this chapter will describe the steps for corner construction when using green materials.

First, the wall system for this example building will be placed on the subfloor as explained in Chapter 8, section **11.** However, here there will be no corner posts, and the walls will stop *four* feet (1220 mm) short of the chalked centerline. This is done to accommodate the notched corners. The chalked centerline refers to the perimeter line inset 4″ (100 mm) from the edge of the subfloor. The walls will be centered on this line and provide an overhang of approximately 1″ (25 mm) for a drip cap. The notched corners will be taken from a small 8′ × 8′ (2440 × 2440 mm) square building (walls only) constructed in the center of the subfloor (or elsewhere). The log materials will be 14′ (4.25 m) lengths to allow for the curved log ends. The logs described here have a 12″ (300 mm) mean diameter, but may be either larger or smaller, to match the size of the other wall logs. The directions for construction of the notched corner building follow.

1. How to prepare and place the first logs.

The objective here is to flat-surface the bottoms of the first logs so they will sit flat on the subfloor. Since we are working with an average of 12″ (300 mm) logs (butt size), simply cut one log in half lengthwise to form the first two sill logs. The next two logs which notch over the top and form the first "round," should be large enough to have a

Figure 9–1. Log post and beam building with round notch corners.

5″–6″ flat surface and still be 12″ (300 mm) thick. For this reason, use 14″ (355 mm) logs. Before notching these first logs together, chalk an 8′ square (2440 × 2440 mm) on the subfloor deck. The centers of the first logs will be positioned on these lines, as shown in Figures 9–2 and 9–3.

Tools: Chalkline, tape measure, level, hammer.

Materials: Flat-surfaced logs, nails.

Procedure:
1) Using one of the methods described in Chapter 6, flat-surface the first logs approximately to the sizes shown in Figure 9–3.
   Note: The dimensions may vary, depending on the size of the logs in your building, but the procedure remains the same.
2) Mark chalklines on the subfloor to form an 8′ square (2440 × 2440 mm), taking diagonals. Leave the extended lines to aid in placing the first logs, as shown in Figure 9–2.
3) Chalk centerlines on the flat under-surface of each log.
4) Position the two "halved" sidewall logs on the centerlines, and toe-nail them to the subfloor to prevent movement.

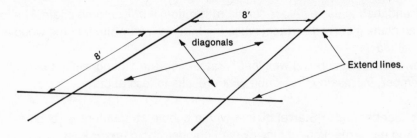

Figure 9-2. An 8′ square chalked onto the subfloor.

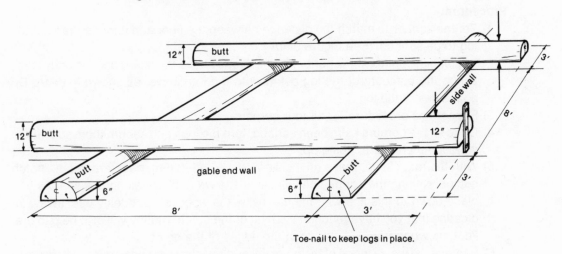

Toe-nail to keep logs in place.

Figure 9-3. Flat-sided logs positioned on chalklines.

5) Position the next two gable wall logs on top of the first two, so that their centerlines are directly over the chalked lines on the floor. The flat under-surface of these logs should be level and parallel with the floor. (See Figure 9-3.)

6) The butt ends of the logs should be aligned as shown.

7) This first round is now ready to be scribed and notched together.

2. Scribing and cutting the first bottom log notches.

It will be necessary to notch the two top logs down over the logs below so that their under surfaces lie flat on the subfloor. The process of scribing and cutting out the notch waste wood can be done in either one or two steps, depending on the accuracy of your scribing technique. Since there is no lateral groove to contend with at this time the process can usually be accomplished in one step.

A good chainsaw, when handled correctly, becomes a precision instrument. With a little practice, you will find it no great feat to actually split the wood along a pencil line, and cut out an entire round notch using ony the saw and no chisels. The trick to cutting out a round notch with a chainsaw is to first "knife" the scribe line with utility razor knife, and then to use a *chipper* chain rather than a *chisel*-tooth chain. The former can cut and plane a curved surface, while the latter will only bite into the wood and rip in a straight line.

However, if the scribing was inaccurate, accurate cutting will not correct the error. Remember, increasing the scribe width results in less accuracy.

Tools: Scriber (a #85 Starret divider with a bubble attachment is recommended), eye and ear protection, chainsaw with chipper chain, razor knife, level.

Procedure:

1) Set the scriber to match the distance between the floor and under surface of the log to be scribed. (See Figure 9–4A.)
2) Keeping the points of the scriber vertical (one above the other) and the body level, scribe the contours of the log below onto the log above, as shown in 9–4A. Do both sides of the log.
3) Repeat this procedure for all four corners.
4) Once all the corners have been scribed, turn the logs and secure them so that the scribed notches are facing up.
5) With the razor knife, make an incision $1/8''$–$1/4''$ (3–6 mm) deep around the notch outline. Knifing the scribe line will sever the wood fibers along this line. As you plane down to this line with the chainsaw the wood will suddenly peel away, indicating that you have reached the limit of the notch. Knifing will also help to prevent the wood from splintering at the edges of the notch.
6) Remove the waste wood of the notch by cutting, carving, and planing, as shown in Figure 9–4B and C. Refer to the procedures for rough and finish notching detailed in sections **4** and **5,** below. All notches should be slightly concave so that the edges only will bear the weight of the log.

Figure 9–4. Scribing and cutting the bottom log notches.

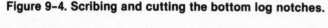

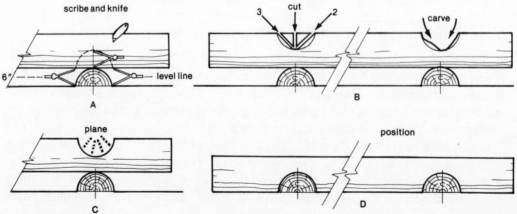

7) Repeat the foregoing cutting procedure on all the notches, and position the logs so that their chalked midlines align with the centerline on the subfloor.

8) Toe-nail these two logs to the subfloor to prevent movement.

3. Placing the wall logs.

The aesthetic impression of a building will be better if each course of horizontal logs is on the same plane. (For example, if the third log in one wall is set at the same height as the third log in all the wall panels of the building.) The builder should strive to match wall logs so that they are on the same plane for each entire wall of the building.

If your log materials are fairly uniform in diameter, and you remain aware of the need to maintain levels as you work, there will be no difficulty in doing so. A method of checking and maintaining equal wall log heights on the construction jig was described at the beginning of Chapter 8. But as these notched corners are not prefabricated in a jig, it will be necessary to take frequent measurements and make the appropriate adjustments.

As the walls are going up, always alternate the direction of butt ends on every course round. (See Figure 9–5.) When positioning a log on the wall always place it over the center of the wall. Remember that markedly bowed logs should be placed with the bow facing *outside* the building. It is unlikely that with such short length walls any logs will be discarded due to excessive bowing. However, a log considered too bowed or bent would be one with the preponderance of its weight not resting over the center of the wall. During the scribing process secure the log so it will not move. Finally, where curved log ends are desired, the log ends lateral groove must be prepared as the wall is constructed. Refer to the layout and cutting procedures for arched opening in Chapter 12, section **5**.

Figure 9–5. Placing wall logs with bows facing outward, and alternating built ends direction on each course.

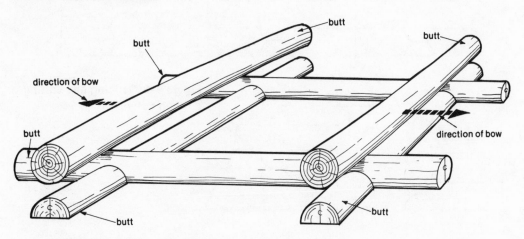

4. Scribing and cutting a rough notch.

"Rough" notching is the term used to describe the initial notching that sets the top log down close to the log below, prior to finish scribing the entire log. However, it does not mean that the notch is loose and rough. On the contrary, the rough notch demands a great deal of accuracy due to the large amount of wood removed initially. It must be noted that the closer the logs lie to each other after rough notching, the more accurate the finish scribe will be. Large inaccuracies near the corners of the notch cannot usually be scribed out at the finish scribe stage.

Tools: Eye and ear protection, chainsaw with chipper chain, utility knife, level, axe, indelible pencil, scriber (with bubble attachment recommended), peavey.

Procedure:
1) Align the log on the building, alternating the butts and tops.
2) Adjust the scribers to within 1"–2" (25–50 mm) of touching the log below and scribe the log on both sides of the notch, as in Figure 9-6A. Readjust the scriber and repeat this procedure for opposite end of the log.
   Note: Do not move the log during the scribing process, and hold the scriber in a perpendicular and level position.
3) Turn the log upright and make an incision $\frac{1}{8}$"–$\frac{1}{4}$" (3–6 mm) deep with a utility knife around the notch outline. This cut-line will help to identify the boundary of the notch when brushing down to the line with the chainsaw. It also helps to keep the notch edges from splintering and fraying. Some builders prefer to take less wood out for the rough notch and to increase the scriber distance for the finished scribe. Where this is done the utility knife cut can be omitted.

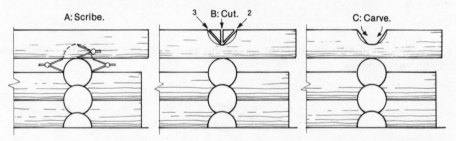

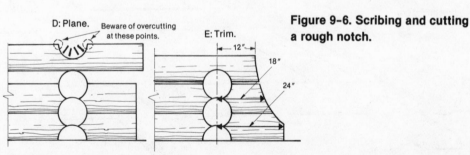

Figure 9-6. Scribing and cutting a rough notch.

4) To cut the notch make straight cuts in the sequence 1, 2 and 3, as shown in Figure 9–6B, using the full length of the chainsaw bar. This will remove bulk of waste wood.

5) Carve out the side portions close to the scribe line, working the full length of the chainsaw bar from the top of the notch to the bottom. (See Figure 9–6C.)

6) Plane the notch to the scribe line, as shown in Figure 9–6D, keeping the bar at right angles to the wood surface. Criss-crossing the planing cuts produces a smoother surface. This planing is only necessary at the top of the notch where a minimal amount of wood will be removed during the finish scribe. Be aware that there is a danger of overcutting at this point. Use the full length of the chainsaw bar when cutting the notch.

7) Repeat this cutting procedure for the opposite end of the log.

8) After the two notches of the log are cut roll the rough notched log back into position and realign it, with its weight over the wall. Trim any large knots so that the logs sit close to each other in preparation for finish scribing.

9) Prior to finish scribing the log ends must be trimmed, or curved, if desired. See the view of a rough notched log in Figure 9–6E, showing the ends trimmed in preparation for finish scribing. Measure the degree of curve using the vertical centerline on the log ends as reference.

5. Finish scribing a wall log.

The process of scribing transfers the shape and contours of one surface onto another surface, using a scriber. Here the shape of the bottom log is reproduced onto the undersurface of the log above it. During the finish scribe the whole length of the log is scribed, on both the inside and outside of the wall. Every curve and knot must be identified so that, when the waste wood of the lateral groove and notches is removed, a self-draining, tight, chinkless fit will join the two logs together. The scriber must be held level and vertical, with the points one above the other. It becomes increasingly difficult to achieve accuracy as the scriber setting is widened.

Tools: Scribers.

Procedure:

1) Determine the scriber setting by locating the widest gap between the two logs and then increase the scriber distance $1/8$" to $1/4$" (3–6 mm). The purpose of this procedure is to mate the two surfaces completely, and, to do so, a continuous length of waste wood will have to be removed. Of course, the scriber setting will be only for the gap in the walls themselves. The log ends will be outside the living area, and so not have to keep out the elements.

2) Scribe the full length of the log, up and over the notches, around the log ends and down the other side of the log. Make sure that:

a) The scribers are held level and vertical with one point directly above the other.
b) The scriber setting is *not* changed until the entire log is completed.
c) A good, readable scribe line is visible. Wetting the scribe path with a fine spray of water will make an easily readable line when an indelible pencil is used.
d) The entire log is scribed, even the log ends.
e) The log is *not* moved until it has been completely scribed.

scriber distance = widest gap + ¼ "

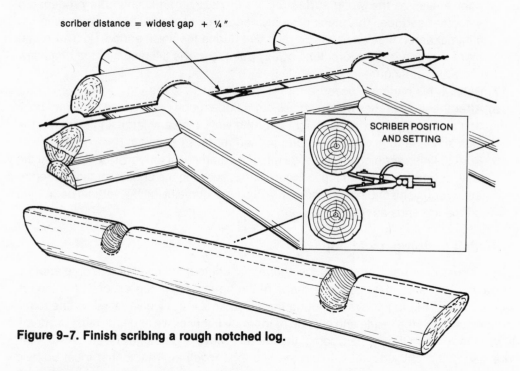

SCRIBER POSITION
AND SETTING

Figure 9–7. Finish scribing a rough notched log.

6. Cutting a round notch.

Removing the waste wood in a notch is accomplished with either an axe or a chainsaw. The steps for cutting a round notch with a chainsaw are described here. Just as important as one's cutting technique and practice is the choice of a cutting chain. I have never seen a satisfactory round notch cut with anything but a chipper chain. The rounded back of the tooth promotes the carving and brushing action necessary for cutting a round notch.

Tools: Eye and ear protection, chainsaw· with chipper chain, utility knife, peavey, straightedge (level).

Procedure:
1) Wedge or dog the log, with the notch upright, so it will not move.
Using the utility knife make a ¹/₈"–¼ " (3–6 mm) incision around the notch

outline. This cut-line helps to identify the boundary of the notch when planing down to the line with the chainsaw, while also preventing the notch edges from splintering and fraying. If the wood is extremely dry and hard, a chisel and mallet will do the job. Follow the scribe line exactly during this step. (See Figure 9–8A.)

2) The notch is worked in quarters, sawing half the wood out from one side of the log, then sawing the remainder out from the other side of the log.

3) Working from the bottom of the notch and on up the sides, carve the bulk of the wood out close to the scribe line. (See Figure 9–8B.) The nose of the bar should be slightly deeper than the outer lip of the notch. To keep from overcutting the scribe line, use a pivoting action, keeping the bar nose stabilized at the center of the notch and carving with the portion of the bar that is 6″ (150 mm) or so from the nose.

4) Plane down to the scribe line until the wood breaks cleanly away from the knife cut. The planing action is from the top of the notch down toward the bottom. Use the nose of the bar, keeping it perpendicular to the wood's surface. This action should resemble a sweeping motion. Criss-crossing these plane cuts with a light pressure produces a smoother outer lip surface. (See Figure 9–8C.)

5) Complete the notches and use a straightedge (level) to check that the notch is concave. The center of the notch should be approximately ½″ (12 mm) below the outer lips. (See Figure 9–8D.)

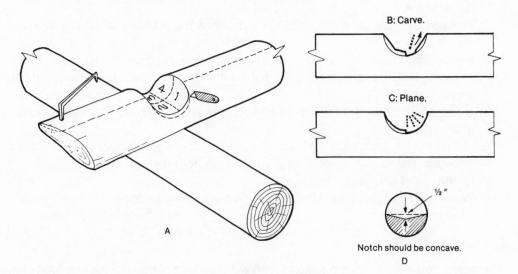

B: Carve.

C: Plane.

½″

Notch should be concave.
D

A

Figure 9–8. Cutting a finish round notch with a chainsaw.

7. Cutting a lateral groove.

The lateral groove, if properly scribed and cut, provides a self-draining, chinkless join between the logs, which, when insulated, prevents wind and weather from entering and

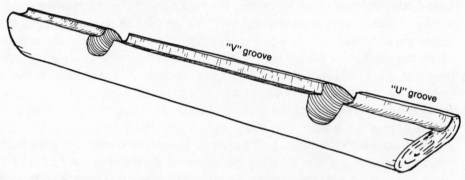

Figure 9–9. A log with completed notches and lateral groove.

heat from escaping the building. (This groove and the notch are insulated at a later stage.)

Tools: Eye and ear protection, chainsaw, pencil, round axe, peavey.

Procedure:
1) Pencil the desired angle of cut (normal or wide scribe) on the inside of the notches, as shown in Figure 9–9. For a description of the lateral cuts, see Chapter 8, section **4.**
2) Position, then wedge or dog the log so your saw blade enters at the proper angle and depth.
3) Keeping the blade 1/8″–1/4″ (3–6 mm) inside the line, cut down the length of the log between the notches. Repeat the cut for the opposite scribe line and remove waste wood.
4) Using an axe, pare with the grain down to the scribe line. *Do not remove scribe line.*
5) Round the log ends back 12″ (300 mm) or so to avoid the unsightly "V" groove showing. This is easily accomplished working from the end of the log using the length of the chainsaw bar.
6) When this has been done, position the log back on the building and check for any gaps in fit.

8. Leveling the walls.

Alternating butt and top ends on each round will take care of most of the leveling work, as in a building of such small size there is little chance the wall heights will deviate very much. Nevertheless, it is important that all the walls are level, especially when approaching the last logs on the top. Below is the procedure for taking level readings and adjusting for any discrepancies.

Log walls can only be leveled on "even" rounds, there being an equal number of butt

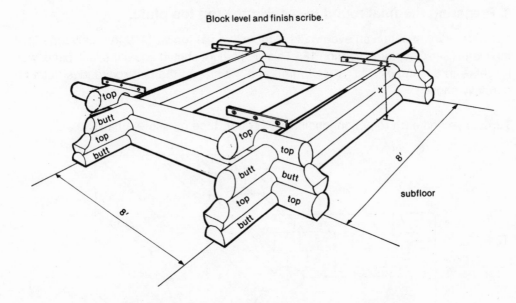

Block level and finish scribe.

Figure 9-10. Leveling the wall height on an even round.

and top ends per corner. On a four-sided building only two logs can be leveled at one time. Since the subfloor is already level, this surface will be used to take measurements from.

Tools: Eye and ear protection, chainsaw, tape measure, level, scriber, peavey, pencil.

Materials: Small spacer blocks for leveling.

Procedure:

1) Work with an even round and from the level foundation or floor measure up each end of the wall. Determine which of the two walls is lowest, and place the larger of the two logs on the low wall.

2) Rough notch the logs in place, then take a measurement at each corner and note heights. (See Figure 9-10.)

3) Block the low corner of each log until it is level.
   Note: If there is a large height discrepancy it may be necessary to finish the leveling procedure on the next even round to avoid taking too much wood from one end.

4) Scribe the entire log. Do not adjust the scriber or move the log during the scribing process.

5) Continue with the construction of the walls, leveling when necessary on the even rounds.

9. Preparing the final round to receive the log top plate.

It is necessary to obtain an even wall height with a flat top surface to receive the final top plate. (See Chapter 8, section **18.**) This wall height should equal the infill panel wall heights—in this case, 7'11" (2413 mm), and the size of the last round logs must be carefully chosen.

Tools: Eye and ear protection, chainsaw, scriber, tape measure, chalkline.

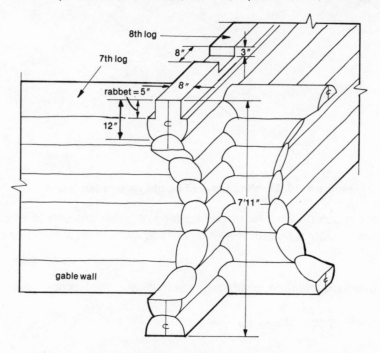

Figure 9-11. Preparing the final side wall log.

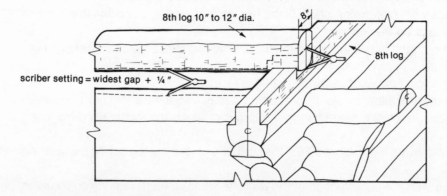

Figure 9-12. Scribing and fitting the gable wall log.

Procedure:

1) Upon its completion, the wall height should contain an even number of logs (i.e., 8 or 10). The last two logs must cap the ones below, and the entire top surface must be flattened. So that these last two logs will not have their notches cut off during the flat-surfacing process, the log below must also be notched. (See Figure 9–11.) Since these two sidewall logs must be notched to accept the last two gable wall logs and still provide a 6″–8″ (150–200 mm) flat top surface, they must be of substantial size. If you are working with 12″ (300 mm) ± size logs, these two logs would be 14″–15″ (355–380 mm) in diameter. Scribe and fit these two large sidewall logs in place.

2) Measure an equal distance from the floor—in this case, 7′11″ (2413 mm) to match the infill wall height—chalk a horizontal line, then cut a flat surface along the length of each log. (See the flat-surfacing procedures described in Chapter 6.)

3) Working from chalked centerlines lay out and cut square notches 3″ (75 mm) deep by 8″ (200 mm) wide, as shown in Figure 9–11.

4) In final preparation, cut 5″ (125 mm) deep rabbets down the length of each log, inside and outside. These rabbet grooves will be required for the application of skirting boards after the top plate is in place.

5) Obtain a 10″–12″ (250–300 mm) diameter log and flat surface two sides to an even 8″ (200 mm) thick. (See Figure 9–12.) Place this log into the square notches on the building and scribe it in place.

6) Flat surface these last gables wall logs to produce a flat, even surface for the log top plate. (See Figure 9–13.)

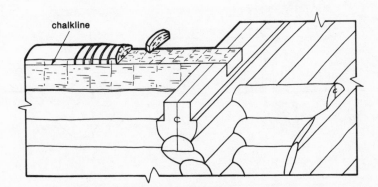

Figure 9–13. Flat-surfacing the gable wall in preparation for the top plate.

10. How to plumb-cut and spline-groove the notch corners.

After flat-surfacing the top log members to receive the top plate the walls can be cut into four equal segments. These segments will form the corners of your building. The procedure for plumb-cutting is identical with the one described in Chapter 8, section **6,** or by using a mini mill like the one described in Chapter 6, section **8.** Spline-grooving the plumb-cut ends is identical to the procedure outlined in Chapter 8, section **7.**

Tools: Eye and ear protection, chainsaw, router with ¾ " (19 mm) straight bit, level, tape measure, hammer.

Materials: Plumb-cutting jig, 1 " × 4 " (19 × 89 mm) straightedge, nails, pencil.

Procedure:
1) Using the plumb-cutting jig, set up and then cut the notched building into four equal corner segments. (See Figure 9–14.)
2) Number the corner pieces, dismantle, and assemble one of the notched corners on the building subfloor nearest a door opening.
   Note: Cut the spline groove of the first bottom log prior to assembly, since when it is placed it will be difficult to cut the groove without accidentally cutting the floor.
3) After the notched corner is in place, rout the spline groove, attach a post, and continue assembly of infill wall panels and posts as described in section **11,** below.

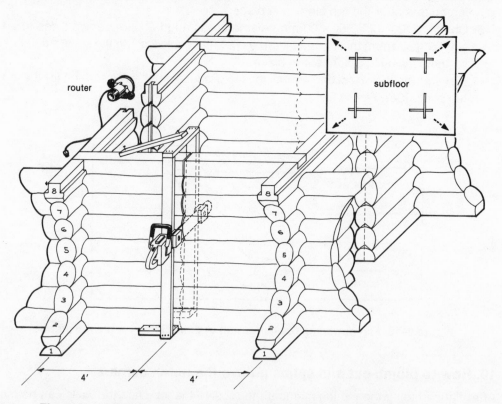

Figure 9–14. Plumb-cutting and spline-grooving the notched corners.

11. Assembling the notched corners and placing the top plate.

Assembling the notched corners on the building subfloor is done by following the procedure for placement, insulating, pinning, and drilling for electrical wiring outlined in Chapter 8 sections **14** and **15,** and Chapter 14, sections **1** and **2.** In this case, however, the top plate should be log in order to withstand the cantilevered stresses of the roof weight.

Tools: Electric drill with ½ " (12 mm), ⅝ " (16 mm) auger bits, chalkline, 4' (1220 mm) level, sledge hammer, hammer, knife.

Materials: Numbered notched corners, wall panels and posts, 1 " × 8 " (19 × 200 mm) skirting boards (rough cedar), insulation, ¾ " × 3 " × 8' (19 × 75 × 2440 mm) marine plywood strips, nails, foam roll or tar, 2 " × 6 " (38 × 140 mm) bracing.

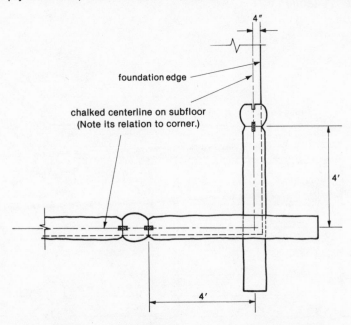

Figure 9–15. Top view of notched corner assembly.

Procedure:

1) Chalk a 4 " (100 mm) inset centerline around the perimeter of the subfloor as shown in Figure 9–15. The centerline of the wall logs will be positioned on this line.

2) Place the bottom, flat-surfaced corner logs on the subfloor with a layer of foam roll or tar between the two surfaces. Secure these first logs as described in Chapter 8, section **13.**

3) Assemble the notched corners, insulating, pinning, and drilling for electrical wiring as you go. (See Chapter 8, sections **14** and **15;** Chapter 14, sections **1** and **2.**) Make sure the plumb-cut ends are flush. Rout the spline groove after the corners are completed, if they are not already routered.

4) Position a post and assemble the wall panel as previously outlined. The procedure of starting at one corner nearest a doorway and working simultaneously toward the doorway and around the building is identical to the procedure described in Chapter 8.

5) After all the walls are in place, position the top plate as shown in Figure 9–16, then insulate and nail the skirting boards to the plate.
Note: Prior to placing the roof system tie beams may be needed or desired to tie the walls together or provide support for second storey floor joists. Tie beams are placed in the same manner as girder beams, following the procedures described in Chapter 7, section **6.**

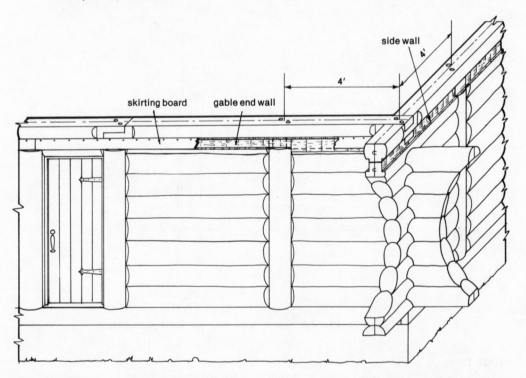

Figure 9–16. Assembly of notched corners, wall panels, and log top plate on the subfloor.

CHAPTER TEN

Timber
Post and Beam Walls

This chapter is intended for those who prefer the appearance of hewn timbers to that of round logs. The following procedures describe methods of joinery commonly practiced hundreds of years ago. However, with simplified template and jig construction these methods become more realistic for today's builder.

1. Preparing the post tenons and slots.

Traditionally, the squared timber posts were fashioned with a tenon on either end which mated into mortises in the foundation sill and top plate. Generally, the male portion of a joint is prepared first, and the female portion is cut to match the male piece's dimensions. Whenever possible the female layout should be traced rather than measured. Cut the mortise for a tight fit, then shave the tenon if necessary.

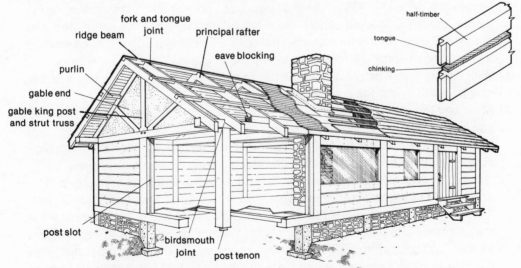

Figure 10–1. Timber post and beam with half-timber infill.

The traditional method for joining the infill wall half-timbers to the posts is by tongue and slot. The half-timbers have a tongue which fit into a groove or slot in the posts. Below are diagrams and procedures showing how to prepare a corner post. The procedure will be the same for a midpost, except for the placement of the slot.

Tools: Eye and ear protection, chainsaw, carpenter's square, tape measure, chalkline, hammer, crosscut handsaw, chisel or slick, pencil.

Materials: Posts.

Procedure:
1) Hew or mill the post materials till they are of equal dimensions. They can be square or rectangular, but usually they are the same width as the sill and top plate. Test for a right-angled surface on the corner posts by using a carpenter's square. By using two squares, as shown in Figure 10–2A, any twist in the post, will be revealed. If possible, the posts should be dry, and without any spiral grain.
2) Cut the post to overall length. If the wall height is to be 8' (2440 mm) then the overall length should be 8'8" (2642 mm) to include the 4" (100 mm) tenons.
3) Lay out the tenons on the post ends. Chalk a centerline down both sides of the post, as shown in Figure 10–2B. Working from this centerline lay out the tenon length, thickness, and width, using a carpenter's square. The 2" (50 mm) body of the square works as a template for the tenon's thickness. Alternatively, use the template described in section **2,** below.
4) Remove the waste wood of the tenon layout. The result is a full shoulder tenon, which can be left as it is or narrowed, if desired.
5) Layout a 2 1/8" × 2 1/8" (53 × 53 mm) deep slot (groove) down the midline of the timber, using the chalked centerline as the reference. Since the completed post shown in Figure 10–3 is for a corner, the slots are at a right angle to each other. If this were to be a midpost the slots would be on opposite sides of the timber.
6) With a pencil mark on the side of the bar to serve as a depth gauge, use a chainsaw to carefully cut the post slots.
7) An alternative method for cutting accurate post slots is to use a modified chainsaw of the type which incorporates an abrasive wheel for cutting concrete and steel. This tool may not be suitable for the one-time homebuilder due to its high cost. The chainsaw, however, can be adapted back to wood cutting use by attaching the regular bar and chain. It is included here simply as another option.

Figure 10–4 shows the abrasive wheel replaced with conventional dado blades. It will be necessary to redrill the dado blade holes to fit the ¾" (19 mm) shaft of the chainsaw. The blade guard restricts the width of dado blades to ¾" (19 mm) as well. To regulate the depth of cut a wood or metal piece is attached to the blade guard. A wood straightedge is used to guide the slot cut. When additional width is required simply move the straightedge to accommodate.

A: Checking a post for squareness and twists.

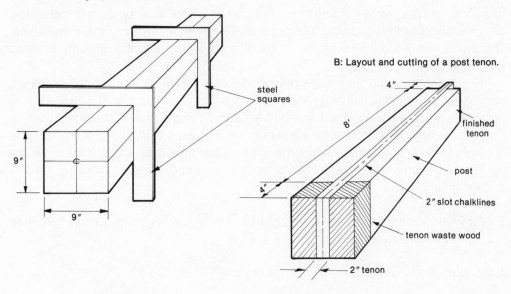

B: Layout and cutting of a post tenon.

steel squares

9″

9″

4″

8′

4″

finished tenon

post

2″ slot chalklines

tenon waste wood

2″ tenon

Figure 10-2. Laying out the post tenon and slots.

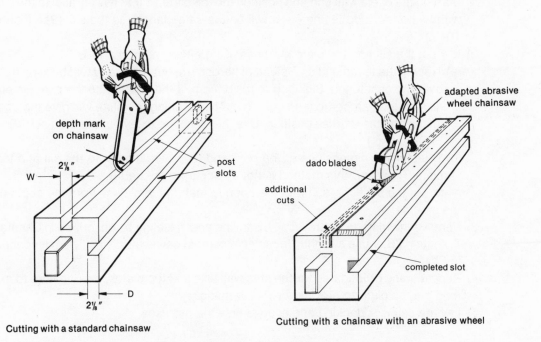

depth mark on chainsaw

2⅛″

W

post slots

2⅛″

D

Cutting with a standard chainsaw

adapted abrasive wheel chainsaw

dado blades

additional cuts

completed slot

Cutting with a chainsaw with an abrasive wheel

Figure 10-3. Two methods of cutting the post slot.

2. Laying out the post mortises on the sills and top plates.

In standard timber frame building, the structural members (sills, posts, and top plates) are assembled on the building's subfloor in wall sections and then raised into position. This procedure is followed because of the timbers' weight and the difficulty of fitting them together.

In traditional post and beam construction the posts are raised into position on the sill, and the top plate is left off until the wall infill half-timbers are in place. This procedure is necessary so as to place the wall half-timbers from the top and slide them down, which could not be done if the top plate were in position. However, initial fitting of the top plate mortises to the post tenons requires much less effort than to do so once the walls are up. The procedures below show how to lay out the post mortise locations on the sills and top plates.

Tools: Chainsaw and mortising jig (optional), brace and ¾ ″ (19 mm) bit, 1½ ″ (38 mm) chisel, mallet, tape measure, knife, pencil.

Materials: Posts, sills and top plates, hardboard.

Procedure:
1) Start on the gable wall end and position the top plate so that it is parallel to the sill, with its bottom side facing up. It will be the same length as the sill. (See Figure 10–5.)
2) Lay out the sill and top plate mortises using either method A or B.
    (a) Tracing the tenon end on a piece of hardboard, cut it out, and test by slipping it over the post tenon. Slip it up to the bottom of the post, trace the post dimension on the hardboard, and cut it out. The resulting template will give the post image and the mortise position. Use this template to lay out the mortises. (See Figure 10–6.)
    (b) Transfer the dimensions of the post and tenon location onto the sill and top plate. However, this method is not as accurate as the first.
    Note: On the subfloor, subtract the flooring material thickness from the depth of the mortise.
3) Remove the mortise waste wood by drilling and chiseling as described in Chapter 7, section **7B** or use a slightly modified electrical cavity mortising jig as described in Chapter 14, section **2**.
4) Repeat these procedures for the side wall sills and top plates, making sure to extend the top plate to provide a roof overhang.
5) Lay the subfloor decking and expose only the mortises.

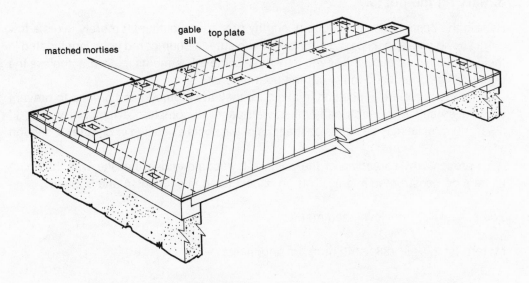

Figure 10-4. Matching the top plate to sill for mortise layout.

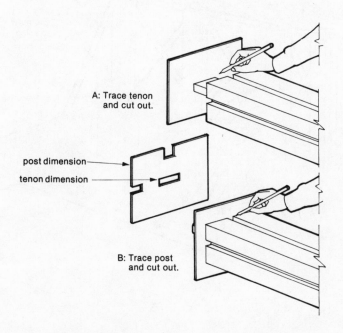

Figure 10-5. Constructing a post mortise template.

3. Raising the posts.

Raising the posts does not require a lengthy procedural outline. It merely takes a few extra strong backs to help with the work. Make sure the numbered posts are located in their respective sill mortises or you may have some adjustments to do later (unless the template has been used to lay out the post tenons).

Once the posts are in position, make sure they are plumbed and braced to prevent any movement. After each half-timber wall panel is complete a temporary 2″ × 6″ (38 × 140 mm) tie may be nailed on the tops of the posts as shown in Chapter 8, section **11.**

To prevent any spreading of the posts it is recommended that the wall infill half-timbers be constructed in a jig. This jig is described in sections **4** and **5,** below.

Tools: 4′ (1220 mm) level, hammer.

Materials: 2″ × 6″ (38 × 140 mm) bracing, nails.

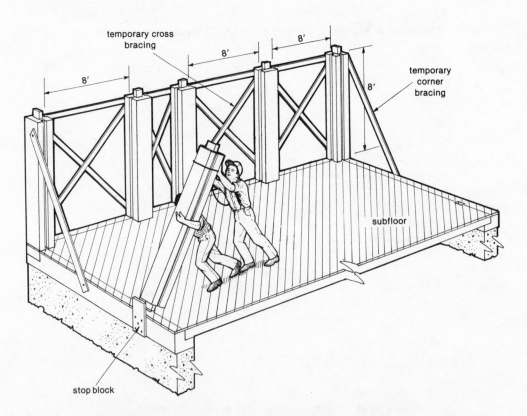

Figure 10-6. Positioning, plumbing, and bracing the posts.

4. Constructing the half-timber infill walls using a jig.

Custom cutting and fitting each wall half-timber in place between the vertical posts can be a difficult and lengthy procedure. If the walls are to be scribe-fitted, a jig like the one described in Chapter 8 would do the job. However, since here the walls will be chinked and not scribed, another type of jig must be constructed to simplify the job. Now, instead of cutting a groove in each end of the wall to be keyed with a spline to the posts, you would instead fashion a ''tongue'' at either end. Below is an inexpensive jig, with a quick method for mass-producing half-timber infill panels. The example given is for an 8′ × 8′ (2440 × 2440 mm) infill wall with a 2″ (50 mm) tongue. For an illustration of an alternative jig-type, see section **5,** below.

Tools: Eye and ear protection, chainsaw, tape measure, chalkline, hammer.

Materials: Wall timbers, 2″ × 6″s (38 × 140 mm), 2″ × 4″s (38 × 89 mm), 1″ × 4″s (19 × 89 mm), nails.

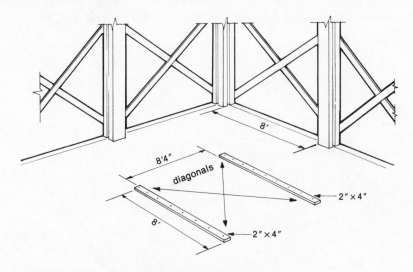

Figure 10–7. Jig layout.

Procedure:

1) Working on the flat subfloor surface nail two 8′ (2440 mm) long 2″ × 4″s (38 × 89 mm) to the subfloor. They should be parallel to each other and 8′ 4″ (2540 mm) apart to include the tongue lengths. Check their parallel spacings by taking diagonals. (See Figure 10–7.)

2) Nail a 2″ × 6″ (38 × 140 mm) to the inside of the 2″ × 4″s (38 × 89 mm) and a 1″ × 4″ (19 × 89 mm) ledger strip, as shown in the Figure 10–7 inset. See also Figure 10–8.

3) With the jig complete, the wall half-timbers (hewn on two sides) can be cut to overall length. In an 8′ (2440 mm) wall the overall length would be 8′4″ (2540 mm) to include the 2″ (50 mm) tongues.

4) Place the wall half-timbers on the jig as shown in Figure 10–8. The ledger 1″ × 4″ (19 × 89 mm) will hold them in position while the 2″ × 6″ (38 × 140 mm) suspends them off the floor. The butts and tops should be alternated as shown in Figure 10–8.

5) Trim any high spots between the half-timbers with an axe so that they lie close to one another.

6) Lay out the tongue lengths by chalking a line 2″ (50 mm) in from each end. Chalk another two lines on the ends to give a 2″ (50 mm) wide tongue. (See Figure 10–8.)

7) Make vertical and horizontal cuts with the chainsaw to remove half of the tongue's waste wood.

8) It will be necessary to turn the members to complete the tongues. Repeat the layout and cutting procedure, referring to Figure 10–9.

9) Set the completed wall half-timbers in place between the vertical posts. The bottom log should be flat-surfaced to sit on the floor, with a layer of foam roll or tar between.

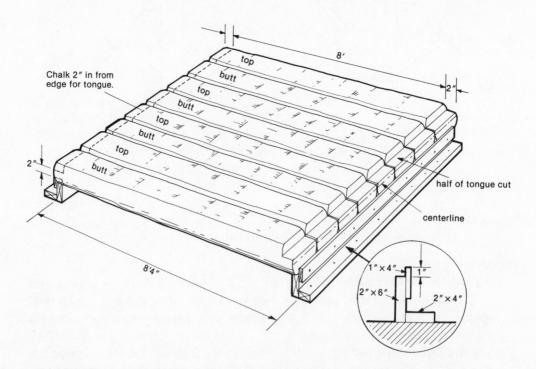

Figure 10–8. Jig in use.

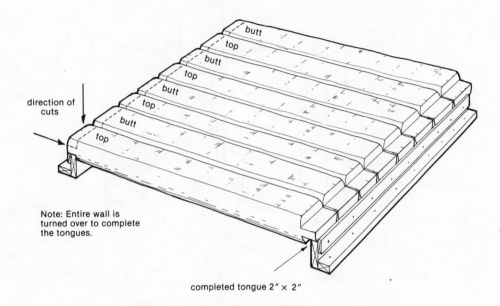

Note: Entire wall is turned over to complete the tongues.

direction of cuts

completed tongue 2″ × 2″

Figure 10–9. Completed half-timber wall tongues.

5. An alternative wall construction jig.

Figure 10–10 is an illustration of a jig that some builders have used in the past to test the fit of wall pieces before they are carried to the building. The diagram speaks for itself. Essentially it is a model of a sill and two vertical posts. The posts are slotted to receive the wall half-timber tongues, and the entire assembly is adjustable to accommodate wall panels of different lengths. Notice that a section exposing part of the slot has been cut away on both verticals. This is to facilitate the stacking of the wall half-timbers while allowing for the bottom one to be removed. This is advantageous if the walls are to be scribed. As this jig is somewhat antiquated, it is included here largely as a point of interest, or in case a reader might wish to adapt or improve on it.

6. Placing the top plate.

Now that the wall half-timbers are placed and leveled to an even height (i.e., 8′ or 2440 mm), the top plate can be positioned. Since the mortises of the top plate members were laid out and cut at the same time as the sills, this procedure needs no explanation. Once the top plate is in position and level, it can be drilled and pinned to the vertical posts. Any settling which does occur can be concealed by chinking or by the installation of a skirting board as described in Chapters 8 and 9.

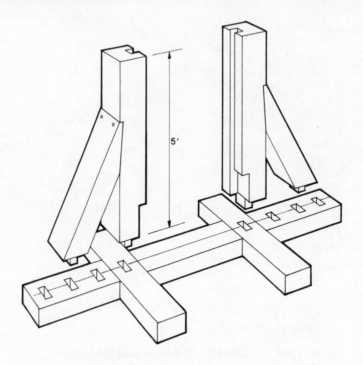

Figure 10-10. Alternative wall jig.

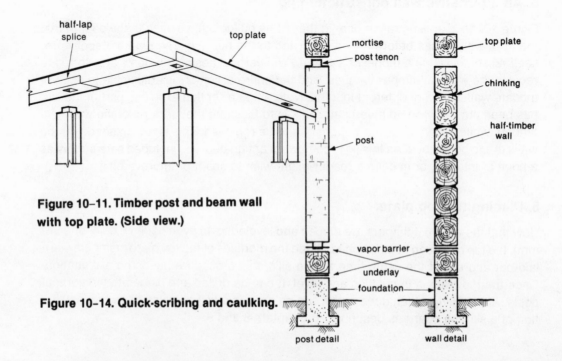

Figure 10-11. Timber post and beam wall with top plate. (Side view.)

Figure 10-14. Quick-scribing and caulking.

7. Applying chinking to the wall half-timbers.

The term "chink" refers to a small crack or fissure. In the context of timber or log construction it refers to the gap between any two horizontal wall members. The term "chinking" loosely describes the entire process of filling this opening, which is part of a dual process: chinking with a material to form the bulk fill between wall members and caulking to provide a weather-tight seal.

In Chapter 8 the construction of the walls involved a scribing process to eliminate the gap and preclude any chinking. The identical scribing process may be used for half-timber wall members as well.

A chinked building has both advantages and disadvantages. The construction process will be easier and faster if the wall members do not have to be scribed and custom fitted together. Also, the contrast of tan or grey timbers with white chinking between is very attractive. The major drawback with a chinked wall is that any runoff water can become trapped between the chinking materials and the wood, eventually resulting in rot. For this reason it is wise to have plenty of roof overhang to prevent chinked walls from becoming rain soaked.

For some I suggest a combination quick-scribe and chink. This method is for those individuals who do not have the patience or inclination to do a perfect scribing job, as well as for use with very uneven logs which would require a lot of time to scribe. The aim here is to make a very quick scribe and lateral groove so that the wall members will lie close to each other. The remaining minor gaps would then require a minimal amount of caulking material.

The chinking process is described below.

Tools: Handsaw, knife, hammer, large spoon, caulking gun (optional), 1½ " (38 mm) paint brush.

Materials: Oakum (tar impregnated hemp rope), poles or wood or metal lath chinking, shingle nails, barbed wire (optional), stucco mortar, powdered acrylic, whitewash, caulking compound (optional).

Procedure:
1) Figure 10–12 shows three ways to chink half-timber infill walls. In A, sapling poles are nailed on the inner and outer surfaces with oakum insulation (or a substitute) sandwiched in between. In B, the sapling poles are replaced with wood quarter round material. In C, wood or metal lath material is used. The metal lath should be used in conjunction with a mortar caulking mix.
2) Wherever needed, apply some form of anchorage. If metal lath is used during the chinking process, the mortar or caulking will have sufficient holding surface. But if poles or wood laths are used some sort of anchorage will have to be secured to the chinking before the mortar can be applied. Methods of anchorage include

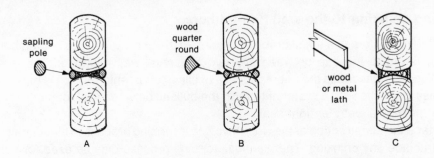

Figure 10-12. Chinking with poles or lath.

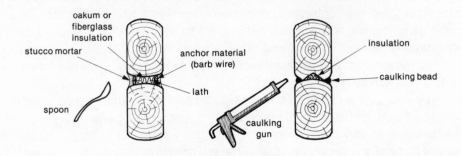

Figure 10-13. Applying mortar.

shingle nails, barbed wire, or metal lath nailed to the chinking material down the length of the opening both inside and out.

3) Figure 10-13 shows how the stucco mortar mix is applied with a spoon. The rounded back of the spoon makes a slightly concave surface. As mortar mixes are brittle and will crack as the wood expands and contracts, it is important to make the mix as plastic as possible. For this purpose acrylic powder combined with the dry mix works well. Trial experimentation will discover the best proportions for providing the most plastic mix. Alternatively, there are synthetic caulking compounds available which remain pliable.

4) Figure 10-14 shows a quick-scribing method which eliminates pole or lath chinking by closing the gap enough so that a bead of caulking compound can be used. The shallow lateral groove is then stuffed with insulation or oakum, and the gap is caulked with a petroleum-based compound. These compounds retain their elasticity and can be purchased in a variety or colors. Application is usually done with a caulking gun which extrudes the mixture from a tube. If the weather is cold it may be necessary to warm the caulking tubes before application can begin. For hard-core traditionalists a method using old socks as chinking and dung daubing as caulking is illustrated in Figure 10-15. It is most important to have a high-fiber

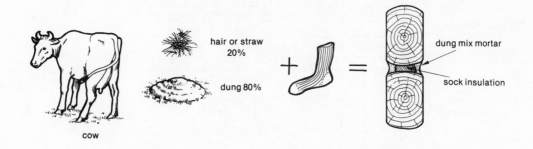

Figure 10-15. Traditional chinking method.

content in the dung to give it elasticity, so a random sampling of the cow pasture may be in order. Or one can mix one's own good batch by combining 80 percent cattle dung and 20 percent cattle hair. This is then applied with a large spoon, allowed to dry, and whitewashed.

8. An alternative method of wall construction.

When time saving is a factor the builder may forego the infill wall pieces and construct the roof directly on the building's frame. These wall infill pieces may then be placed between the posts and keyed to them by means of a ''pieced spline''. Heretofore, the methods described have required that the top plate be placed after the wall infill pieces are in position and completed.

When using the pieced-splined method it is recommended that the wall infill pieces are scribed rather than chinked. This is because a segmented spline does not afford the degree of lateral shear strength provided by a full length one. Furthermore, a chinked wall does not afford the degree of lateral strength of a scribed and pinned wall. Combining these two weaker elements would create a weaker wall.

It is intended that these wall infill panels will be constructed in a prefabrication jig like the one described in Chapter 8. The reason a jig is recommended is because a log is a tapered cylinder. If logs are fitted individually they will sit on a slight angle, causing a gap at either end where the horizontal half-timbers meet the posts, while an entire panel can be plumb-cut to the dimensions imposed by the vertical posts. As an alternative to solid wood infill another infill medium such as stackwall, or rock and mortar, can be used, as described in Chapter 11. However, because there is no integral cross-bracing in post and beam construction, a framework must be temporarily braced until the infill wall material is in place.

Tools: Eye and ear protection, chainsaw, (router with ¾ ", or 19 mm, straight bit), hand-saw, tape measure, chalkline, hammer, level.

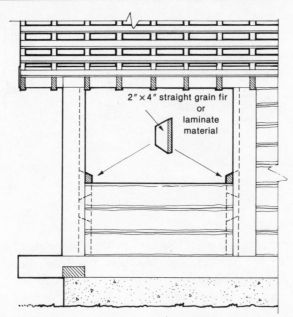

Figure 10-16. Assembling timber wall infill pieces after the roof is in place.

Materials: Posts, wall timbers, spline material to be straight grain fir or laminate material.

Procedure:

1) Mill the posts then lay out and cut a spline groove so a 2″×2″ (38×38 mm) or 2″×4″ (38×89 mm) spline will fit. The groove can be cut with a chainsaw or a router.

2) Erect all posts and top plates; plumb and brace them securely. The roof may be constructed at this point if desired. (See Chapter 13.)

3) Build the wall panels in a jig, then plumb cut them to fit between the posts. Cut the spline grooves, disassemble the panels and erect the pieces between the posts.

4) Insert the spline in the matched grooves, locking the post and wall timbers together. The spline should protrude part way into the next wall timber as shown in Figure 10-16, and should fit tightly into the groove.

5) Insulate the timbers, pin, and drill for electrical wiring as required. (See Chapter 8 for detailed instructions.)

9. An alternative method of top plate construction.

To provide lateral wall strength as discussed above, the following type of top plate construction is recommended for a scribe fitted wall. The top plates described in Chapter 8 incorporate a method for concealing the settling space which develops after the horizontal wall members have finished their shrinkage. In each of those cases the roof weight rests entirely on the posts, and the walls are free-floating. In this alternative method the roof weight rests primarily on the walls, and the settling space is dealt with at the posts with the use of lengthened tenons. The top plate is tied to the posts by the tenons and secured to the walls. This has the advantage of applying pressure to the wall pieces, causing the lateral grooves to fit more tightly. In addition, the skirting boards are done away with. It is recommended that tie-beams are placed to prevent the slight increase in wall instability. These may span between and lock the two sidewall top plates, or a truss system may be used which incorporates a tie-beam.

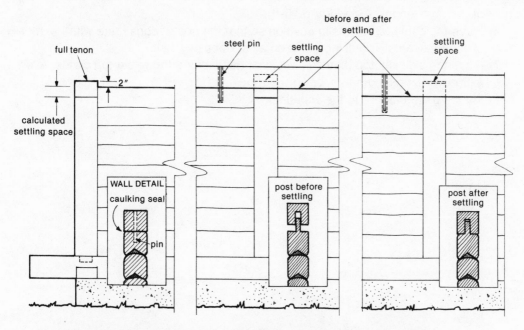

Figure 10–17. Alternate method of post and top plate construction.

Tools: Eye and ear protection, chainsaw, tape measure, electrical mortising jig (optional), electric drill with $9/16$ " (14 mm) auger bit, $1\frac{1}{2}$ " (38 mm) chisel, slick, scribers, carpenter's square, 3 lb (1.5 kg) sledge hammer, $\frac{1}{2}$ " (12 mm) drift pin, chalkline, pencil.

Materials: Top plate and post members, $\frac{1}{2}$ " (12 mm) steel pins, caulking compound.

Procedure:

1) Cut the posts to overall length. (See Figure 10–18.) Cut full shouldered tenons on all the posts, with the length of the top plate tenon equal to the calculated settling space plus 2 " (50 mm). If using green wood calculate $\frac{1}{2}$ " (12 mm) settling space

per vertical foot (300 mm). (In an 8', or 2440 mm, wall there would be 4", or 100 mm, settling.)

2) Lay out the mortise locations on the top plate as described in section **2,** above. Cut the mortises.

3) Raise, plumb, and brace the posts in position. A temporary top plate tie will help to prevent the posts' spreading during installation of the wall's infill pieces.

4) Construct the wall panels on a jig as described in Chapter 8 section **2.** Plumb-cut, number, and assemble the panels between the posts.

5) Flatten the tops of all the wall panels so they are an even 1" (25 mm) below the top of the post tenons. (See Figure 10–18.)

6) Place the gable top plates in position so that the post tenons mate with the mortises. Apply ample caulking between all surfaces.

7) Place the sidewall top plates in position, half-lapping the gable top plates. Allow extra overhang length to support the roof.

8) Pin the plate timbers to the wall timbers.

CHAPTER ELEVEN

Alternative Wall Infills

The purpose of this chapter is to acquaint the reader with stackwall and insulated frame wall with a stucco or siding finish—some of the many different wall infill varieties that are possible in post and beam construction. Along with design flexibility, the use of alternative infills allows this method of construction to be adapted in a great variety of climates and geographic regions. Other infill materials might include rock and mortar, glass, or adobe—or practically anything that affords protection from the elements. Of course, on the inside of the building's walls one can really put one's imagination to work.

Stackwall Infill

Where stackwall originated is anyone's guess, but it is easy to imagine that someone, somewhere, looked at a stack of stovebox cordwood and decided that filling the spaces between the posts with it would make an attractive and substantial wall. From this idea grew a new method of house construction, which has changed only slightly since it was popularized in early eastern Canada. Its inherent problem then was that it could not keep the wind and elements out for any length of time. For as the cordwood expanded and contracted with variations in atmospheric moisture content, it left gaps between the wood and inert filler, and these gaps had constantly to be recaulked. Today's generally accepted stackwall construction involves a double wall system with an inner cavity filled with an insulative material. This provides a warmer wall, and one less prone to air infiltration. A newly constructed house must still be caulked around the cordwood after a year or so, but this is usually a one-time job. If the caulking compound is the petroleum-based type, it will retain its plasticity and allow for the wood's dimensional fluctuations.

Stackwall used for exterior walls should be a minimum of 12″ (300 mm) thick. This allows for 3″ (75 mm) of mortar at either end of the wood and a 6″ (150 mm) cavity. If the wall were thinner, the inner cavity would have to be reduced (causing a cooler wall), for

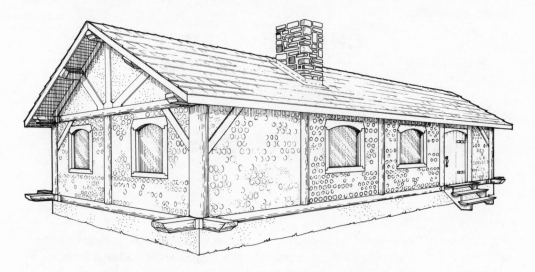

Figure 11-1. Post and beam house with stackwall infill.

a mortar bedding of less than 3″ (75 mm) is likely to crack. To reduce the likelihood of water saturating the walls a large roof overhang will be needed.

Stackwall interior walls need not be double walled, and so can be less than 12″ (300 mm) thick. I have seen some beautiful mosaic walls using colored bottles with stackwall construction. Note, however, that stackwall construction gains strength and rigidity with thickness. Where wall thickness is reduced there should be a reduction in the span between structural supports, or cross-bracing must be installed.

1. Placing knee braces.

A post and beam frame by itself is not rigid without some form of bracing. Log and timber infill give the frame rigidity through the stability of its mass which provides a form of internal bracing. Rock and mortar is another infill medium with sufficient mass stability by itself. Glass, on the other hand, is a low mass material which does not provide significant stability for the framework. Nevertheless, such low mass materials may occupy large floor to ceiling wall areas if some form of bracing maintains the rigidity of the frame, at the building corners—the hinge-points of a frame. Stackwall infill may be considered a medium mass material. It adds some stability to the frame, but where wall lengths exceed 20′ (6 m) additional bracing should be provided.

Common stud framing relies on external sheathing as a form of bracing. The most common method of bracing a timber or log frame is to use knee braces. These are short length timbers which bisect the corner framed by a post and beam at a 45° angle. The resulting triangle will strengthen the corner against horizontal forces applied by wind. Two methods of installing knee bracing within a post and beam frame follow.

Tools: Eye and ear protection, circular saw and/or chainsaw, combination square, tape measure, chalkline, electric drill with $^5/_8$″ (16 mm) auger bit, 1½″ (38 mm) chisel and mallet, slick, pencil.

Materials: Knee brace material, $^5/_8$″ (16 mm) dowels.

Procedure:
1) Figure 11–2 gives the mathematical equation for determining the hypotenuse length of a 45° triangle.

$$y = x \times 1.414$$

Example: Where distance x is 36″ (1000 mm), find the length of the knee brace needed (less any tenon allowance, if applicable).

Knee brace length y = 36″ (1000 mm) × 1.414
$$= 50\,^7/_8″\,(1414\,mm)$$

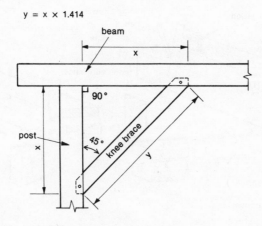

Figure 11-2. Determining the length of the knee brace.

Butt joint knee brace method
Figure 11–3 shows a simple butt joint knee brace.
   After it is cut it is fastened in place with pins or dowels.

1) Prepare the log or timber brace material and cut to rough length, including waste allowance.
2) Using a combination square, lay out the 45° angles as shown in Figure 11–3.
3) Cut the knee brace and pin it in place.

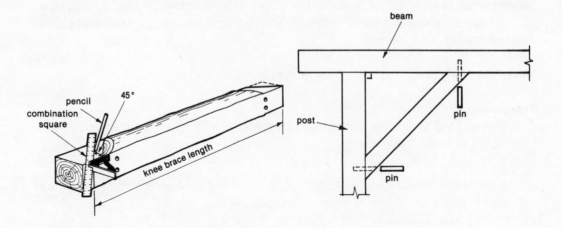

Figure 11-3. Butt joint knee brace method.

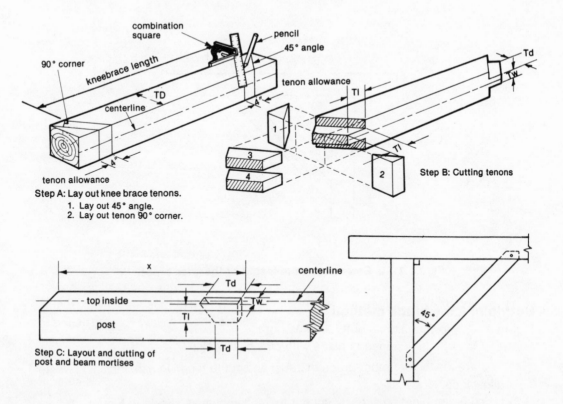

Figure 11-4. Mortise and tenon knee brace.

Mortise and tenon knee brace method

In the case of a free standing frame, where the frame will not be housing an infill material, the mortise and tenon joint is recommended to increase the holding capacity of the brace. Figure 11–4 shows the layout and cutting sequence for executing this joint.

1) Prepare the log or timber brace material and cut to rough length, including tenon and waste allowance.
2) Lay out the knee brace and tenons as shown in step A.
3) Cut the knee brace tenon as shown in step B.
4) Lay out and cut the post and beam mortises as shown in step C. Make sure that the layout distance x is accurate. If it is not, the frame will be out of square. The knee brace has a tapered tenon. Note that the distance TD represents the tenon depth at its widest portion, while Td represents its narrowest.
5) Assemble and dowel the braces in place.

2. Preparing the frame for stackwall infill.

As the stackwall infill will be 12″ (300 mm) thick, the timber or log framework must have broad, flat surfaces of at least 12″ (300 mm) to provide the necessary support. In constructing the log or timber frame, do not cut a spline groove in the post. Instead, rabbeted cuts will provide a better recess for the mortar bedding. (See Figure 11–5.)

Tools: Eye and ear protection, chainsaw, electric drill with ⅝″ (16 mm) and ¾″ (19 mm) auger bits, level, hammer, tape measure, pencil.

Materials: Electrical conduit, electrical wire to local code specifications, bracing material, shingle nails.

Procedure:

1) Construct the log or timber infrastructure, plumb, and brace securely. There should be a post on each side of door or large window openings. Note the rabbeted cuts on the posts in place of spline grooves. (Figure 11–5.)
2) Mark on the frame where any electrical outlet receptacles are to be located. (Refer to building code.) Drill access holes through the sill and run metal conduit piping to feed these outlets, as in Figure 11–5. Later, the electrical wire will be pulled up through the conduit with an electrician's fish tape, beginning from the basement or crawlspace. Note that switches are nearly always located near doorways. The wire to service these switches can be recessed in a groove running inside the doorway. Later this groove will be covered by the door frame. (See Chapter 12 for rough opening specifications.)
3) Embed shingle nails on all surfaces which will be in contact with the mortar; they should protrude ¾″ (19 mm). These nails will help to anchor the mortar to the wood frame.

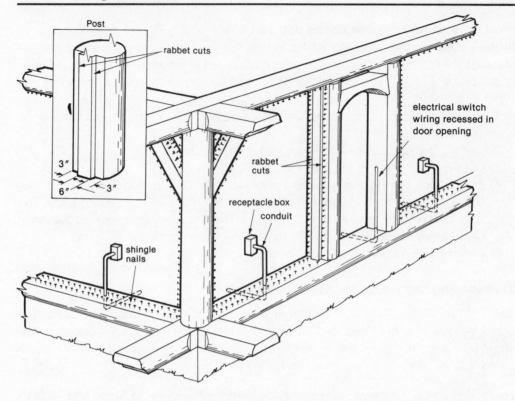

Figure 11-5. Preparing the post and beam frame to receive a stackwall infill.

3. Placing the stackwall infill.

During construction of the wall, rain or snow must not be allowed to wet the insulation and render it useless. To prevent this, cover the open wall every night with a sheet of polyethylene plastic. If your construction schedule will take you into the winter it would be wise to place the roof on the building first leaving the walls till later.

Tools: Eye and ear protection, chainsaw, tape measure, level, drawknife, shovel, mortar mixer, trowel, jointer, stringline, pail, hammer.

Materials:

Cordwood: Use any low density, softwood species such as poplar, pine, tamarack, alder, or cedar, with diameters ranging from 3″–5″ (75–125 mm). Since the logs should be dry, local fire-kill areas are an ideal source for material acquisition. The cordwood will be cut into 12″ (300 mm) lengths, and the bark removed. Note: Heartwood will undergo less dimensional change than sapwood. To estimate the amount of wood needed, use the following formula:

Number of sq. ft. of wall area × .015 = cords of wood required.

Number of sq. meters of wall area × .16 = cords of wood required.

Mortar: A mortar mix contains water, masonry cement, and sand, but no coarse aggregate. Since the house walls will be subject to vibration from time to time, it is recommended that acrylic powder or its equivalent be added to the dry ingredients to make the mix more plastic. A good, workable mixture can be recognized when it will readily adhere to vertical surfaces and to the underside of horizontal surfaces. The dry mix is 5 parts sand to 2 parts masonry cement. Add water to attain the proper plasticity.

Sand: Number of sq. ft./meters of wall area × .18 = cu. ft./meters of sand required.

Masonry cement: Number of sq. ft. of wall area × .1 = bags of cement required.

Number of sq. meters of wall area × 1.08 = bags of cement required.

Insulation: A sawdust and lime mix is inexpensive but does not have as high an insulative factor as regular granular insulation such as vermiculite.

Procedure:
1) Stretch a taut stringline parallel to the outside wall surface section where you will be working. This string will serve as a guide to keep the wall from wavering as you build. The string will be moved up as the wall progresses.
2) Start by applying a 1″ (25 mm) mortar bedding to the surface of the sill. The first row of cordwood will be placed in this bedding. Since mortar sets fast, work only in 2′ (600 mm) sections.
3) Embed this first row of cordwood into the mortar by positioning its outside face ¼″ (6 mm) from the stringline and then tapping it level. There should be a distance of at least ½″ (12 mm) between the cordwood pieces.
4) When the first row is complete begin at one end, and, working in 2′ (600 mm) sections, lay 3″ (75 mm) of mortar on the inside and outside edge of the wall. This mortar will cover the first row of cordwood. Place the second row of cordwood on the mortar bedding, adjust its face to the stringline, then press down to embed it. Maintain its level. Clean up the wall face inside and out where the mortar has become squeezed out.

   The cordwood layers should be staggered for maximum strength.
5) Place the insulation in the wall cavity after finishing each layer.
6) Finishing the mortar is done just as it starts to dry when it can be smoothed without changing its shape. Finish the mortar face so it is flush with the cordwood face, or by pointing, so that a ¼″ (6 mm) recession appears around each cordwood piece. The pointing can be done with a jointer as described in the section on tools, or by using a spoon.

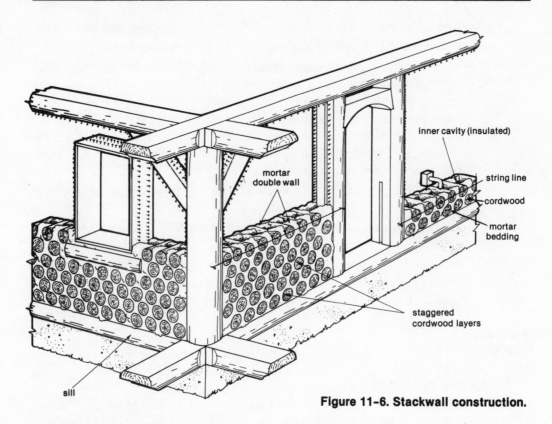

inner cavity (insulated)

string line

cordwood

mortar
bedding

mortar
double wall

staggered
cordwood layers

sill

Figure 11-6. Stackwall construction.

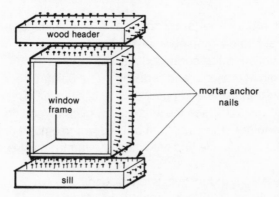

wood header

window
frame

mortar anchor
nails

sill

Figure 11-7. Window box frame.

7) Continue building up the stackwall infill until the window sill height is reached. (Chapter 12, below, covers openings in detail.) In Figure 11-1 the timber window frame incorporates both sill and header. A simpler approach is to make a simple box frame into which the window unit will fit. Figure 11-7 shows a box frame and its accompanying sill and header.

Note: The box frame should be constructed ½ ″ (12 mm) longer and wider than the window unit to allow for a ¼ ″ (6 mm) shim clearance between the frame and window. This space can then be insulated, caulked, and trimmed, once the window is installed.

8) To install the window frame, first place the window sill in a 1 ″ (25 mm) bedding of mortar, and make sure that it is level. Apply another mortar bedding to the top of the sill and set the window box frame in place. Make sure that it is level. Build up the wall to the top of the window box frame, then apply a mortar bedding and set the header in place. Provide a flashing or drip cap allowance above and below the window unit to prevent water from seeping into the wall.

4. Finishing the stackwall infill.

A stackwall infill will, in time, reveal small gaps encircling the cordwood. Though certain procedures can reduce this effect, some gaps will still appear due to shrinkage of both the wood and mortar.

Beginning with the mortar mix, the addition of acrylic powder into the dry mix will increase plasticity and reduce its tendency to shrink. This coupled with slow curing produced by wetting the wall, or else sealing it to prevent moisture loss, will do much to prevent excessive shrinkage.

Since dry wood will both absorb and release moisture in its effort to attain atmospheric equilibrium, even the use of dry cordwood will eventually result in slight gapping. Green wood will undergo a reduction in overall girth as it dries, and then will expand and contract with seasonal changes in the ambient moisture content. As a result, significantly larger gaps will occur than with dry wood. Clearly, then, it is better to use dry cordwood for stackwall infills.

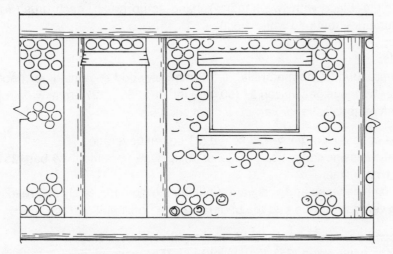

Figure 11-8. Window unit installed in a stackwall building.

Applying a wax sealer or its equivalent to the ends of the pieces, both inside the building and out, will prevent these seasonal changes affecting the wood. Rather than sealing the mortar and wood separately, it is simpler to purchase a sealer which will work for both. Any gaps that do occur should be caulked with a petroleum-based non-hardening compound which retains its elasticity. An obvious precaution is to prevent the wall's being continually rain soaked by extending the roof overhang.

A design alternative would be to stucco most of the wall leaving only the occasional cordwood ends exposed, as shown in Figure 11–8.

Frame Infill with Stucco Finish

Another type of wall infill utilizes a stud frame with a stucco exterior finish. Although many other exterior materials can be applied to a frame wall, stucco is described here because of its attractiveness, simplicity of application, low cost, and its suitability for areas where wood materials are scarce. Moreover, the plastic nature of stucco allows for easy finishing to contoured surfaces such as around curved windows. A stucco surface can also be finished in a variety of ways: smooth, rough, or brushed, or even sculptured in relief, or set with mosaic patterns or glass inlay. It can also be colored. Inside the building, to obtain the same effect, building plaster is coated over drywall.

The surfacing described below is known as a "California finish." It is smoothed over textured facing and is slightly off-white or yellow so as to highlight the wood frame.

Tools: Chainsaw (optional for rabbet cut), level, tape measure, hammer, handsaw, circular saw (optional), chalkline, combination square, wire cutters, utility knife, pencil, mortar trowel, shovel, cement mixer, darby float (48", or 1220 mm, board or metal blade with two handles), hand scrub brush, dash brush (one with a natural rice root pad works best).

Materials:

Frame: Stud frame materials, ³/₈" (9 mm) plywood sheathing, tar paper, stucco wire (16 gauge galvanized 2" (50 mm) mesh × 50" (1270 mm) wide roll), interior finish materials, vapor varrier, insulation, nails.

First coat stucco mix for 25 sq. yd (21 sq. m) coverage:
20 shovels fine sand; 1 bag (88 lb, or 40 kg) type 10 cement; ½ bag (25 lb, or 11.3 kg) type S lime.

Combine these and add water until the mix spreads easily and readily adheres to a vertical surface and the underside of a horizontal surface.

Second coat stucco mix for 50 sq. yd (42 sq. m) coverage:
4 bags white sand (353 lbs, or 160 kg). (For white colored stucco use "China White oo"; for yellow colored stucco use "Valley Yellow oo." Additional colors

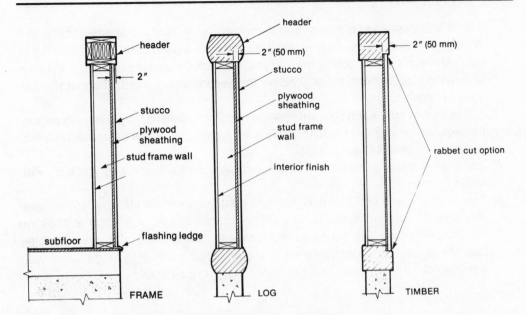

Figure 11-9. Stud framed stucco exterior in a standard frame, and in log and timber post and beam buildings.

739-4
i

may be obtained with colored oxide agents. Instead of white sand you can use a mix of #20 and #30 dolomite coarse and fine sand.); 1 bag white cement (88 lb, or 40 kg) "Federal White" or "Onada" brands; 1 bag Type S lime (50 lb, or 22.7 kg).

Combine and add water until the mix spreads easily and readily adheres to a vertical surface and the underside of a horizontal surface.

Procedure:

1) Construct the stud frame wall infill using one of the methods shown in Figures 11-9. Cutting a 2" × 2" (50 × 50 mm) rabbet groove around the exterior face of the post and beam frame will ensure a more airtight seal. However, if the stud frame is properly nailed to the framework and caulked this will not be necessary.

   Note the installation of horizontal bracing of the stud wall where spacings are greater than 16" (400 mm). This is a precaution against warpage of the plywood sheathing, which provides the actual bracing.

2) Sheath the exterior surface to the stud wall. Apply tar paper and then stucco wire, as shown in Figure 11-10. Stucco wire is nailed to the wall with roofing nails every 12" (300 mm) to supply the anchorage for the stucco.

3) Apply the first coat of stucco with a trowel. Work in one direction without allowing the stucco to dry at the edge. Wherever possible, work the full width of the wall at one time. Any joining should occur at a natural division of the surface, such as at a window or door.

The first coat should cover the stucco wire to a depth of approximately ¼″ (6 mm), and must be thoroughly troweled to insure a good bond. Use the darby to aid in leveling and smoothing the surface. Scratch the surface with a scrub brush to provide a good mechanical bond for the second stucco coat. Then let the wall cure for seven days.

It is best to cure each coat with periodic water sprinkling, together with protection against the elements with tarpaulins. Stucco should never be applied in freezing weather as it is likely to fail.

4) Just before applying the second finish coat, saturate the first coat completely with water.

5) Trowel on the second finish coat mix to a depth of approximately ¼″ (6 mm) and then smooth out. To obtain a textured appearance use a 6″ × 6″ (150 × 150 mm) square dash brush. Dip the brush into a pail of mix and use it to "throw" a facing over the second coat. Complete the entire wall, then very lightly smooth over with a trowel. Cure and protect this final coat as described above.

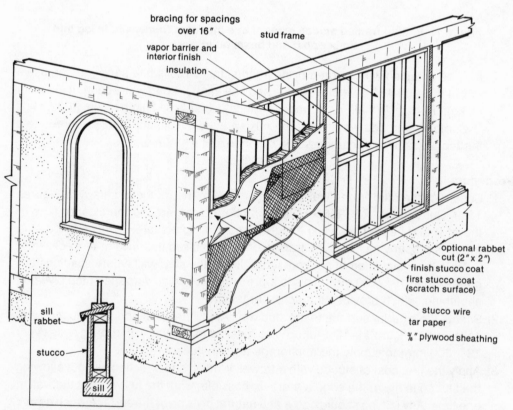

Figure 11-10. Stud framing with stucco infill walls.

6) Complete the wall by insulating, then applying a vapor barrier, and an interior finish, as shown in Figure 11–10.

Stud Framed Wood Exterior Siding

If wood siding is preferred for the exterior, the same stud frame infill method described for a stucco finish would be employed here. Application of the wood siding is a simple matter of nailing it to the face of the plywood sheathing with a layer of tar paper stapled between. (See Figure 11–11.) The style of application can be designed to suit the taste of the builder. (See Figure 11–12.) Exterior wood siding should be cut with a tongue and groove or lapped edge joint, since a butted joint is likely to leave gaps between the boards as a result of hot, dry weather shrinkage and/or buckling during wet weather expansion.

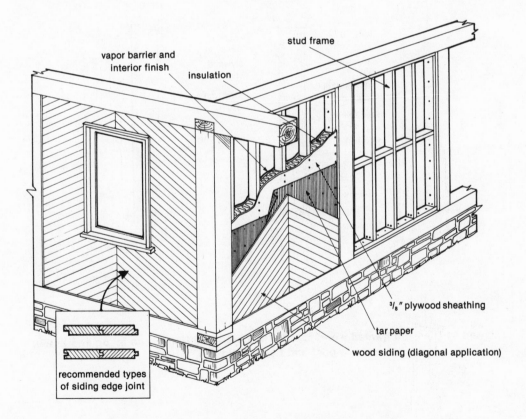

Figure 11-11. Stud framing with wood siding infill.

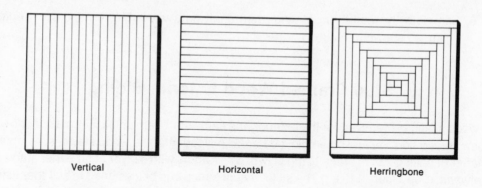

Vertical   Horizontal   Herringbone

Figure 11-12. Alternative patterns of wood siding.

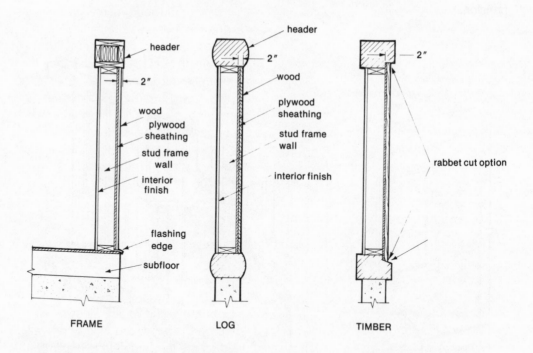

FRAME   LOG   TIMBER

Figure 11-13. Stud framed wood exterior in a standard frame, and in log and timber post and beam buildings.

CHAPTER TWELVE

Openings

Openings are needed to gain access into the building or between rooms, as well as to provide ventilation, illumination, and a view of the outdoor environment. What such openings should not do is to allow too much adverse weather in, or to let precious heat out. They will always, however, be weak links in terms of heat loss because they have less insulative capacity than do solid walls. Doors and windows are responsible for approximately thirty percent of a building's heat loss through thermal conduction, and another ten percent due to air infiltration. It is, therefore, well worth taking time to plan and install doors and windows to maximize the benefits and minimize the drawbacks. Post and beam buildings present no special difficulties in installing doors and windows, but the work may take longer in some cases than it would in a conventional frame building. A list of guidelines for planning openings, doors, and windows follows.

Door and window design factors.

- In case of fire there should be at least two door exits. Exit doors should open inwards so they cannot be blocked by snow.
- At least one exit door should be 36″ (914 mm) wide for furniture movement in and out of the house.
- Doors should be situated on the leeward side of prevailing winter winds.
- Windows to be used for ventilation should be on the windward side of prevailing summer winds, and smaller windows situated on the leeward side to maximize air flow.
- In the northern hemisphere south-oriented windows will maximize solar heat gain. Large, north-oriented windows would be a major source of heat loss during the winter. Generally, this would mean that the larger windows face south, and the smaller ones (or none) face north.
- Glass area should be between seven and fifteen percent of the floor area in the room. If the house is oriented to maximize solar heat gain this will affect this percentage.

- Single large windows provide more illumination than a series of small ones.
- Doors and large windows should be placed between vertical posts in post and beam buildings.
- Outside doors should be insulated and, in cold climates, should incorporate a cold porch to block winter winds.
- Glass is a poor insulator. In double or triple glazed windows it is the dead air space between the panes which serves as insulation. Insulated shutters which close at night are cheaper and afford better protection.
- Wood frame windows or doors will not conduct cold into the house as do metal frame ones.
- Windows are manufactured in standard sizes for round figure openings; non-standard sizes cost more.
- Actual manufactured window dimensions are ½″ (12 mm) undersize to facilitate ¼″ (6 mm) shim clearance within the rough opening.
- Window sizes are listed width first, height second.

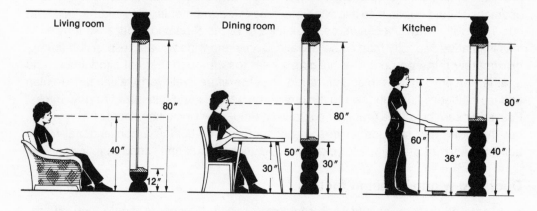

Figure 12-1. Standard window heights.

Rough openings for doors and windows.

A rough opening is an opening in a wall into which a window or door unit will be placed. A door unit consists of the actual door plus its 1½″ (38 mm) frame. In order to place the unit within the rough opening and maintain a "shim clearance" for leveling, the opening should be ½″ (12 mm) larger than the entire window or door unit. Standard door heights are usually 80″ (2032 mm) high. Standard door widths vary depending on their location.

Standard door sizes

Exterior front	36″ × 80″ (914 × 2032 mm)
Exterior rear	34″ × 80″ (864 × 2032 mm)

Exterior service	32″×80″ (813×2032 mm)
Interior doors	30″×80″ (762×2032 mm)

To obtain the rough opening size add 2″ (50 mm) to both width and height. Note that the *exterior* doors will be an extra 1½″ (38 mm) higher to allow for the threshold thickness. (See Figure 12–2.)

Rough opening sizes for doors

Exterior front	38″×83½″ (965×2120 mm)
Exterior rear	36″×83½″ (914×2120 mm)
Exterior service	34″×83½″ (864×2120 mm)
Interior doors	32″×82″ (813×2083 mm)

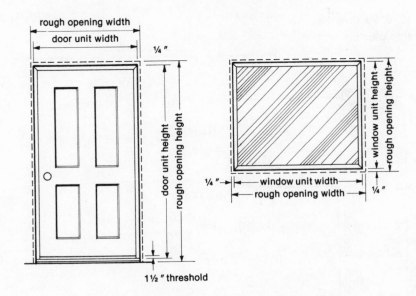

Figure 12-2. Rough openings for doors and windows.

1. Installing doors between posts.

When placing a door between two posts it is important that the post spacing be equal to the rough opening width. For example, the post spacing for a front entrance door would be 38″ (965 mm) wide. After the door unit is installed, plumbed, and leveled the space above it to the top plate can be either framed or of the same infill as the rest of the walls. The door need not contain a structural header as the roof will exert no weight upon it.

Tools: 48″ (1220 mm) level, tape measure, chalkline, handsaw, square, hammer, nail set, pencil, eye and ear protection, chainsaw, 1½″ (38 mm) chisel, and mallet.

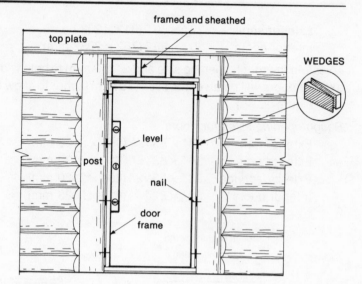

framed and sheathed

top plate

WEDGES

level

post

nail

door frame

Figure 12-3. Making the door frame plumb.

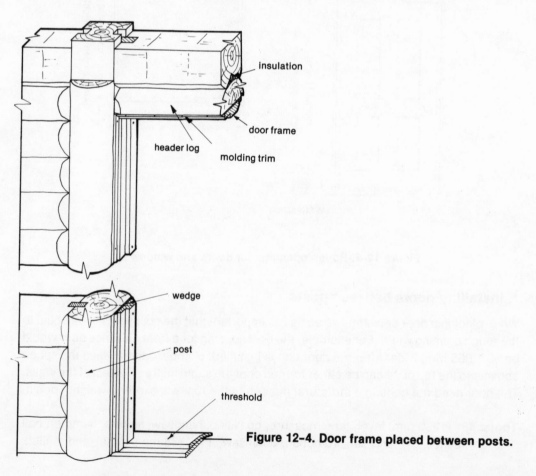

insulation

door frame

header log

molding trim

wedge

post

threshold

Figure 12-4. Door frame placed between posts.

Materials: Door unit, cedar shim wedges, insulation, caulking compound, molding trim, nails, wall infill material.

Procedure:
1) Insert the door frame between the posts.
2) Plumb and level the frame as shown in Figure 12–3. Shim the frame in the rough opening with the wedges, then nail through the frame and wedges into the post.
3) The space above the door can either be framed or built up with whatever wall infill material (i.e., log, half-timber, stackwall) you are using. (See Figure 12–4.)
4) Provide adequate drip edge or flashing protection above the door.
5) Insulate the spaces around the door, then caulk to prevent any air leaks, and apply molding strip. (See section **4,** below, for additional molding trim methods.)

2. Installing windows between posts.

Placing windows between posts rather than within a solid log of half-timber infill wall saves on chainsaw work and eliminates the need for a settling space above the unit. Basically, installing a window between posts follows the same procedure as for installing a door—the post spacing will be equal to the rough opening width of the window unit. It will be necessary to either frame or build up wall infill to the level of the window sill and from the header to the top plate. As with the door it is not necessary to provide a structural header as the roof weight will not bear on the header.

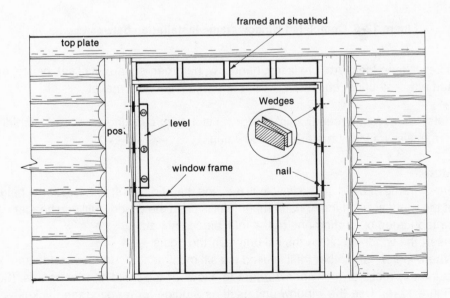

Figure 12–5. Making the window frame plumb.

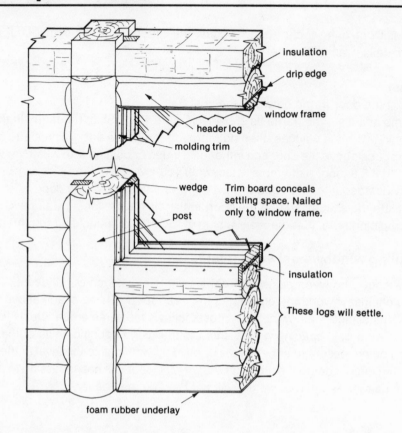

Figure 12–6. Completed window frame installation between posts.

Tools: Level, tape measure, chalkline, handsaw, hammer, square, nail set, pencil, eye and ear protection, chainsaw, 1½″ (38 mm) chisel, and mallet.

Materials: Window unit, cedar shim wedges, insulation, caulking compound, molding trim, nails, wall infill material, window unit.

Procedure:
1) Either frame or build up the wall infill (i.e., log, half-timber, stackwall) to the height of the window sill. If log or half-timber infill is used the window sill and header can be fabricated by cutting one of the infill pieces in half.
2) Insert the window unit on the sill between the posts.
3) Where log or half-timber infill is used the sill must be flat-surfaced inside and out to the thickness of the window frame to allow for the molding trim boards. (See Figure 12–6.) Use the window unit itself as a guide for marking the thickness of the sill.

4) Plumb and level the window, then wedge and nail it to the posts, as shown in Figure 12-5.

5) Frame or place wall infill over the space above the window. Provide adequate drip edge or flashing protection above the window.

6) Insulate the spaces around the window caulk to prevent any air leaks, and apply molding strip. (See section **4,** below, for additional molding trim methods.) Note that the trim boards nailed to the bottom of the window frame are used only when log or half-timber infill is used. These trim boards will conceal any settling space caused by shrinkage of the infill pieces.

3. Installing windows in a solid wood infill wall.

Placing a window within a solid wood wall requires cutting a rough opening. The *width* of the rough opening will be equal to the window unit plus a ½″ (12 mm) shim clearance. The *height* of the rough opening, however, will be equal to the window unit's height plus the amount of settling the logs or half-timbers are calculated to incur. For green wood the amount of settling is ½″ (12 mm) for every 12″ (300 mm) of vertical wood. For example, a window height of 48″ (1200 mm) will require a settling space of 2″ (50 mm).

After the rough opening is cut out, a wood spline is recessed into each side of the opening. These splines will prevent the infill pieces from being jarred out of alignment, and also serve as backing onto which to nail the window. The spline material should be 2″×2″ (38×38 mm) fir and can be easily installed using a router and ¾″ (19 mm) straight carbide bit to cut the groove. There should also be a settling space allowance above the spline.

Plumbing and leveling the window uses the same procedure as those described in section **2,** above. Trimming the window can be done in a number of ways, four methods are outlined in section **4,** below.

Tools: Eye and ear protection, chainsaw, router with ¾″ (19 mm) straight bit, tape measure, chalkline, level, hammer.

Materials: 1″×4″ (19×89 mm) straight edge material, 2″×2″ (38×38 mm) fir splines, nails, window unit.

Procedure:

1) Lay out the rough opening width by plumbing and nailing 1″×4″ (19×89 mm) straight boards to the wall where the window will be placed. The inside distance between the parallel boards will be equal to the window's rough opening width.

2) Measure the window height (80″, or 2032 mm) up from the floor, and add the calculated settling space. (See Figure 12-7.) Chalk a level line between the boards at this height to obtain the header height.

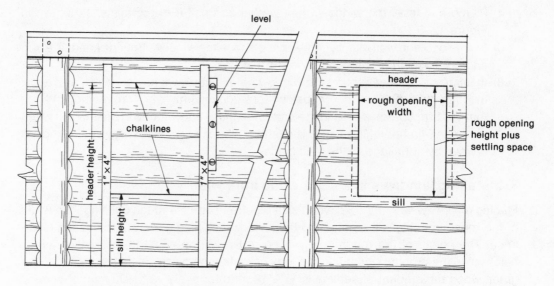

Figure 12–7. Laying out and cutting a rough window opening.

Note: The header and sill log (or half-timber) should have a portion of wood remaining after the rough opening is cut. This may necessitate moving the window unit up or down a couple of inches/centimeters. This is done to provide wide bearing surfaces at the header and sill. It will also ensure that the spline effectively locks the header to the sill. (See Figure 12–7.)

3) From the header measure down the height of the window unit plus the settling place allowance and chalk a level line between the boards, to obtain the sill height.

4) Cut out the rough opening with a chainsaw. Make the vertical cuts first, using the boards as guides. Remove the waste wood pieces.

5) Remove the sill waste wood by either making bread-slice cuts to the line and cleaning, or by plunging the saw bar horizontally through the wall and cutting along the line.

6) Remove the header waste wood by plunging the chainsaw bar horizontally through the wall and cutting along the line. Alternatively, if the top plate is not in position, the header can be removed from the wall and cut.

7) To cut the spline groove use a straight 1″ × 4″ (19 × 89 mm) as a guide, and rout the groove as shown in Figure 12–8.

8) Install and trim the window using one of the methods described in section **4,** below.

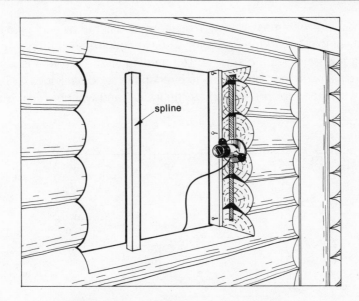

Figure 12-8. Routing the spline groove.

4. Installing and trimming windows.

The following procedures are only for the installation and trimming of windows. Doors are usually placed between posts and so do not require a settling space. However, if a situation arises where a door is to be placed within a log or half-timber infill wall, it will have to be installed and trimmed in the same manner as a window.

There are a variety of methods for installing and trimming windows. The procedures and advantages and disadvantages of each are discussed below. Trim styles may be varied according to the builder's preference. Flashing or a drip cap should be provided in each case.

Tools: Eye and ear protection, chainsaw, tape measure, chalkline, axe, level, adze, handsaw, square, hammer, nail set.

Materials: Windows, trim boards, insulation, caulking compound, finishing nails, vapor barrier.

Trim method A (See Figure 12-9.)

This method sandwiches the opening between trim boards. It necessitates sawing or axing the logs back 5″ (125 mm) from around the opening, on both the inside and outside, to produce a flat surface for the trim boards. Because of the thickness of the wall, the width of the window frame will have to be increased either by adding to the existing frame or by building a box frame around it. The window frame is then placed into the rough opening and nailed to the splines. The settling space above it is insulated and trim boards are nailed to the frame so as to overlap the axed-back logs. This method of installation is very good for preventing air infiltration and will not require any further maintenance.

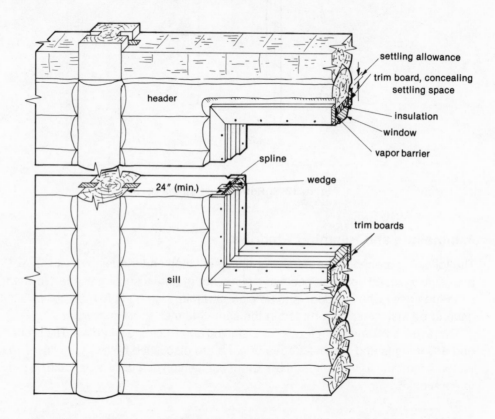

Figure 12-9. Window installed in wood infill wall: trim method A.

Procedure:

1) Insert the widened frame into the rough opening and trace around its inside and outside edge.

2) Remove the frame, then chainsaw or axe the wood, using the outside of the trace lines, back 5″ (125 mm) around the rough opening to accommodate the trim boards. A contoured curve can be made to the header with the header in place. This is done by making successive bread-slice cuts, holding the chainsaw bar in a vertical position, so that the rounded bar nose produces the curve. Next remove

the bulk of the waste wood with an adze, then feather to a smooth curve with a chainsaw. This method is less difficult than it sounds.

3) Replace the frame and nail it only to the splines and sill. Insulate the settling space and caulk any gaps between the logs and frame. (See Figure 12–9.)

4) Finish nail the trim boards to the window frame so that they overlap the logs.
Note: If the logs are small in diameter it may not be necessary to increase the width of the window frame.

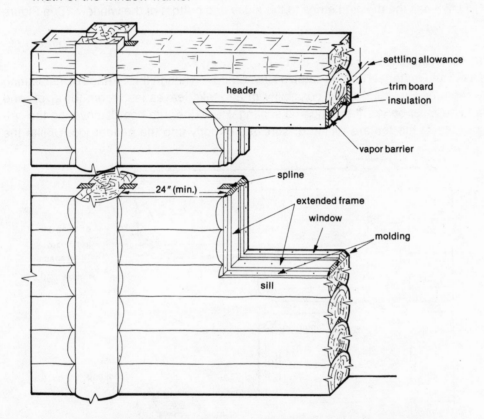

Figure 12–10. Window installed in wood infill wall: trim method B.

Trim method B (See Figure 12–10.)

Tools and materials are the same as in method A. The procedure here is similar to the one used in method A and can be employed where very large logs are used. In this case the window is nailed to the outside of a frame so as to increase its width. The header is traced out and cut back, using the method described in A. The difference here is that instead of trim boards on the sides or bottom, a molding strip is nailed to the window frame instead. There is little room for error in this method, especially on the sides and bottom where air might penetrate.

Procedure:

1) Insert the widened frame into the rough opening and trace its top inside and outside edge.
2) Remove the frame and cut the header log back to accommodate the trim boards. For a better appearance, also bevel the sides of the logs back.
3) Replace the frame and nail it only to the splines and sill. Insulate the settling space, and caulk any gaps between the logs and frame.
4) Finish nail the molding strips to the sides and bottom of the window. (See Figure 12–10.)

Trim method C (See Figure 12–11.)

The tools and materials are the same as in method A. Though this method of installation may seem easier, the greater possibility of air leaks leaves less room for error, and more time must be spent cutting and sealing. Here, the trim boards covering the settling space at the top are nailed or screwed directly into the header log. Unlike the

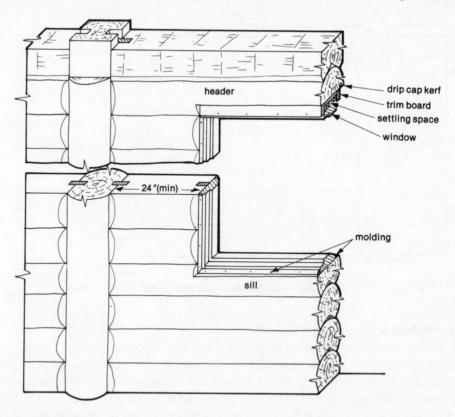

Figure 12-11. Window installed in wood infill wall: trim method C.

previous methods, they then slide down on either side of the window casing during set-tling. Any overcutting at either the header or rough opening sides will necessitate filling with caulking. The header must be cut perfectly straight and sanded to receive the straight trim board. This requires precutting the header or scribing the trim board to fit any curves. Any place where two surfaces only butt against each other instead of overlapping will be difficult to seal against air leaks. This method also involves follow-up maintenance, for as the trim boards settle down over the window (or door) casing they must be removed and planed.

Procedure:
1) Ensure that the rough opening has been cut straight, and is properly sanded.
2) Bevel back the logs on either side of the window.
3) Position the window and nail it to the splines and sill.
4) Insulate the settling space and caulk any gaps between logs and frame.
5) Nail molding strips to the bottom and sides of the window. The side strips should be the length of the window.
6) Cut a rabbet at each end of the settling space trim board, then nail or screw the board into the header on both the inside and outside. During settling the trim board will slide down over the vertical molding strips. (See Figure 12–11.)
7) Caulk any gaps between the window trim and log work.

Trim method D (See Figure 12–13.)
Arched windows add a touch of grace and elegance to a log or half-timber house un-matched by rectangular windows or doors. The procedures for cutting an arched open-ing are described in section **5,** below. Note that the arched window is attached firmly to the header, and the settling space is left at the sill. It is important that the calculated amount of settling space be left at the base of the nailer spline, as shown in the dia-gram. Tools and materials are the same as in method A.

Procedure:
1) Lay out and cut the rough opening according to the methods described in section **5,** below. In this case it would be simplest to merely trace out the window.
2) Insert the window frame into the opening and trace its width onto the log work.
3) Remove the frame, then cut back the log work to accommodate the molding and trim boards.
4) Replace the frame and nail it to the splines and header. Make sure the splines have a settling space allowance at their base. Insulate and caulk any gaps be-tween logs and frame.
5) Finish nail the molding strips and the trim boards as shown in Figure 12–12.

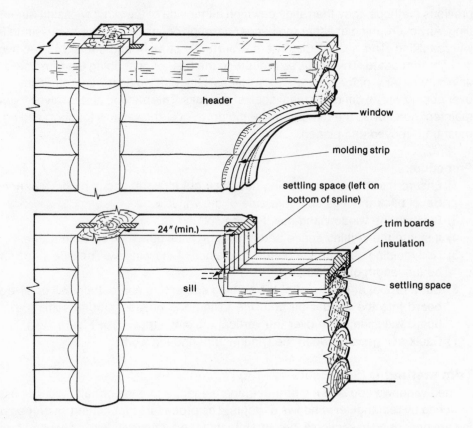

Figure 12-12. Arched window installed in wood infill wall: trim method D.

5. How to lay out and cut an arched opening.

Sweeping archways dividing living areas inside a home add elegance and individuality to the entire structure. If you can make or afford to buy arched windows and doors, it is well worth the extra time for the resulting amount of visual effect.

This section explains the steps for cutting arched openings in log or half-timber infill walls. The main preparation is the lateral groove which, when cut, should expose a flat or cupped face rather than an unsightly ''V'' groove. To cut a curved arch with the chainsaw will require the round-backed cutting tooth of a chipper chain. (A chisel chain with a straight-backed cutting edge cannot initiate a curved cut.)

Tools: Eye and ear protection, chainsaw with chipper chain, disc sander, tape measure, chalkline, level, hammer, axe, pencil or crayon.

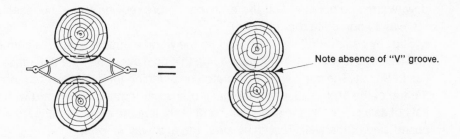

Note absence of "V" groove.

Figure 12–13. Flattening between top and bottom scribe lines will give flat, mated surfaces for arched openings.

Materials: Length of single strand wire, nails.

Procedure:

1) After an archway is cut its log or half-timber face surfaces will be exposed. Unsightly "V" grooves between the scribed pieces will look unfinished and amateurish. Instead, as the infill walls are being constructed, prepare the lateral grooves where the opening will be cut out (usually 3"–4", or 75–100 mm, on either side of the cutline), to reveal either a cupped or flat mated surface.

   However, cupping the lateral groove is a hit-or-miss procedure as it is difficult to remove just the right amount of wood: too much and there is a gap, too little and the scribed logs or half-timbers will not fit together exactly. The cutting procedure requires the rounded nose of the chainsaw bar. An easier, more exact method of preparing the lateral groove is to flatten the area between the scribe lines, as shown in Figure 12–13.

2) In order to prepare the lateral grooves it is necessary to know the parameters of the arched opening. Figure 12–14 shows how to lay out the archway using a wire and pencil in a modified compass arrangement. A wire is used rather than a string, because the latter will stretch. Note that lowering the focal point reduces the amount of curvature. These diagrams indicate with a broken line where the lateral grooves will have to be cupped or flattened.

3) Lay out the archway on both sides of the wall using the illustrated compass.

4) Cutting the sides of the opening is quite straightforward; the use of guide boards is recommended. After the sides are completed cut the curved header by one of the following:

   a) Remove the header from the wall and cut the curve.

   b) Cut the entire arch within the wall.

   The second method is easier than it sounds and is the one recommended. It requires a chainsaw with a sharp chipper chain. The arch is cut from the top downwards, completing half the archway before moving to the opposite side of the wall to complete the other half.

Start by penetrating the bar nose into the wood a couple of inches/centimeters and tracing the arch line. Continue doing this until about half the thickness of wall has been cut. The cut is then completed by plunging the chainsaw bar through at the top of the arch, and, using the *back* of the bar, cutting downward with the initial cut as a guide. Do the same for the other half of the arch, working from the opposite side of the wall. Then disc sand the archway smooth.

Note: Some builders keep a modified chain on hand for cutting arches. Removing every second cutting tooth on one side of the chipper chain will result in a curved cut.

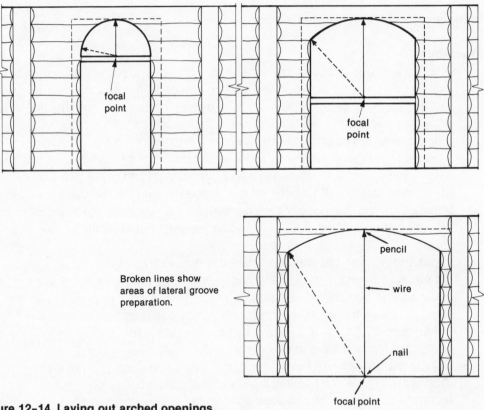

Broken lines show
areas of lateral groove
preparation.

Figure 12-14. Laying out arched openings.

CHAPTER THIRTEEN

The Roof System

If many people shy away from constructing an open timber or log roof structure it's with good reason: The conventional architecturally drawn exposed beam and trussed roof structures all employ metal plates instead of joinery. Carpentry books offer only basic knowledge, and the few other information sources are either painfully confusing or leave much to the imagination. In this chapter I hope to unravel the mystery and difficulty of structural exposed beam roof construction in a simple and logical manner. The confusion often associated with joinery layout procedures will be avoided by graphic planning, template use, and step-by-step instruction.

Heavy roof members are laid out and cut into their component parts on the ground or on the building's subfloor prior to final placement. With this approach the builder will have the information to construct a number of roof structures and the means with which to create variations. While only the common gable roof is described here, the method remains the same for other roof styles as well.

This chapter begins with illustrations of the various roof structures. These are followed by the terms and geometry of roof layout, and then by the actual construction of the roof. Any and all types of roof coverings may be applied to these roof structures. The internal strength of these roof systems allows for the inclusion of insulated sod roofs as another option. This roof covering originates in northern Europe, and is very durable, most attractive, and complimentary to log and timber post and beam buildings.

Strict adherence to the structural beam sizes and code requirements must be observed throughout the entire roof construction. As well, the strength of the roof structure depends upon the execution of the joinery. Therefore these stress joints must be tight fitting in order to be effective.

Roof Structures

Conventional trussed roof systems

This type of roof framing uses either factory or site manufactured 2″ × 4″ (38 × 89 mm) or 2″ × 6″ (38 × 140 mm) frame trusses. Such a style of roof framing is common in stud frame construction today. It is included here to show that such a common method of roof framing is also possible for post and beam buildings.

Figure 13–1 shows a roof framed with conventional trusses. The building's top plate is also of the dimensional type (as described in Chapter 8) to simplify truss placement and soffit framing. The ceiling in this house is closed and no structural beams are exposed. Such a closed ceiling is often employed for kitchens, and in many cases houses will have a combination of closed and open beam ceiling combinations.

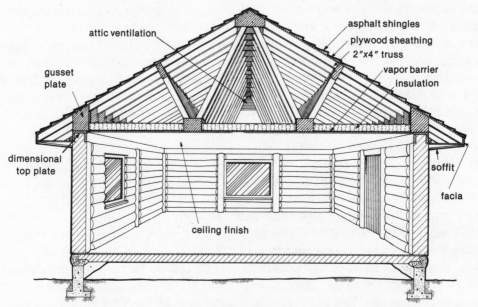

Figure 13–1. Conventional trussed roof for closed ceilings.

Conventional raftered roof systems

Another option using conventional framing material is to use 2″ × 10″ (38 × 235 mm) rafters. The air space between the plywood roof sheathing and the insulation is needed to ventilate the roof and keep it cold, so as to prevent accumulated snow from melting. If snow were to melt during freezing temperatures, water will run down to the cold eaves where it will freeze, causing ice damming, water backup, and possible inside leaks. Roof ventilation also prevents water vapor saturating the insulation and rendering it useless.

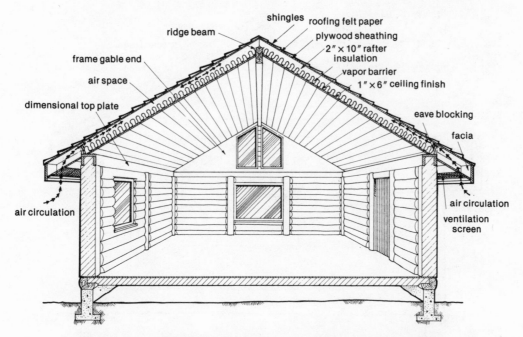

ridge beam

frame gable end

air space

dimensional top plate

air circulation

shingles | roofing felt paper

plywood sheathing

2″ × 10″ rafter
insulation

vapor barrier

1″ × 6″ ceiling finish

eave blocking

facia

air circulation

ventilation
screen

Figure 13–2. Conventional raftered roof system for open ceilings.

The open ceiling shown here in Figure 13–2 has the finish material attached to the underside of the rafters. The top plate is again of the dimensional type to simplify rafter placement and soffit framing. (Although Figure 13–2 shows a ridge beam, the corresponding directions are for a rafter layout using both a ridge beam and ridge board.)

Timber raftered roof systems (with collar-tie truss)

By relying on the size and strength of timbers one can replace the many smaller conventional frame rafter components with fewer but larger timber principal rafters, and can then join these together with ridge and purlin beams. Incorporating a collar-tie beam half-way up the principal rafter, as shown in Figure 13–3, will keep the rafter legs from spreading or sagging due to excessive roof loading. The roof covering illustrated here is insulated sod, common to northern Europe. As sod is heavier than the more conventional coverings, the roof structure should include a tie-beam to further arrest any spreading forces. (See section **13,** below, for sod roof construction.) Open beam timber framing gives an impression of both strength and finesse unattainable by conventional framing methods. The steps in sections **4** and **5,** below, which correspond to Figure 13–3, describe two methods of principal rafter joinery, as well as a method for collar-tie truss construction. The top plate must be a solid wood log or timber to allow for wood removal joinery. The gable end incorporates a king post truss with struts. (See section **6,** below, for details.)

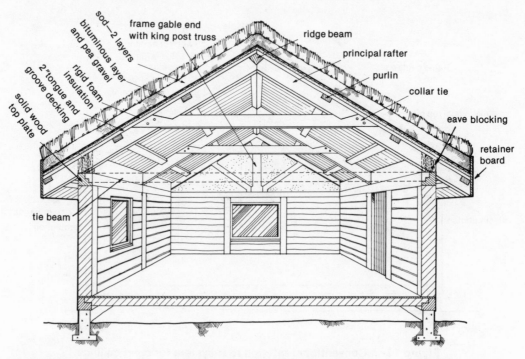

Figure 13-3. Timber raftered roof system with trussed rafters and frame gable ends for open ceiling.

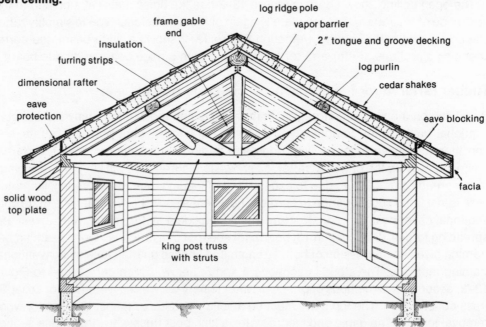

Figure 13-4. Timber trussed roof system with log ridge pole and purlins.

Timber trussed roof systems (with log ridge pole and purlins)

Figure 13–4 shows a king post with strut roof midspan truss supporting log (or timber) ridge and purlin beams. An understanding of this truss construction provides the basis for constructing many other types of roof. The steps for this and other forms of joinery are simplified with the use of hardboard templates. As long as the support beams conform to the tables in Appendix III, a roof structure such as this is very strong. Included in the procedural instructions are three methods of frame gable end construction which will accommodate the ridge and purlin beams.

Log ridge pole and purlin roof systems (with log gable ends)

This type of open beam ceiling is common to many log homes. Figure 13–5 shows a log ridge pole and purlins supported by log gable ends. The corresponding directions beginning in section **9,** below, give two methods for log gable end construction, and for ridge pole and purlin placement.

This building also shows a log tie beam, which serves to counteract the spreading forces exerted by the roof on the walls. To function correctly the intersecting joint at the top plate should be a locking dovetail or else be securely pinned. Note also that the rafters do not touch at the ridge. A 2″ (50 mm) space provision has been made to prevent binding at the peak after settling of the log gable ends. A 7′ (2 m) high gable end constructed of green logs will settle an anticipated 3½″ (90 mm) causing a slight change in the roof slope. The peak gap is incorporated for this reason.

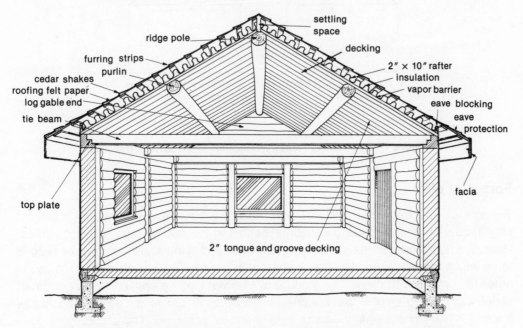

Figure 13–5. Log ridge pole and purlin roof system with log gable ends.

The log materials for gable ends should be thoroughly seasoned, in addition to the settling factor, there is a natural accumulation of heat near the roof peak, as heat rises. This heat will cause rapid drying of green, short log lengths, resulting in excessive checking.

The handling of short log pieces unsupported on the ends, at break-neck heights, is awkward and sometimes dangerous. For this reason, the log gable end construction methods outlined in this book involve building them on the ground. Afterwards the finished gable end can be dismantled and reassembled on the building's top plate.

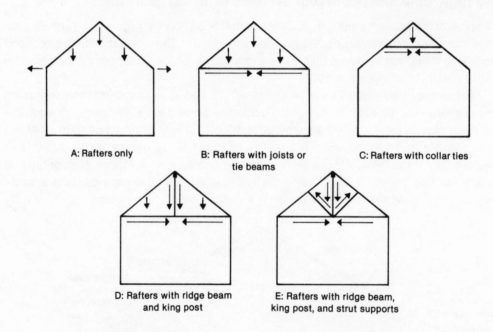

A: Rafters only B: Rafters with joists or tie beams C: Rafters with collar ties

D: Rafters with ridge beam and king post E: Rafters with ridge beam, king post, and strut supports

Figure 13-6. Loading forces in relation to structural framing.

Forces at play

The roof is subjected to two loading forces while the rest of the house frame is subject only to one. Vertical posts and horizontal beams in the house frame support vertical loads. Roofs, because of their sloping rafters, change this vertical loading into a second force which tries to spread the frame apart. It is important to visualize these forces in order to contend with them. The amount of external loading applied to a sloped roof varies with the degree of slope. The chart in Appendix III, *Defining loads,* shows that as the roof increases in slope, the snow load becomes correspondingly less.

Moreover, massive structural members alone will not guarantee that the building is structurally sound. If the crucial joinery points are not tight fitting the entire framework becomes weak, in the same way that a chain is only as strong as its weakest link. Any structural area, where loading forces come into play, must be correctly constructed.

Figure 13–6 illustrates how vertical forces create horizontal spreading forces on a sloped roof. These forces can be dealt with by using various ways of tying the rafters together or redirecting the force.

In A, a gable roof is shown with lone rafters. The forces created are forcing the walls apart, with no method for arresting these forces.

In B, the spreading forces are arrested by tying the walls together with the addition of joists or tie-beams. However, if the rafters are over 16′ (4.8 m) long, they could sag under snow loads.

C shows a collar-tie arresting both the spreading forces and the vertical load forces which cause rafter sag.

In D, the spreading forces are redirected vertically. Here the ridge beam is supported by a kingpost, and the rafters virtually hang from the ridge beam. The rafters therefore exert no spreading force, but if they are over 16′ (4.8 m) long, they will sag due to vertical load force.

E shows the same arrangement as D, but with strut supports. These struts redirect some of the vertical force back upwards to support the rafter and prevent sagging.

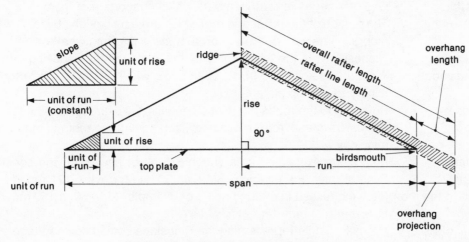

Figure 13–7. Gable roof terminology.

Basic roofing principles and terms

Before one can begin construction of the roof frame the basic roofing principles and terms must be understood. Though Figure 13–7 shows a gable roof with two sloping sides, all other roof types use the same principles and terms. A roof is a combination of right-angle triangles, and the gable roof shown here employs two triangles joined back-to-back. In roofing, the altitude of the triangle is called the "rise". It is measured from the building's top plate to its peak or "ridge." The base of the triangle is called the "run." It is half the "span" or width of the building. To increase a roof slope the rise is increased while the run stays constant, rather like raising the roof of a tent. The triangle's hypotenuse is called the "line length." It is equal to the rafter length, less any overhang projection. In order to frame a roof you must know what the run and rise distances are, and these are easily taken from the building's blueprints. You must also know the line length distance of the rafter plus the overhang allowance in order to purchase the materials with which to frame the roof.

Roofing terms

Span: The horizontal distance between the outer edges of the top plates; the width of the building.

Run: Half the span distance.

Rise: The vertical distance measuring from the building's top plate to the peak. The roof's steepness increases as the rise is increased.

Line length: The hypotenuse of the triangle, equal to the length of the rafter less the overhang length.

Rafter: One of a series of roof members which supports roof loads.

Overhang: The portion of the rafter and roof which projects past the building walls (approximately 3', or 1 m) to protect the walls from weather.

Ridge: Highest part of the roof formed by the joining of the opposing rafters.

Birdsmouth: A notch resembling a bird's open beak, which is cut in the rafter for joinery to the top plate.

Slope: Referring to the roof's angle of steepness it is expressed as "pitch" in standard imperial roof terminology, and "cut of the roof" in metric terminology.

Pitch: Roof slope expressed as a variable "unit of rise" over the constant "unit of run." For example, 8/12, an 8″ rise for every 12″ run.

Cut of the roof: Pitch expressed in metric units. For example, 150/250, a 150 mm rise for every 250 mm run.

Unit of rise:⎫
Unit of run:⎭   A small triangle representing the roof slope scaled down for use on a rafter square.

1. Methods for determining rafter length.

Pythagorus' theorem for determining rafter length
This theorem is useful for finding the hypotenuse (line length) of a right angle triangle, but it will not lay out the rafter ridge and birdsmouth cuts. As explained in Chapter 5,

section **1,** in determining the diagonals for a building's foundation layout, the following mathematical formula is used: $a^2 + b^2 = c^2$.

Examples below are for both standard and metric. (See Figure 13–8.)

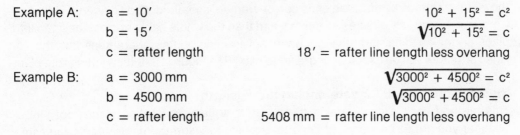

Example A:	$a = 10'$	$10^2 + 15^2 = c^2$
	$b = 15'$	$\sqrt{10^2 + 15^2} = c$
	c = rafter length	$18'$ = rafter line length less overhang
Example B:	$a = 3000$ mm	$\sqrt{3000^2 + 4500^2} = c^2$
	$b = 4500$ mm	$\sqrt{3000^2 + 4500^2} = c$
	c = rafter length	5408 mm = rafter line length less overhang

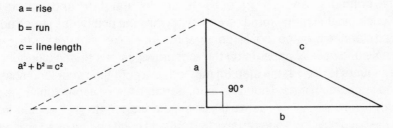

Figure 13–8. Determining the rafter line length with Pythagorus' theorem.

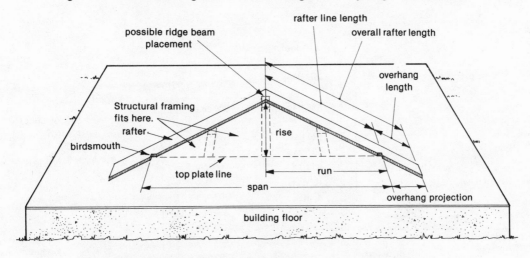

Figure 13–9. Full scale drawing of roof's shape on subfloor.

Lofting method for determining rafter length

This method involves drawing the roof shape full scale on the building's subfloor, after which the rafter dimensions and joinery details can be measured directly from the lofting plan. It is a particularly useful method for heavy log and timber truss construction, or for log ridge pole and purlin layout, where the framed gable ends must accommodate the ridge pole and purlins. For example, in section **7,** below, the lofting method is used for framing the gable ends. In fact, if there is a machine on site capable of lifting the entire framework, the gable ends can be framed, sheathed, and finished—including windows—using the loft lines as guides, and then the whole gable end can be lifted into place on the building. In heavy member roof framing, lofting guarantees that the finished structure will be exactly according to plan. See Figure 13–9 for a lofting roof plan.

Stepping-off method for determining rafter length

This method uses a carpenter's metal rafter square to duplicate the roof slope. Whether you are using standard imperial building measurements or metric, the same fundamental principles apply. Figure 13–10 shows standard and metric framing squares. In each the unit of run remains constant while the unit of rise varies according to the desired steepness of the roof slope. A representation of the roof slope is noted as a small triangle and usually appears on the roof drawings of a house blueprint.

The rafter square is used in the step-off method to lay out the rafter length, as well as the ridge and birdsmouth cuts. Though a more portable method than lofting, it is not as fool-proof. It will help to try to visualize the completed rafter as it will appear in its final position on the building. Once one rafter is laid out and cut it can be used as a pattern to lay out the others.

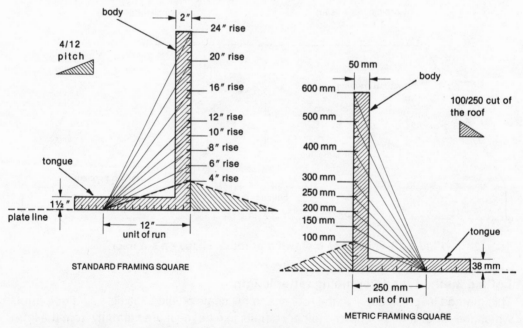

Figure 13-10. Rafter framing square simulating roof slope.

The following two examples give standard and metric roof rafter layouts respectively.

Example A: standard measurement

Run = 15′
Slope = 6/12
Overhang projection = 3′

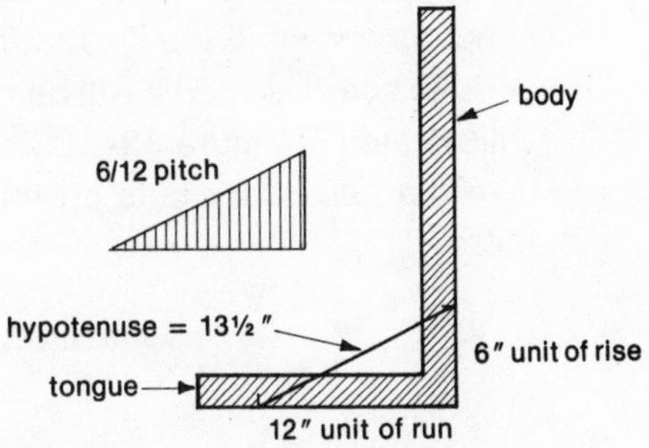

Figure 13–11. Measuring the hypotenuse off a standard rafter square.

Procedure:

1. Determine the number of units of run from the total run of the building.

    Total run 15′ = 15 units of 12″ run.

2. Determine the overall length of the rafter material needed. If the roof rise height is known, the line length of the rafter can be found using Pythagorus' theorem, $a^2 + b^2 = c^2$. If not, the hypotenuse can be measured directly from the square, as shown in Figure 13–11 (i.e., 13½″), and the rafter length can be found by multiplying the hypotenuse by the number of units of run.

    Rafter line length = 15 units × 13½″ = 202½″

The length of rafter overhang can be found by multiplying the overhang projection (expressed in units of run) by the hypotenuse.

    Rafter overhang length = 3 units × 13½″ = 40½″

Adding together the rafter line length, the overhang length, and a wastage allowance of 6″ will give the overall length of the rafter material needed.

        rafter line length = 202½″
        overhang length = 40½″
            wastage = 6″
    overall length of rafter = 249″

3. Select a straight length of rafter material and chalk a line offset by 2″ parallel with the bottom edge, as shown in Figure 13–12A. In post and beam construction the roof rafters are often large timbers with dimensions that are not strictly uniform. This offset chalked line will serve as an exact line of reference, while also setting the depth of the rafter birdsmouth.

4. Begin stepping-off by aligning the units of rise and run of the square on the chalked line, and marking the ridge cut line as shown in Figure 13–12A. Continue stepping-off the square 15 times down the rafter until the birdsmouth is reached, then mark the birdsmouth as shown in the illustration.

5) To step-off the overhang turn the square over as shown in Figure 13–12B, and step-off an additional three 12″ units for the desired 36″ projection. Complete the tail cut as shown in the illustration.

6) If a ridge board is used it will be necessary to shorten the rafter half the thickness as illustrated in Figure 13–12C.

7) Make the necessary cuts on this pattern rafter and use it to lay out the other rafters.

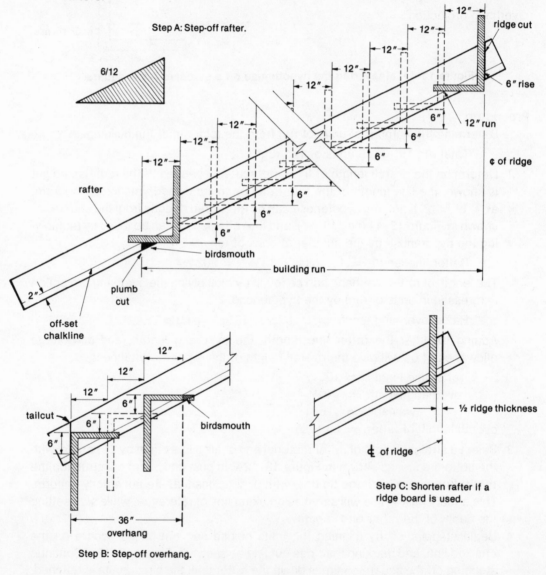

Figure 13–12. Standard measurement roof rafter layout.

Example B: metric measurement

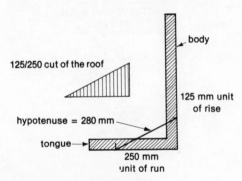

Run = 4572 mm
Slope = 125/250
Overhang projection = 1000 mm

125/250 cut of the roof

body

125 mm unit of rise

hypotenuse = 280 mm

tongue

250 mm unit of run

Figure 13-13. Measuring the hypotenuse off a metric rafter square.

Procedure:

1) Determine the number of units of run from the total run of the building.

   Building run 4572 ÷ 250 = 18.28 units of 250 mm run.

2) Determine the overall length of the rafter material needed. If the roof rise height is known, the line length of the rafter can be found using Pythagorus' theorem, $a^2 + b^2 = c^2$. If not, the hypotenuse can be measured directly from the square, as shown in Figure 13-13, (i.e., 280 mm), and the rafter length can be found by multiplying the hypotenuse by the number of units of run.

   Rafter line length = 18.28 units × 280 mm = 5118 mm.

   The length of rafter overhang can be found by multiplying the overhang projection (expressed in units of run) by the hypotenuse.

   Rafter overhang length = 4 units × 280 mm = 1120 mm.

   Adding together the rafter line length, the overhang length, and a waste allowance of 150 mm will give the overall length of the rafter material needed.

   rafter line length = 5118 mm
   overhang length = 1120 mm
   wastage = 150 mm
   overall length of rafter = 6388 mm

3) Select a straight length of rafter material and chalk a line offset 50 mm parallel with the bottom edge, as shown in Figure 13-14A. In post and beam construction, the roof rafters are often large timbers with dimensions that are not always uniform. The offset chalked line serves as an exact line of reference, while also setting the depth of the rafter birdsmouth.

4) In order to step-off the rafter square 18.28 times it will be necessary to obtain the .28 portion of the run. When you multiply .28 × 250 (unit of run), the result is 70 mm, and is referred to as the "odd unit." To begin stepping-off, align the unit of rise and run of the square on the chalked line, as shown in the inset in Figure 13-14A, and mark the ridge cut line. Next, slide the square up the ridge cut line

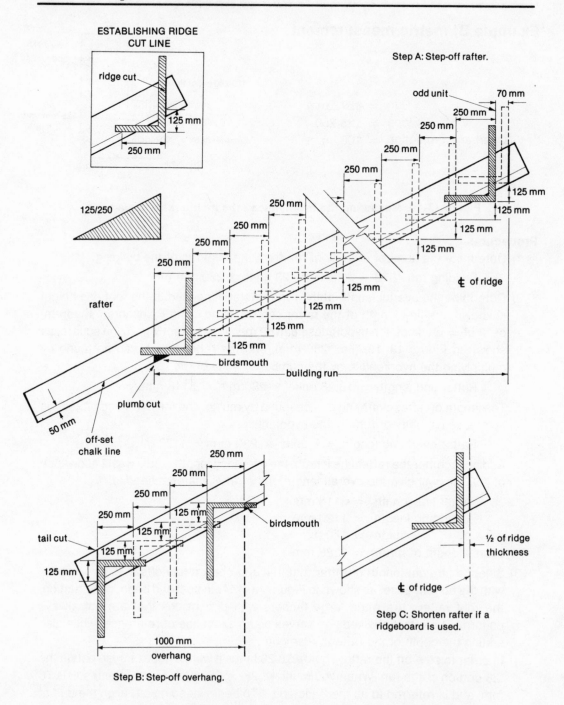

ESTABLISHING RIDGE
CUT LINE

ridge cut

125 mm

250 mm

Step A: Step-off rafter.

odd unit

70 mm

250 mm

250 mm

250 mm

250 mm

125 mm

125 mm

125 mm

125 mm

125 mm

250 mm

125/250

250 mm

250 mm

₵ of ridge

250 mm

125 mm

125 mm

rafter

125 mm

125 mm

125 mm

birdsmouth

building run

plumb cut

50 mm

off-set
chalk line

250 mm

250 mm

250 mm

250 mm

125 mm

125 mm

birdsmouth

tail cut

125 mm

½ of ridge
thickness

125 mm

₵ of ridge

1000 mm
overhang

Step C: Shorten rafter if a
ridgeboard is used.

Step B: Step-off overhang.

Figure 13-14. Metric measurement roof rafter layout.

until 70 mm on the tongue of the square intersects the chalked line, as shown in Figure 13–14A. Mark this odd unit, then continue stepping-off the square 18 times down the rafter, using the regular rise and run units, until the birdsmouth is reached. Then mark the birdsmouth as shown.

5) To step-off the overhang turn the square over, as shown in Figure 13–14B, and step-off an additional four 250 mm units for the desired 1000 mm projection. Complete the tail cut as shown.

6) If a ridge board is used it will be necessary to shorten the rafter half the thickness as illustrated in Figure 13–14C.

7) Make the necessary cuts on this pattern rafter and use it to lay out the other rafters.

Part 1: Transverse Framing

In the following methods of roof framing, rafter and truss construction are explained. This type of roof construction is called "transverse framing" (where structural members run at right angles to the ridge line). The structural members provide the strength of the roof while their form gives the roof its slope. See Part 2 of this chapter for methods of longitudinal roof framing.

2. Placing conventional framed trusses with a close ceiling.

Where an open, vaulted ceiling is not desired, conventional framed trusses allow for a simple, quick to construct roof system. The structural members comprising these

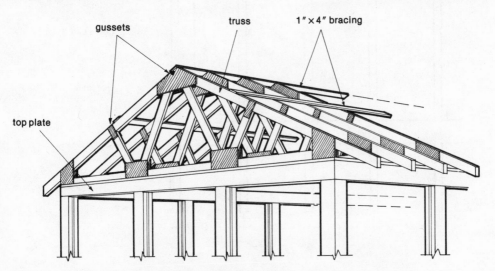

Figure 13-15. Conventional framed truss for a closed ceiling.

trusses are either 2″ × 4″ (38 × 89 mm) or 2″ × 6″ (38 × 140 mm), depending on the span and roof slope of the house. Either plywood or metal gussets sandwich all butt-joined locations and are essential to the strength of the truss. See Appendix V for specifications for constructing a ''W'' truss. The following procedure describes how the trusses are placed on the building. The top plate of the building will be a dimensional one. As there is no joinery involving wood removal a log or timber top plate is unnecessary. There is, however, no gable end roof projection allowance with this dimensional top plate. This necessitates a ''ladder'' framework to support the roof covering, should the house design call for one. For two methods of ladder and gable end construction, see section **3**, below. Figure 13–1 shows this type of roof.

Tools: Tape measure, level, hammer, handsaw, pencil.

Materials: Trusses, 1″ × 4″ (19 × 89 mm) bracing, nails.

Procedure:
1) Ensure that the building's top plate is level and square.
2) Beginning from the outside edge of the top plate at one gable end, lay out the first truss so that its position will be flush with this outside edge. Layout all the other trusses on 24″ (600 mm) spacings, as shown in Figure 13–16. The opposite gable end truss will be set flush with the outside top plate edge, regardless of the spacing outcome.

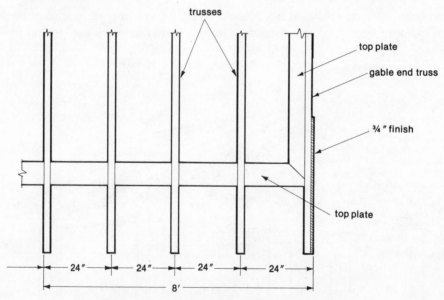

Figure 13-16. Conventional truss spacing.

3) Position and plumb the trusses on the layout marks, as shown in Figure 13–15. Nail the trusses to the top plate, and provide bracing to the structure.
4) Apply roof sheathing and covering. (See Figure 13–1.)
5) The ceiling's finishing material is applied to the under surface of the trusses' bottom cords. Then a vapor barrier and insulation are put in place. (See Figure 13–1.)

3. Constructing a conventional frame rafter roof: two open ceiling methods.

Another roof construction method using conventional framing materials is the raftered roof. Unlike the previous method, this roof allows for an open ceiling. The cavity between the rafters contains the insulation and for the previously mentioned reasons, it must be ventilated.

The raftered roof may employ a ridge board or beam. As well as the difference in their appearance, there is a difference in direction of the roof loading forces. With a ridge board the vertical load forces exert a spreading force on the rafters, which in turn transmit these forces horizontally to the side walls. With a ridge beam, however, the rafters virtually hang from the timber, and the load forces are exerted vertically through the gable support posts, under the beam, and along the rafter's length. Unlike a ridge board, the ridge beam now serves as a structural support, and its size will be dependent upon the loading and span factors, just as for a floor girder. Appendix III contains information on roof beam sizes.

The dimensional top plate here described does not allow for a gable roof projection. If an overhang is desired, as is usually the case, a ladder must be constructed. This ladder can be made in two ways, just as the gable end itself can be built in two ways, depending on whether a ridge board or ridge beam is used. Two methods of rafter frame construction are explained below. Figure 13–2 provides a useful reference for these procedures.

Tools: Rafter square, tape measure, chalkline, level, circular saw, handsaw, hammer, pencil.

Materials: 2″ × 10″ (38 × 235 mm) rafters, 2″ × 6″ (38 × 140 mm) gable end material, 2″ × 8″ (38 × 184 mm) ridge board or ridge beam (see Appendix III), nails.

Procedure: Ridge board method.
1) Ensure that the building's top plate is level and square.
2) Lay out the rafter spacing according to Figure 13–18 on both the top plate and ridge board.
3) Lay out and cut the rafters. (See the stepping-off method described on page 192.)
4) Construct the gable ends according to Figure 13–19 and position them on the building. Gable end layout and construction can be simplified by being lofted on the subfloor.

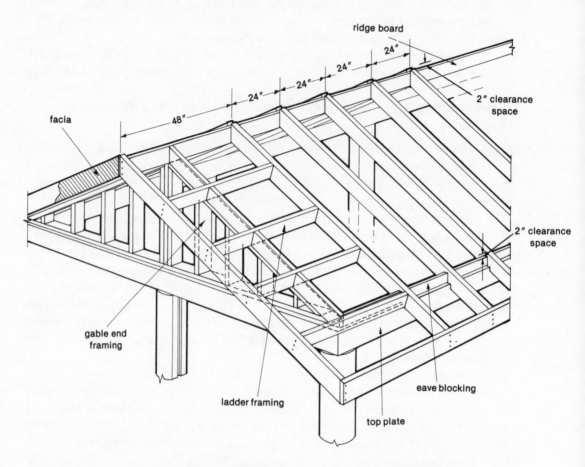

Figure 13-17. Constructing a raftered roof: ridge board method.

5) Position the ridge board, making sure it is straight and level.

6) Nail the rafters to the ridge board, maintaining a gap at the ridge for air circulation. (See Figure 13–17.) Construct the gable end ladder at this time also.

7) Apply roof sheathing and covering. The ceiling's finishing material is applied to the under surface of the rafters.

Procedure: Ridge beam method.

1) Erect and brace the ridge beam on gable support posts, as shown in Figure 13–20. The height of the ridge beam can be determined from Figure 13–19.

2) Lay out the rafter spacings, as shown in Figure 13–21.

3) Lay out, cut, and place the rafters. To lay out the ridge beam notch refer to the Figure 13–20 inset.

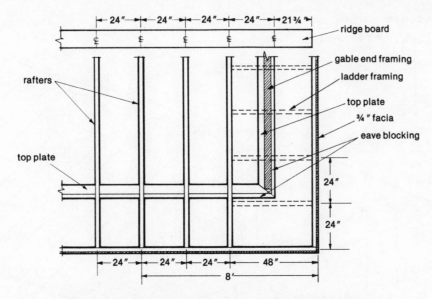

Figure 13-18. Rafter layout for the ridge board method.

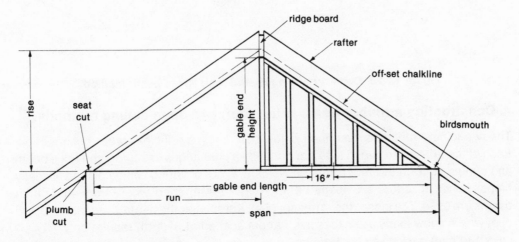

Figure 13-19. Determining gable and dimensions for a raftered roof: Ridge board method.

4) Construct the gable end ladder, and fill in the gable end framing as shown in Figure 13-20. The length of the ladder may vary depending on the amount of overhang desired.

5) Apply roof sheathing, covering, and interior finish.

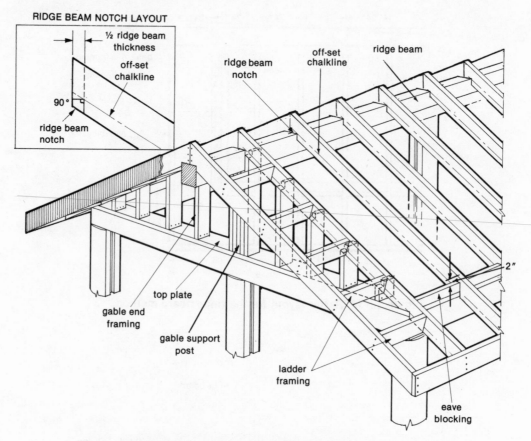

RIDGE BEAM NOTCH LAYOUT

½ ridge beam thickness

off-set chalkline

90°

ridge beam notch

ridge beam notch

off-set chalkline

ridge beam

ridge beam notch

off-set chalkline

ridge beam

2″

top plate

gable end framing

gable support post

ladder framing

eave blocking

Figure 13–20. Constructing a raftered roof: Ridge beam method.

4. Constructing a timber frame rafter roof: two open ceiling methods.

The two joinery methods described below both involve principal rafter construction. Each of the rafters are joined together either by a continuous or segmented ridge beam and purlins, to form the roof frame on which the roof covering will be placed. Usually timber principal rafters are spaced 6′ to 10′ (2 to 3 m) apart where ridge and purlin beams are used. The closer the rafter spacing, the smaller the beam sizes required. Except where snow loads are excessive, rafters spaced at 3′ (1 m) require only 2″ × 6″ (38 × 140 mm) decking to tie them together, instead of ridge beams and purlins. (See Appendix III.)

The first method of principal rafter construction employs simple lap joinery at the ridge and plate. The second method employs a variation of the mortise and tenon joint, called a fork and tongue, at the ridge and a tenoned birdsmouth at the plate. The latter method is stronger, especially at the plate location, since the rafter is tenoned into the top plate. In the former, pinning or pegging is very important since the rafter birdsmouth

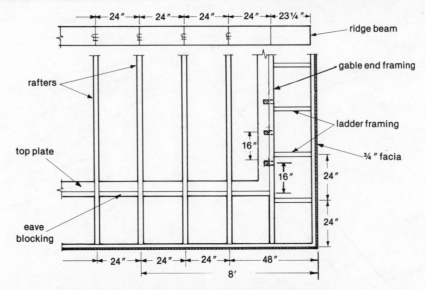

Figure 13–21. Rafter layout: Ridge beam method.

is merely lapped on the top plate, and roof thrust could cause it to slip. Steel pins or hardwood pegs are used as fasteners at the joinery locations. The top plate for both of these methods must be either log or timber to allow for wood removal and pinning.

Since neither of these principal rafters relies on a mechanism of restraint (i.e., collar-tie, truss), excessive roof loading could cause an outward thrust of the rafters, and possible spreading of the side walls. Where such loading could occur, a tie-beam should be included, such as the one described in Chapter 7, section **6.** To simplify joinery layout, hardboard templates are used. The same templates will also be used for more complicated joinery layouts. This type of roof is shown in Figure 13–3.)

Tools: Eye protection, circular saw, cross-cut handsaw, electric drill with ⅝″ (16 mm) or 1″(25 mm) auger bit, rafter square, chalkline, 3 lb (1.5 kg) sledge hammer, tape measure, slick or 1½″ (38 mm) chisel, pencil.

Materials: ⅛″ (3 mm) hardboard, rafter material, ⅝″ (16 mm) steel pins or 1″ (25 mm) hardwood dowels.

Procedure: Method A.

1) Lay out and cut the ridge template out of a piece of ⅛″ (3 mm) hardboard, as shown in Figure 13–23.
2) To lay out the rafter a rafter square is used to "step-off" the number of run units down its length. Figure 13–24 shows the method of layout, beginning at the ridge. It is important to make use of the offset chalked line during this procedure. Make sure that both the ridge plumb line and the plate birdsmouth are marked out. Note

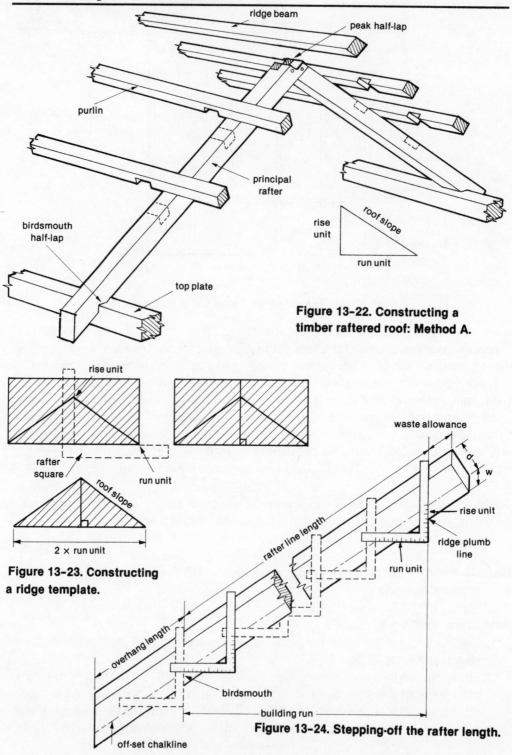

Figure 13-22. Constructing a
timber raftered roof: Method A.

Figure 13-23. Constructing
a ridge template.

Figure 13-24. Stepping-off the rafter length.

the additional material allowance at the ridge; this extra material is for the joinery.

3) Figure 13–25 shows the layout of the ridge half-lap using the ridge template. Begin by aligning the slope of the template to the top surface of the rafter, and align the center ''rise'' line of the template with the ridge plumb line. Mark line *a*.

Next, slide the template down the distance of the rafter depth, *d,* and mark line *b*. The resulting parallel lines identify the half-lap portion.

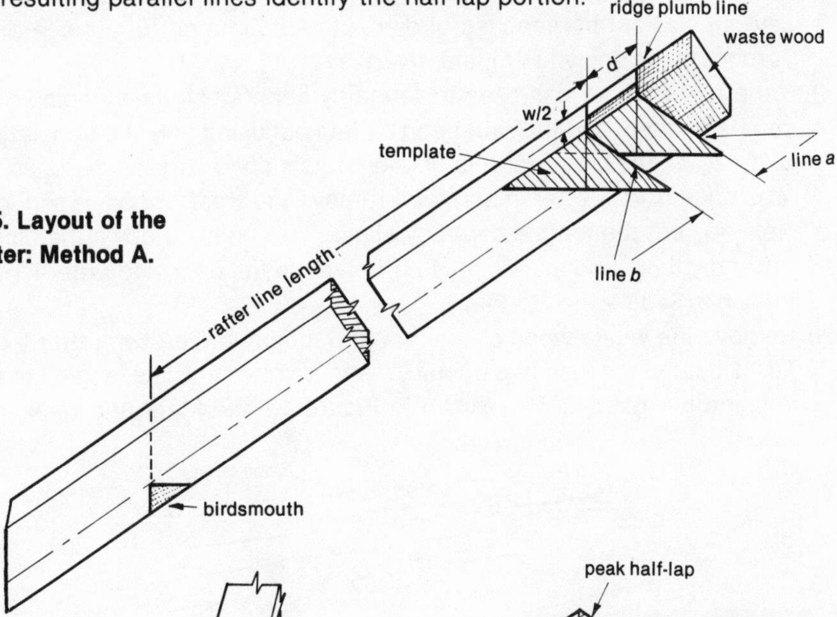

Figure 13-25. Layout of the principal rafter: Method A.

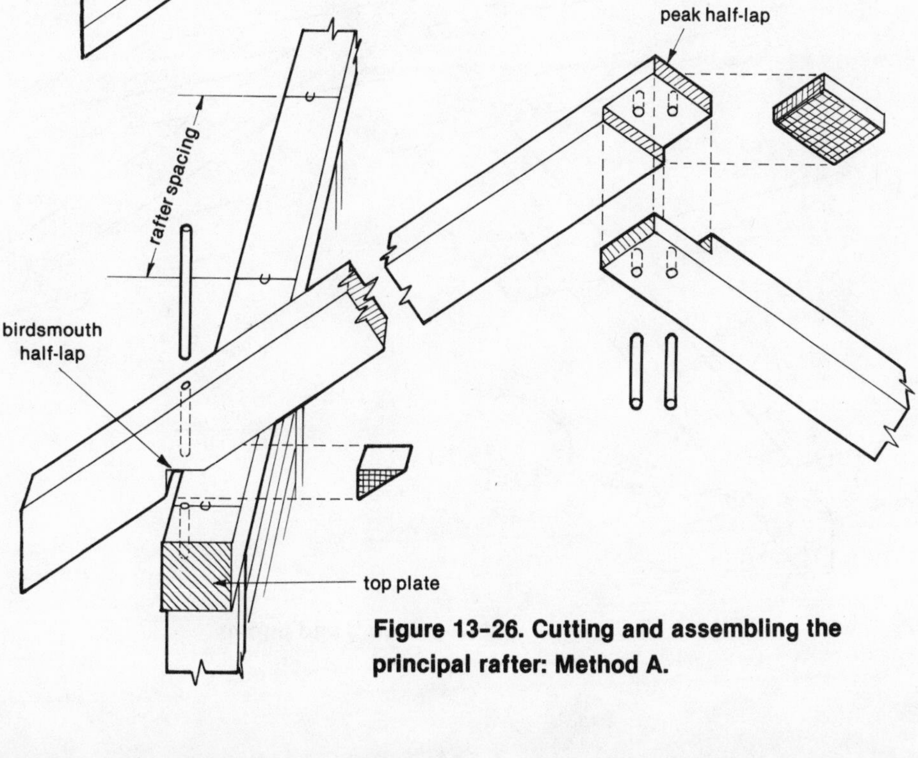

Figure 13-26. Cutting and assembling the principal rafter: Method A.

4) Remove the waste wood and lay out the half-lap, as shown in Figure 13–25.

5) Figure 13–26 shows the completed birdsmouth and ridge half-lap joints. Repeat these procedures for all rafters, pin or peg them, and position on the building.

6) After all the principal rafters are in place, brace firmly, then install ridge beam and purlins, as shown in Figure 13–22. Pin or peg these beams to the rafters.

Procedure: Method B.

1) Lay out and cut the tenoned birdsmouth template out of a piece of ¹/₈″ (3 mm) hardboard, as shown in Figure 13–28.

2) If the rafter timber has been milled fairly accurately, the stepping-off procedure can be omitted, and the rafter can be laid out using only the templates. To do so, begin by aligning the ridge template so its sloped surface matches with the top face edge of the rafter, mark, then remove the waste wood. (See Figure 13–29.)

3) Next, lay out the tongue depth by sliding the template down the distance of the rafter depth, *d,* and mark. Lay out the fork on the opposing rafter leg in the same manner. (See Figure 13–29.)

4) Remove the waste wood of the fork and tongue on the two rafter legs.

5) To lay out the tenoned birdsmouth, measure down the line length of the rafter and position the template as shown in Figure 13–29. Mark and remove the waste wood.

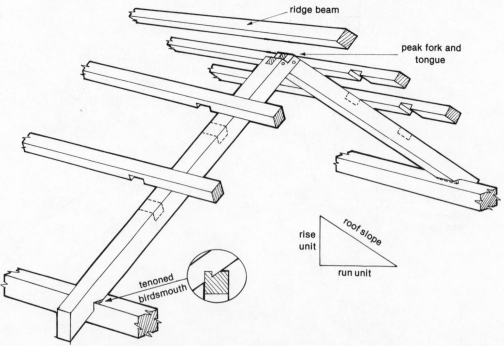

Figure 13-27. Installing ridge beam and purlins.

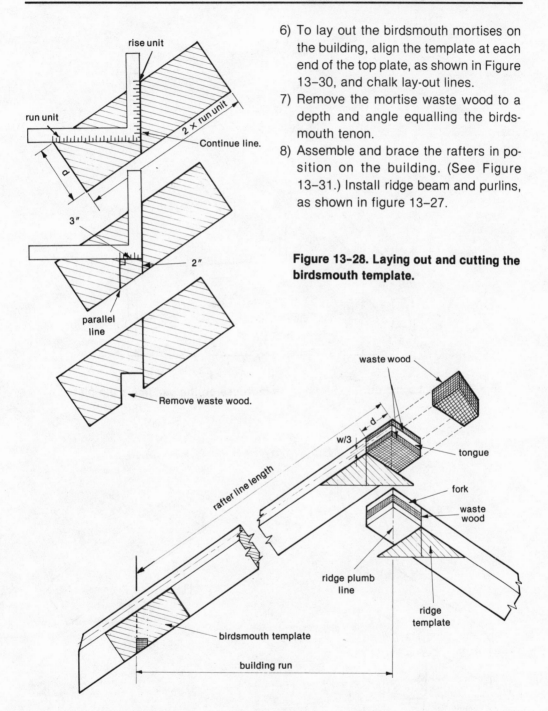

6) To lay out the birdsmouth mortises on the building, align the template at each end of the top plate, as shown in Figure 13-30, and chalk lay-out lines.

7) Remove the mortise waste wood to a depth and angle equalling the birdsmouth tenon.

8) Assemble and brace the rafters in position on the building. (See Figure 13-31.) Install ridge beam and purlins, as shown in figure 13-27.

Figure 13-28. Laying out and cutting the birdsmouth template.

Figure 13-29. Laying out the fork and tongue with the birdsmouth template on the rafter.

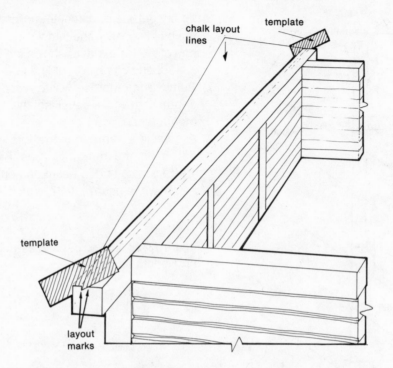

Figure 13-30. Laying out the birdsmouth mortises on the building's top plate.

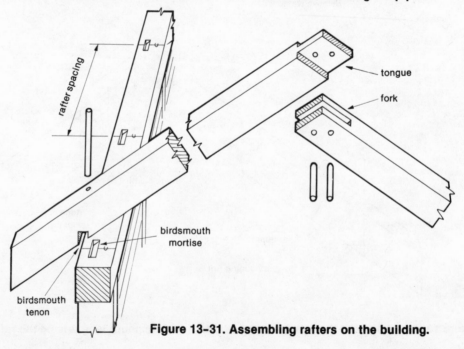

Figure 13-31. Assembling rafters on the building.

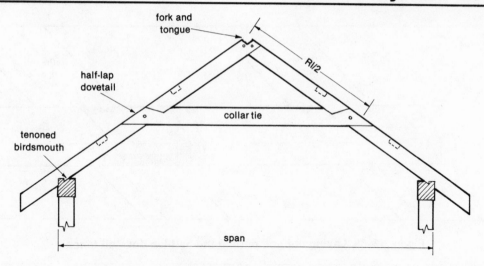

Figure 13–32. Constructing a collar-tie timber truss.

5. Constructing a collar-tie trussed rafter.

Installing a collar-tie half way up the principal rafter will prevent sagging from excessive loads, while at the same time the locking nature of the half-lap dovetail will arrest the spreading forces. This binding of the principal rafter is the reason for the term "trussed" rafter. The joinery at the ridge and plate is the same as in Method B, above. The dovetail joinery of the collar-tie must create a tight fit in order for it to properly do its job. The best way to ensure a tight joint is to trace the tenon dimensions of the collar-tie to produce the rafter mortise. Figure 13–3 shows this kind of roof.

Tools: Eye protection, circular saw, cross-cut handsaw, electric drill with ⅝" (16 mm) or 1" (25 mm) auger bit, rafter square, tape measure, slick or 1½" (38 mm) chisel, pencil.

Materials: Collar-tie material, ⅝" (16 mm) steel pins or 1" (25 mm) hardwood dowels.

Procedure:
1) Construct the principal rafters following the directions for Method B in section **4,** above. Make sure the distances between the rafter birdsmouths are equal to the span of the buliding. (See Figure 13–32.)
2) Lay the collar-tie timber on the principal rafter, so it is half way down the rafter's line length.
3) Lay out the collar-tie dovetail tenon by tracing the rafter sides onto the collar-tie to produce two parallel lines (See Figure 13–33A.) Next drop a distance of 2" (50 mm) on the inside line and join the two parallel lines with this third sloping line.

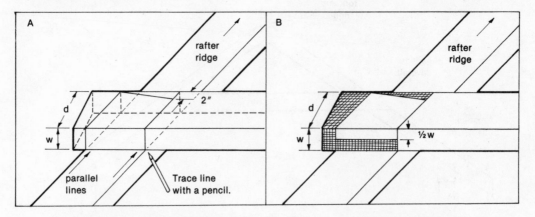

Figure 13-33. Laying out and cutting the half-lap dovetail tenon.

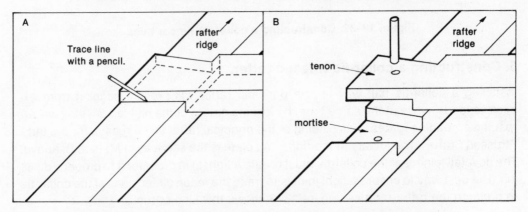

Figure 13-34. Laying out and cutting the half-lap dovetail mortise.

4) Lay out the dovetail half-lap by dividing the width of the collar-tie tenon in half. (See Figure 13-33B.)
5) Remove the waste wood of the tenon.
6) Reposition the collar-tie, and trace around the tenon to produce the female mortise. (See Figure 13-34A.)
7) Remove the waste wood of the mortise, and pin or peg the collar-tie to the rafter. (See Figure 13-34B.)

6. Constructing a king post truss.

A. Lofting and preparing the template

The king post truss construction allows the rafters to hang rather than to exert a spreading force upon the side walls of the building. The struts of the truss redirect this vertical weight force back upward to give support to the rafter and prevent its sagging.

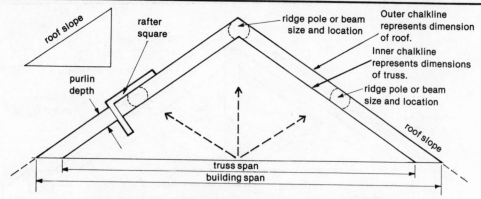

Figure 13-35. Lofting the truss plan on the subfloor.

The configuration of this support truss makes it ideal for roofs where loading is most excessive, as with sod roofs, for example.

In this section the king post truss is shown as a mid-support truss. Although it is possible to ascertain the individual length of each truss component by using any of the methods described in section **1,** above, the use of a lofting plan is recommended. This full-size plan, drawn on the building's subfloor will graphically illustrate all of the member lengths and angles of joinery. It also allows the testing of the two templates that will be used for the joinery layout. The ridge and birdsmouth templates described above in section **4,** Method B, will be used here. However, since the rafter legs of the truss are tenoned into the tie-beam and do not form an overhang, a slight adaptation to the birdsmouth template will be necessary. The tie-beam forms an integral part of the king post truss, and is often used alone in coordination with principal rafters. Its function is to tie or lock the side walls of the building and prevent any spreading forces created by the principal rafters. To serve this function the tie-beam should be joined to the top plate with a housed dovetail in order to provide a locking action while still retaining its strength. The execution of the housed dovetail template and joint are described in Chapter 7, section **6.** (Figure 13-4 shows this kind of roof.)

Tools: Tape measure, rafter square, chalkline, handsaw, pencil.

Materials: Tenoned birdsmouth template. (See section **4,** Method B, above.)

Procedure:
1) Loft the roof plan on the subfloor using chalked lines, as shown in Figure 13-35.
2) Continue the lofting plan to include the size of the truss members, as shown in Figure 13-36. From this completed loft plan the individual member lengths can be measured. (Include tenon and waste allowance.) Check also the accuracy of the templates.
3) Follow Figure 13-37 for the adaptation of the tenoned birdsmouth template.

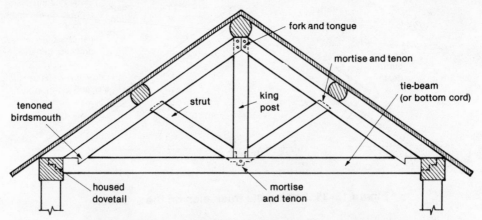

Figure 13-36. Constructing a king post truss with struts.

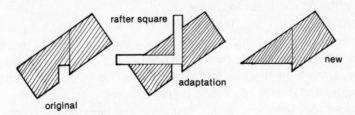

Figure 13-37. Adaptation of tenoned birdsmouth template.

B. Layout out and cutting the truss

The layout of the truss joinery is accomplished with the aid of the ridge, birdsmouth, and housed dovetail templates. These templates rely on the "squareness" of the rectangular beams. If the accuracy of these milled beams is poor it will be necessary to chalk reference lines on the beams to "represent" accurate beam dimensions. In such a case the template would be aligned with the accurate chalkline. Tenon and mortise layout must also always originate from a chalked center line. (See Chapter 6, pages 63–64, for hints for joinery layout and cutting.)

If you are constructing log instead of squared timber trusses, you need only square enough of the log surface to facilitate joinery. The use of chalked centerlines for log truss layout is imperative.

Tools: Eye protection, circular saw, cross-cut handsaw, electric drill with 5/8″ (16 mm) or 1″ (25 mm) auger bit, rafter squre, chalkline, 3 lb (1.5 kg) sledge hammer, tape measure, slick, 1½″ (38 mm) chisel, mallet, pencil.

Materials: Ridge, birdsmouth, and housed dovetail templates, truss materials, 5/8″ (16 mm) steel pins or 1″ (25 mm) hardwood dowels.

Procedure:

1) Begin by laying out the rafter ridge plumb line (step A). Align the ridge template so that its slope matches the rafter's top edge, as shown in Figure 13–38. The center rise line of the template is used to identify the rafter ridge plumb line. Remove the waste wood. Repeat this procedure for opposite rafter.

2) Continue with the ridge fork layout by sliding the template down the distance of d. (Refer to its position on the king post or measure directly from the lofting plan.) Using the center rise line of the template, mark the depth d of the fork joint. Continue these layout lines around the rafter. From the chalked centerline on the rafter lay out the 2″ (50 mm) width of the fork mortise. (The 2″ (50 mm) body of the rafter square works well for such mortise or tenon layout.) Remove waste wood, as shown in Figure 13–38 (step B). Repeat this procedure for the opposite rafter.

3) Measure down the rafter's line length and lay out the birdsmouth, using the tenoned birdsmouth template, as shown in Figure 13–38 (step C). Remove waste wood, and repeat this procedure for the opposite rafter.

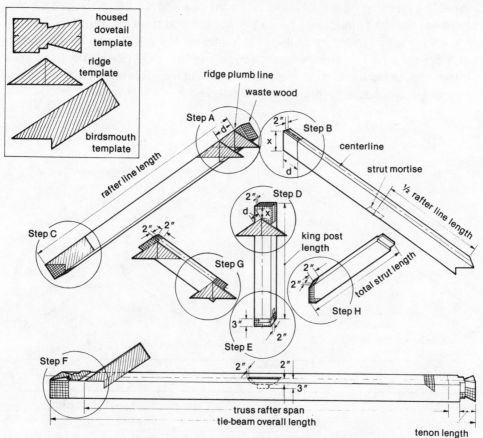

Figure 13–38. Layout of kingpost truss joinery.

4) Next lay out the king post tongue by aligning the peak template on the centerline at a distance marked *x,* equal to the face of the rafter. Mark the layout lines, then lay out the tongue tenon using the 2″ (50 mm) body of the square as a template (step D). Remove waste wood.

5) Measure down the king post's total length, including the 2″ (50 mm) tenon, and cut off any waste allowance. Lay out and cut the 3″ (75 mm) long by 2″ (50 mm) wide tenon (step E).

6) Next, measure and cut the tie-beam to its overall length. (See Figure 13–35.) Then measure and mark onto the tie-beam the truss rafter span, as shown in Figure 13–38. Lay out the tenoned birdsmouth mortise on the tie-beam by aligning the template, as shown (step F). Chalk a centerline on the top of the beam and lay out the housed dovetail tenons on either end, using the template. Remove the waste wood.

7) To lay out the strut joinery, begin at the foot of the member where it joins the king post. Align the ridge template so its sloped edge aligns with the edge of the strut face. The resulting right angle created by the rise and run of the template is then marked onto the strut foot. Remove the waste wood from the strut foot (step G).

8) Measure the overall length of the strut to include the 2″ (50 mm) long tenons at either end, and cut off any waste allowance. Lay out the 2″ (50 mm) long tenons at either end, using the body of a square as a template. Remove waste wood and repeat the procedure for opposite strut (step H).

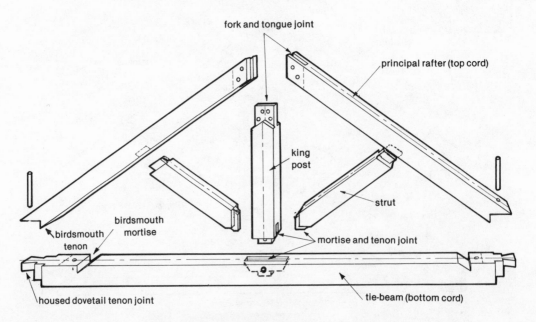

Figure 13–39. King post truss joinery.

9) After all the truss member tenons have been cut, double check their dimensions, then lay out and cut their respective mortises. Always lay out from a chalked centerline.

10) The completed king post truss joinery is shown in Figure 13–39. Assemble all the component pieces, then pin or peg them together. Place the truss on the building.

Part 2: Longitudinal Framing

The seven methods which follow come under another type of roof construction, called "longitudinal framing." Here the structural members run parallel with the ridge line. In this type of construction the roof obtains its sloping form from the shape of the gable end frame. After the gable ends are framed and in place, the longitudinal ridge and purlin beams are installed, locking the two gable ends together, giving the roof its strength and a surface on which to apply the covering. These structural beams (log or timber) must be of sufficient size for the roof weight and span. See Appendix III for the necessary specifications with examples for determining the size of structural beams in a given application.

7. Constructing frame gable ends with log ridge pole and purlins for an open ceiling.

Although it is possible to frame up the gable ends in place on the building, it is easier to construct them by lofting and building them on the subfloor. The frame may be built in two halves, and then manually placed on the top plate. However, if a suitable lifting machine is available on site, the entire gable end can be built to include windows and finish, and then be lifted into place. Lofting the plan will also give the precise size and slope cut of the ridge pole. (Figure 13–4 shows this kind of roof.)

Tools: Rafter square, adjustable T level, chalkline, tape measure, pencil, hammer, handsaw, circular saw (optional).

Materials: Framing materials, sheathing materials, nails, windows (optional).

Procedure:
1) On the subfloor lay out the building's span, run, rise and roof slope lines. (See Figure 13–40A.)
2) Aligning the body of a framing square on the roof slope line, measure down the tongue the specified thickness for the purlins (i.e., 10″, or 250 mm). Mark in several locations and chalk these lines. (See Figure 13–40B.)
3) Locate ridge pole and purlins between these two lines.

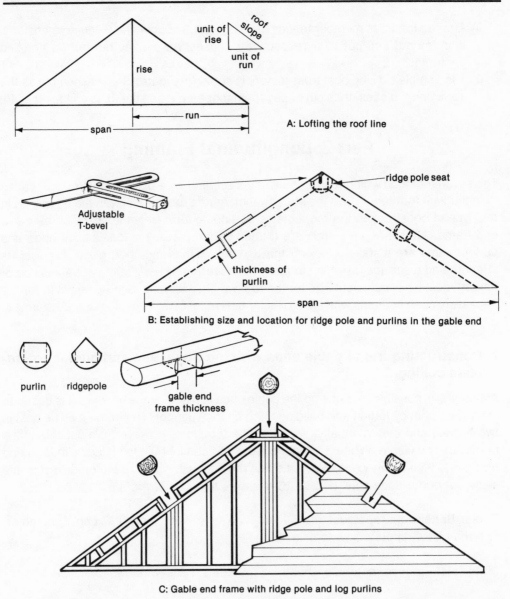

A: Lofting the roof line

B: Establishing size and location for ridge pole and purlins in the gable end

C: Gable end frame with ridge pole and log purlins

Figure 13-40. Constructing frame gable ends with ridge pole and log purlins.

4) Frame the entire gable end on the subfloor, using these lines as guides, as shown in Figure 13-40C.

5) Flat-surface the ridge pole to the angle given on the lofting plan. (Use an adjustable T bevel.) The purlins need only be flat-surfaced and squared where they must pass through the gable end pockets. (See 13-40C inset.)

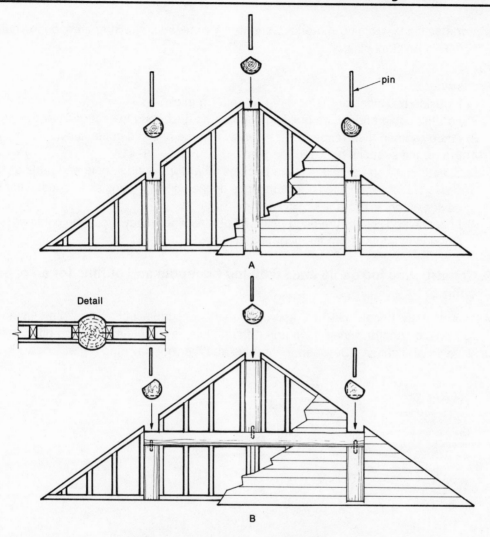

Figure 13-41. Frame gable end with support posts.

8. Installing support posts in a frame gable end.

Posts incorporated within a frame gable end create an interesting design variation, as well as providing structural support. If a lifting machine is available on site no more work is involved in adding posts than there is in straight framing. The lofting method of layout on a subfloor is employed here as well.

Tools: Rafter square, adjustable T bevel, tape measure, chalkline, circular saw, chainsaw, electric drill with ½ " (12 mm) auger bit, handsaw, hammer, pencil, eye and ear protection, 3 lb (1.5 kg) sledge hammer.

Materials: Posts, framing materials, sheathing materials, caulking compound, nails, ½ ″ (12 mm) steel pins.

Procedure:
1) Flat-side two sides of the posts for a uniform thickness.
2) Loft the gable end on the building subfloor as described in section **7,** above.
3) Place posts in their respective places, within the chalked guide lines.
4) Frame the sections between the posts. (See Figure 13–41.)
5) Sheath and apply siding, leaving pockets clear for the ridge pole and purlins.
6) Cross-brace and position the gable ends on the building, using an adequate lifting device, such as a crane or skyline rig.
7) Flat-side and square the ridge pole and purlins where they cross the gable ends. Obtain the angles from the floor layout.

9. Constructing log gable ends with log ridgepole and purlins for an open ceiling.

Although many people like the appearance of log gable ends, it is difficult and dangerous to construct them high up on the building's top plate. It is also difficult to achieve an air-tight seal between the gables and the roof covering. What follows is a

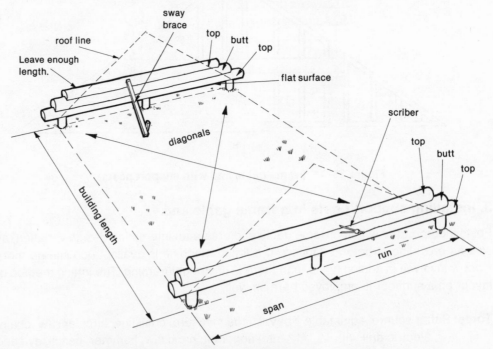

Figure 13-42. Prefabricating log gable end walls.

method for prefabricating log gable ends on the ground where quality can be better controlled and danger avoided. (Figure 13–5 shows this type of roof.)

Tools: Builder's level, tape measure, eye and ear protection, chainsaw, level, chalkline, hammer, shovel, pencil scribers.

Materials: Dry gable end logs, 3′ (1 m) post lengths (6), nails.

Procedure:
1) Lay out and square the building dimensions on the ground. (See Figure 13–42.)
2) At each gable end dig holes and place posts as shown. Level all these posts to an equal height using the builder's level.
3) Chalk a line on the top surface of these posts to represent the outside edge of the top plate.
4) Flat-surface the bottom logs, and place one at either gable end with the butts aligned in the same direction. Toe-nail these first logs so they will not move.

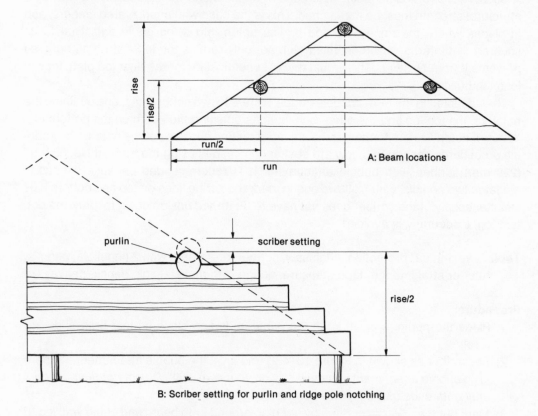

A: Beam locations

B: Scriber setting for purlin and ridge pole notching

Figure 13-43. Placement of purlins and ridge pole.

5) Construct the gable wall, alternating butts and tops on each course. Make sure that the log lengths are long enough to accommodate the roof slope cut. (See Figure 13–42.) Sway brace the gable ends are required for they will be unstable until the beams are in place, locking the two ends together.

6) Build up each wall to the height of the purlin placement, making sure that each wall is progressing equally. Take level heights and adjust on ''even'' rounds.

The purlins and ridge pole can be *notched* into the gable ends, or *inserted* after the gable end walls are built. (For instructions, see section **10** or **13,** below.) In either case, they are positioned in the same way in relation to the rise and run of the roof slope. Figures 13–43A and B show beam location and placement.

10. Laying out and cutting a double-scribed square notch for log gable ridge pole and purlin placement.

A double-scribed square notch has special applications for places where the log's structural strength must be maintained. This is the case with cantilevered timbers, and in places where the ridge pole and purlins notch into a log gable end. Due to its squared, flat internal surfaces, this notch not only retains the log's strength but also prevents it from twisting. (This would make it useful, also, for the final top plate logs in long log buildings.)

The ''double'' in the term ''double-scribe'' refers to two scribe lines, one outlining the notch on the top log and the other identical one outlining the notch on the bottom log. ''Square notch'' refers to the internal squared mating surfaces of the notch. The scribing procedures described below are best accomplished using the Starrett No. 85 – 9″ (228 mm) scriber, with bubble attachment. It is recommended because it accommodates two pencils, which allows one to mark the scribe lines on top and bottom logs simultaneously. If the scriber does not have to be turned upside down to mark the bottom log, inaccuracy is avoided.

Tools: Eye and ear protection, chainsaw, scriber, preferable with 2 (indelible) pencils, ruler or straightedge, tape measure, gouge with mallet, slick, pencil, peavey.

Procedure:
1) Place the purlin in position on the gable ends and block so that both ends are level.
2) Set scriber as shown in Figure 13–43B and level the bubble attachment. (If there is no bubble attachment you must rely on your own skill.) *Do not readjust scribers until both ends of the log are completed.*
3) Mark out the ''double scribe'' by scribing around both beam and gable wall log. If double pencils are not available, turn scribers upside down and repeat the pro-

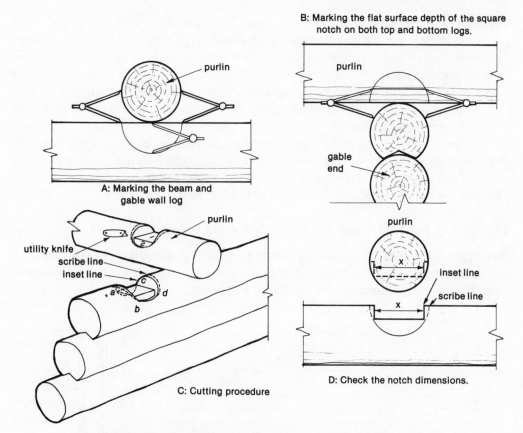

B: Marking the flat surface depth of the square notch on both top and bottom logs.

A: Marking the beam and gable wall log

C: Cutting procedure

D: Check the notch dimensions.

Figure 13-44. Scribing and cutting a square notch.

cess. (See Figure 13-44A.) *Check to see that the scribe line is legible.* A fine spray of water on the scribe's path, together with indelible pencils, will produce a clear line.

4) Mark out the "square notch" portion by positioning the scriber approximately half way down the notch on the top log. (See Figure 13-44B.) Where the two points of the scriber touch each scribe line, mark with a dot. Repeat this process in the four locations on both sides of the log. Then, join these dots together with a straight line on both top and bottom of each log. These lines will indicate the flat, squared portions inside the notch. There is no need to worry if these lines are not exactly level, as each cut surface will still correspond with its opposite surface.

5) Repeat this entire scribing process for the opposite end of the log *before* moving the log or adjusting the scribers.

6) Roll the beam toward the inside of the gable end, and finish laying out the notch by joining points *a-b* and *c-d* with straight, inset lines. (See Figure 13-44C.) Do this on both log ends. This establishes the square portion's layout.

7) With a utility knife, make an incision ⅛″–¼″ (3–6 mm) deep around the notch outline. This cut-line helps to identify the boundary of the notch when "planing" down to the line with the chainsaw. It will also prevent the notch's edges from splintering and fraying.

8) Cut the notch by first removing the waste wood off the top, flat surface portion. This is easily done by making multiple bread-slice cuts to the line, then removing the debris with a slick.

  The curved portion of the notch can be cut to the line using a gouge and mallet.

9) Measure between the finished notch faces for accuracy, as it is difficult to lift and roll the beam once it is positioned. (See Figure 13–44D.)

10) Repeat the entire process for the opposite end of the log.

11. Cutting the roof slope for log gable ends using a jig.

Cutting the gable end roof slope is quick and accurate using the same type of guide rail mill jig as the one described in Chapter 6. For this application it will be necessary to piece the guide rails between the ridge pole and purlins.

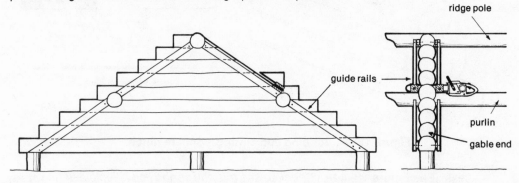

Figure 13–45. Cutting the gable end roof slope using a guide rail jig.

Tools: Eye and ear protection, chainsaw, hammer.

Materials: ½″ (12 mm) carriage bolts, ¾″ (19 mm) plywood pads, guide rails, nails.

Procedure:
1) Attach plywood pads to the chainsaw bar, as shown in Figure 13–45. The spacing may vary according to the size of the gable end logs.

2) Space and nail the guide rails parallel to each other on either side of the gable end as shown. The guide rail spacing will be the same as the chainsaw bar pad spacing.

3) Starting at the peak, cut the gable ends down to the plate. When doing this, have someone else apply moderate pressure to the pads, using two sticks.

12. Inserting the nailing spline for log gable ends.

The nailing spline is an essential part of a log gable end. The roof decking should be nailed into this spline when it passes over the gable ends, so as not to inhibit any possible settling of the gable end.

Tools: Eye and ear protection, chainsaw, chalkline, hammer, tape measure, handsaw.

Materials: Nails, 2″ × 4″ (38 × 89 mm) splines.

Procedure:

Figure 13–46 shows a 2″ × 4″ (38 × 89 mm) spline. Chalk guide lines down the center of the sloped surface equal to the spline width, and cut a groove so that the spline will come flush with the surface. Repeated chainsaw cuts to the correct depth, followed by honing of the groove with the bar nose works well here.

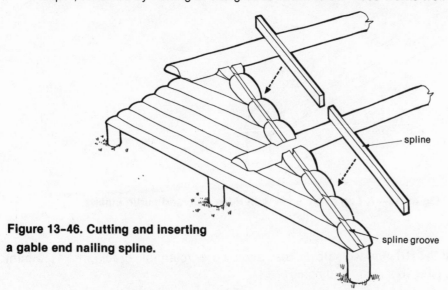

spline

spline groove

Figure 13–46. Cutting and inserting a gable end nailing spline.

13. Placing ridge pole and purlin inserts for log gable ends.

Instead of notching the purlins and ridge pole into the gable ends as they are being constructed, build the gable ends, then cut the roof slope and insert the purlins and ridge pole into their pockets. With this method the purlins and ridge pole can be flat-sided before placing them in the gable ends. It is important to have sufficient sway bracing as the gable ends are very unstable until the purlins and ridge pole are in place.

Tools: Eye and ear protection, chainsaw, tape measure, chalkline, scribers, level, hammer, drill with ⁵/₈″ (16 mm) auger bit.

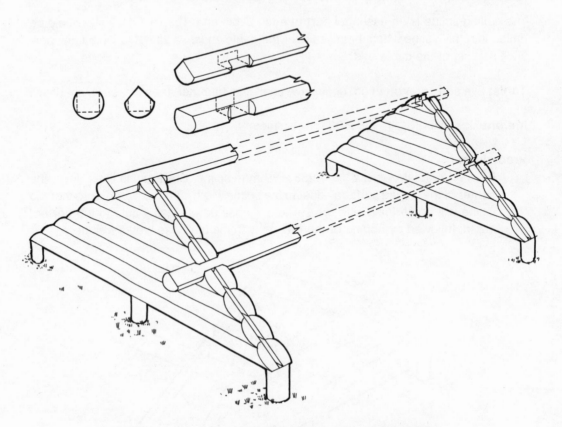

Figure 13-47. Log gable ends with ridge pole and purlin inserts.

Materials: ⁵⁄₈″ (16 mm) lag screws, insulation, tar or foam roll, bracing, ½″ (12 mm) steel pins, roof slope cutting jig.

Procedure:

1) Build up the gable ends, sway bracing as you proceed.
2) Flat-side and square the purlins and ridge pole where they cross the gable ends. (See Figure 13-47.)
3) Cut the roof slope and insert the nailing splines.
4) Cut pockets in the gable ends so the purlins and ridge pole will fit flush with the roof slope surface, as shown.
5) Number the gable end logs and replace them on the building. Add a layer of foam roll or tar and lag screw the first gable end log to the top plate. Put the gable logs in place, insulating and pinning where necessary.

14. Constructing a sod roof.

The visual impact of a solid wood post and beam house built on a foundation of rock, and crowned with the greens and golds of a sod roof is unrivalled. Such a house looks, feels, and is a true embodiment of the environment. The positive psychological effects of living within the protective walls of such a dwelling are little understood by a society which insists on segregating man from nature.

Not so long ago, sod roofs were one of a few primitive protective roof coverings. Then, if it rained for two days outside it rained for a week inside! But the problems and complexities associated with these primitive sod roofs are all solved by the modern materials at our disposal today. Today we have the means for constructing a warm, weatherproof sod roof with double the life of a conventional roof, providing we understand the materials' properties and limitations.

A roof covering composed of two layers of sod is heavier than a conventional covering due both to its physical properties and the increased snow load retained. The average (dead) weight of a conventional roof system is 20 lbs per sq. ft. (100 kg/m²), compared with the 51 lbs per sq. ft. (250 kg/m²) of a sod roof system. Part of this weight increase is due to the increased size and number of roof frame components which are required to support the extra weight.

Sod, like many other roof coverings, has an optimum slope to which it can be applied. The ideal grade for sod is between 20°–25°. Any grade below 18° inhibits rapid water runoff, while a roof grade greater than 25° creates the risk that the sod will slip. Where grades are slightly steeper than 25°, chicken wire can be laid across the ridge and down the roof to prevent this problem. As well, a strong retaining board anchored directly to the rafters will be needed to hold the sod covering, while permitting unobstructed water runoff.

Without additions, the grass and root system of sod is not waterproof. The traditional method was to use birch bark as an underlay between the sod and roof decking. The bark, with its high creosote content, resisted rot and formed a somewhat waterproof membrane. Today its use is impractical in comparison to the various waterproof materials available. A membrane of single or multi-ply rolled roofing (asphalt impregnated), together with either hot or cold process asphalt application (depending upon the product and its requirement) has been used with some success. It effectively waterproofs the roof, but is susceptible to root damage. In its stead, a waterproof, rootproof 2-ply granulated S.B.S. (styrene, butatine, styrene) *modified* bitumen sheet membrane covering is recommended. This material is commonly used underneath indoor gardens and may be obtained through a landscaping supply source. ''Modified'' refers to the chemical conditioning which gives this material flexibility even at low temperatures and also prevents root damage. How to apply this roofing membrane is explained below.

There is some question concerning the insulative value of sod since there is as yet very little recorded data available. Testimony from individuals living under sod roofs in northern Europe and Scandinavia, however, gives sod a very favorable rating. Apparently, the older sod with its established network of roots offers the most loft, and therefore, the most dead air space as compared to younger, denser sod. During the winter the added snow layer contributes to both the overall thermal resistivity and the thermal mass potential. During the summer, the shade of the growing bunch grass together with the substantial root system allows for slow, steady moisture evaporation cooling. Shown graphically, there would be a gradual heat-loss curve much like the one for a solid timber or log wall, due to the time delay factor of thermal mass. The benefits are most evident when the internal heat source fails on a cold winter's night. However, because of today's stringent building regulations, the sod roof will include a 1″–2″ (25–50 mm) layer of extruded polystyrene rigid foam insulation (not the foam bead type) to be sandwiched between roof membrane and sod. As well, to allow moisture transference while preventing organic matter from touching the insulation, a polyolefin woven cloth layer is used to separate the sod from the insulation. Again, this cloth material is widely used in landscaping.

Materials: Preserved retainer boards, anchor bars (galvanized), asphalt primer, asphalt, 2-ply bitumen sheet membrane (described above), rigid foam insulation, polyolefin cloth, 5″–6″ (125–150 mm) thick sod (2 layers), mop, roofing nails, gravel, lead (chimney flashing).

Procedure:
1) Construct the roof frame to accommodate the extra roof weight.
2) Deck the roof. Where tongue and groove decking is used and the seams are not tight there is a possibility the hot tar will seep through. In such a case, apply a fiber board or plywood sheathing over the decking.
3) Fasten the anchor bars to the rafters as shown in Figure 13–48. See Figure 13–49 for retainer boards and anchor bars.
4) Apply an asphalt primer to the roof deck.
5) Starting at the bottom of the eaves, mop a coat of hot asphalt onto the roof deck, and while the asphalt is still wet lay down the first ''sanded'' bitumen sheet. It will be necessary to work a short distance at a time to prevent the asphalt from drying. *Note:* If application of hot asphalt is not feasible, a single ply, slightly thicker bitumen sheet with an asphalt coated undersurface is available. To apply, simply heat the undersurface with a torch until it is soft, then lay it in place on the roof deck.
6) Once the first layer is in place, nail the top edge to the roof deck. Restrict the nailing area to the upper 3″ (75 mm) edge of the sheet. (See Figure 13–48.)
7) Working your way up the roof, mop and lay the next sanded bitumen sheet so its bottom edge overlaps the top edge (and the nail heads) of the first layer by 3″ (75 mm). (See Figure 13–48.) Continue this process until the entire roof is covered with this first ply.

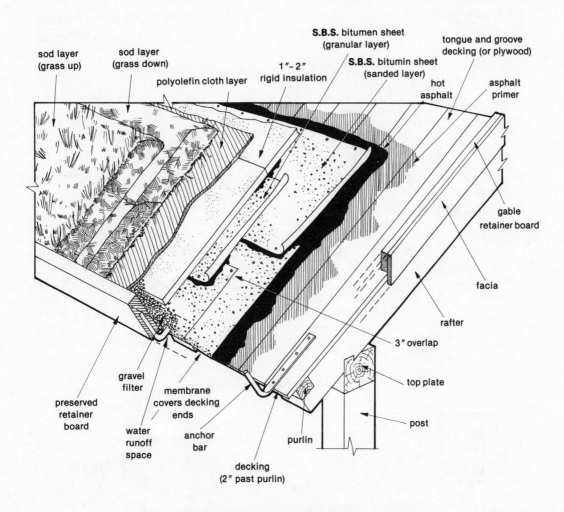

Figure 13–48. Components of a sod roof covering.

8) Begin the next granular ply application by first cutting 12″ (300 mm) from the roll, so that instead of 3′ (900 m), the roll is now 2′ (600 mm) wide. This shortened first roll will off-set the seams, resulting in a "shingled" effect.

9) Wet mop and place this second layer in the same way as the first, nailing the top edge. Continue this process until the entire roof is covered.

10) Position the retainer boards, gravel filter, and insulation as shown in Figure 13–49. Do *not* nail the insulaton to the deck.

11) Place the polyolefin cloth over the insulation, then cover it with two layers of sod, preferably with older, well-established roots. The first sod layer should be placed grass side down with the second layer placed grass side up—staggering all joints.

12) Figure 13–50 is a self-explanatory diagram for the chimney flashing. The flashing material must be lead, as zinc will deteriorate with a chemical reaction to humus water.

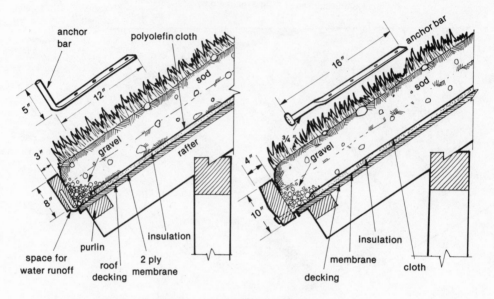

Figure 13-49. Retainer board.

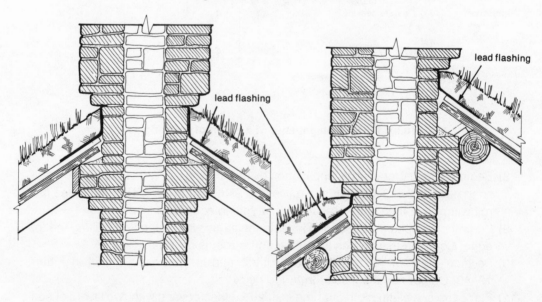

Figure 13-50. Sod roof chimney flashing for timber and log roof systems.

CHAPTER FOURTEEN

Interior Finishing

1. Electrical wiring layout.

It is essential to preplan the electrical work in order to avoid unsightly and dangerously exposed wiring. Such planning should be done in consultation with an electrician and must comply with the local residential building code.

Figure 14–1 shows a typical electrical layout for a solid wood post and beam house. The receptacle outlets, for the most part, are positioned somewhere within 18″ (450 mm) of the floor. In log or timber walls, the receptacles will be in the first or second log or timber, which necessitates predrilling for the supply wires. Kitchen receptacles are located in the counter splash-boards, and rely on the cavities behind cabinets for running the electrical wires. Switches are placed near doorways and their supply wires are set into a groove in the posts which is concealed by the door jamb. Lighting fixtures placed in log or timber walls are positioned near openings which again serve as pathways for the wiring to feed the fixture. Overhead lighting or fans will require access from the ceiling cavity. As the floor, ceiling, and stud partitions conceal the electrical wires as they snake from source to application site, there is very little predrilling required with proper planning. See section **2,** below, for predrilling receptacle outlets, and for a jig for cutting receptacle and switch box cavities.

2. Predrilling and cutting mortise cavities for electrical wiring using a simple jig.

The major part of the predrilling is confined to wires servicing receptacle outlets. Since these outlets are located within 18″ (450 mm) of the floor, or in the first or second wall log or timber, it will be necessary to predrill as the infill wall is being placed on the subfloor. When the drilling is completed, the receptacle box cavity (and switch cavity) is cut, using the mortising jig described below. Electrical wire can then be fed through the access hole to service the box, or a ''fish'' wire can be threaded through, which will later be used to pull through the electrical wire.

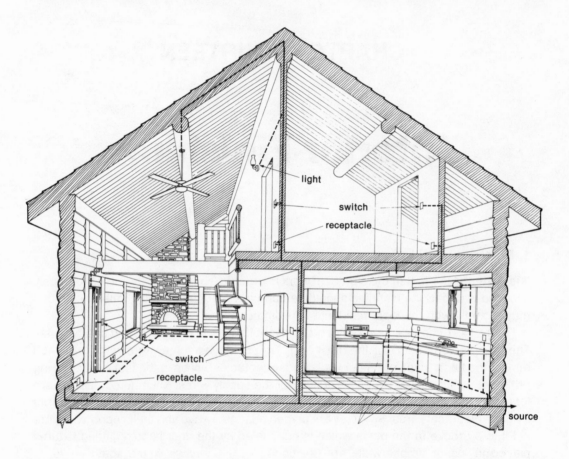

Figure 14–1. Typical electrical layout for a post and beam house.

Tools: Eye protection, electric drill (or hand auger) with 1¼ ″ (32 mm) auger bit, level, pencil.

Materials: ''Fish'' wire (coat hanger wire), strong cord.

Making the jig

Tools: Eye and ear protection, chainsaw, square, hammer, tape measure, brace and 1 ″ (25 mm) bit, cross-cut handsaw, saber saw, pencil, 1 ″ (25 mm) chisel.

Materials: ½ ″ × 1⅝ ″ (12 × 40 mm) long carriage bolts with nuts and washers, ¾ ″ (19 mm) plywood, finishing nails, wood glue, receptacle boxes.

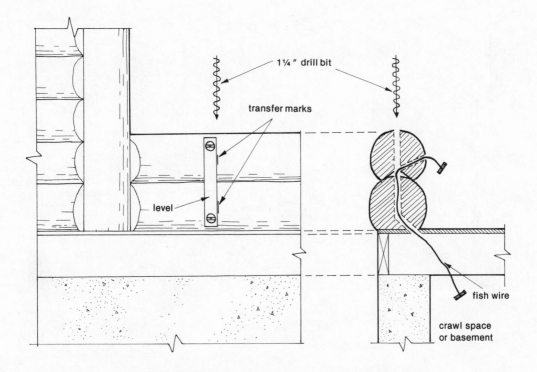

Figure 14-2. Predrilling for electrical receptacle outlets.

Procedure:

1) Place the first log on the subfloor and mark out the drilling locations. Locate wall receptacles no more than 12' (3.5 m) apart and within 6' (1.8 m) from doors or other openings.

2) Drill down through the center of the first log to gain access to the crawl space or basement. The lateral groove of the next log will conceal this hole.

3) Using a level, mark the place where the hole is on the side of the log, then drill a diagonal hole down to meet this first hole. If there is insufficient clearance from the floor, the receptacle outlet can be placed in the second log. In this case, fit this next log in place. (See Figure 14-2.)

4) Using a level, transfer the mark onto the second log, then drill down to meet the hole beneath. The lateral groove will cover the hole if it is drilled on the centerline of the log.

5) On the face of the second log, drill in to meet the vertical hole. The receptacle box will be placed at this junction.

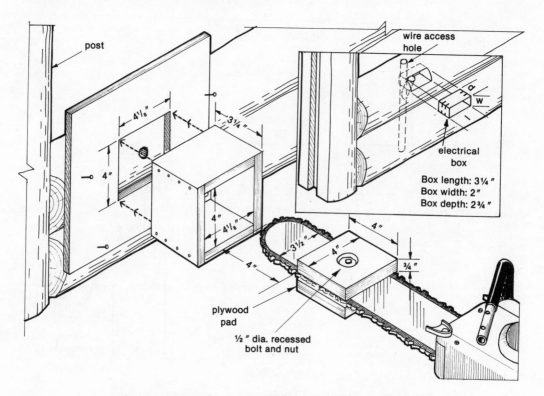

post

wire access hole

electrical box

Box length: 3¼ "
Box width: 2 "
Box depth: 2¾ "

4⅛"

3¼ "

4"

4"

4⅛"

3½"

4"

4"

¾ "

plywood pad

½ " dia. recessed bolt and nut

Figure 14-3. Fabrication and use of the mortising jig.

Constructing the mortising jig

1) Lay out, cut, glue, and nail together a ¾ " (19 mm) plywood box, following the dimensions in Figure 14-3. Then glue and nail the box to the plywood backing sheet.

2) Cut two ¾ " (19 mm) plywood pads and fit them to the chainsaw bar, using the carriage bolt, nut, and washer. The bolt and nut should be recessed.

3) The bar with pads should slide into the plywood box with minimal clearance.

4) Center the mortising jig over the predrilled electrical hole, and cut out a cavity with successive plunge cuts of the chainsaw. For duplex receptacles or switch cavities, simply move the jig box over to create the extra space.

5) Using coathanger wire, "fish" a length of cord from under the floor out through the receptacle hole. Then tie a stick on either end so that the cord cannot pull back through. (See Figure 14-2.) Later, the electrical wire will be taped onto the cord and pulled through to service the receptacle.

6) Alternatively, feed the wire into place now, but do not connect until the official inspection has been made.

3. Plumbing and water lines.

Like the electrical work, the plumbing work requires careful planning. Since it is unrealistic to try to drill a 3″–4″ (75–100 mm) diameter main stack hole through solid log or timber walls, these lines are best placed within a 2″ × 6″ (38 × 140 mm) stud wall. It is wise to align the kitchen and bathroom back-to-back, using this stud wall and a single set of lines to service both areas. In houses with a second floor or basement, the plumbing and water services should be located above and below each other wherever possible.

Drain, vent, and water lines must comply with the local residential code specifications. Figures 14–4 and 14–5 show a typical layout. Because of their ease of installation, most homebuilders use P.V.C. plastic drain and vent lines, and copper water lines. Plastic drain and vent lines must be anchored between floors. This necessitates the installation of an expansion joint to absorb the plastic's thermal expansion and contraction. (See Figure 14–4 inset.)

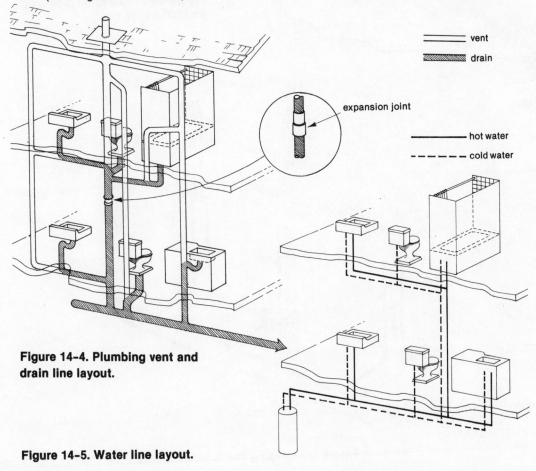

vent

drain

expansion joint

hot water

cold water

Figure 14-4. Plumbing vent and drain line layout.

Figure 14-5. Water line layout.

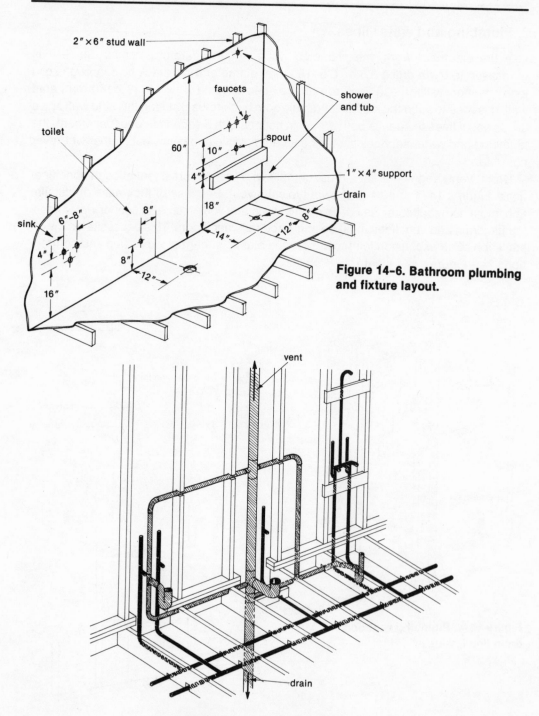

Figure 14-6. Bathroom plumbing and fixture layout.

Figure 14-7. Piping rough in.

Figures 14–6 and 14–7 show a basic drain, vent, and water line rough-in for a bathroom. The dimensions in Figure 14–6 indicate where the pipe and fixture tie together. In most cases new fixtures come with rough-in dimensions and installation instructions. Figure 14–7 shows the piping rough-in complete and ready for the fixtures. For additional information refer to the sources in the bibliography.

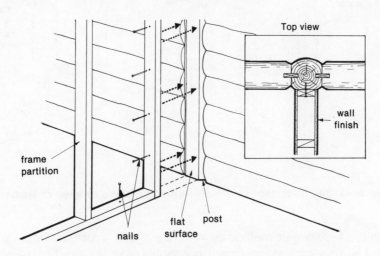

Figure 14–8. Attaching a frame partition to a vertical post.

4. Installing frame partitions.

Any major frame partitions, especially load bearing ones, should be attached to the vertical posts, and not to the wall infill pieces. Attaching a frame partition to a post is a simple matter of flat-surfacing the face of the post and nailing the partition to it. Where a partition wall must tie into the infill wall, there are two methods of attachment. Bear in mind that the horizontal infill pieces must be left free to settle unimpeded by the partition.

Tools: Eye and ear protection, chainsaw, adze, chalkline, level, tape measure, hammer, handsaw.

Materials: 2″ × 4″ (38 × 89 mm), 2″ × 6″ (38 × 140 mm) blocking, 1″ × 6″ (19 × 140 mm) rough cedar, common nails, finishing nails, 6″ (150 mm) spikes with washers, 1″ × 4″ (19 × 89 mm) straightedge.

Procedure:
1) Figure 14–8 and its inset are self-explanatory diagrams for butting and nailing a frame partition to a vertical post.

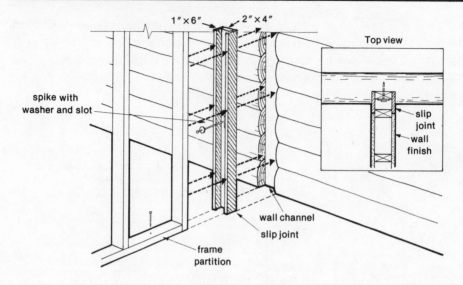

Figure 14-9. Slip joint used to attach frame partitions to a log or timber wall infill.

2) Figure 14-9 shows a method by which a slip joint is recessed into a channel which has been cut into the wall infill. The channel provides a vertical backing as well as eliminating any gaps caused by the curve of the logs. The slip joint allows the infill pieces to settle unimpeded, and provides a finished edge to which drywall or paneling can be butted. Steps 3 to 7 describe how to construct and install this type of frame partition attachment.

Attaching a partition to log or timber infill with a slip joint.

3) Construct a slip joint by nailing a 1″ × 6″ (19 × 140 mm) on either side of a 2″ × 4″ (38 × 89 mm), as shown in Figure 14-9. The length of this slip joint will be the same as the height of the partition.

4) Plumb the slip joint and nail it temporarily in place against the wall where the partition will be located. Temporarily nail in place a 1″ × 4″ (19 × 89 mm) straightedge on either side to be used as chainsaw guides.

5) Remove the slip joint and make three or four chainsaw cuts the length of the wall channel to a depth nearing the lateral groove. Use an adze to remove the waste wood. The result should be a plumb, vertical channel.

6) Position the slip joint and nail the top and bottom to the logs, using a spike with a washer slipped through a slot in the 2″ × 4″ (38 × 89 mm). This will allow the log wall to settle unimpeded.

7) The inset in Figure 14-9 shows a top view of the slip joint, where the finish material butts to the 1″ × 6″ (19 × 140 mm) and nails into the 2″ × 4″ (38 × 89 mm) stud.

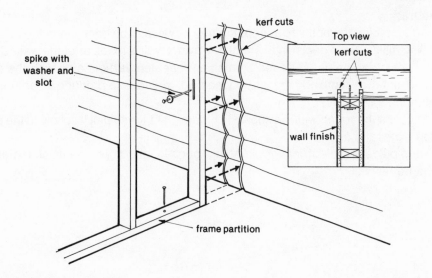

Figure 14–10. Butted and kerfed method of attaching a frame partition to a log or timber wall infill.

Butted and kerfed method for attaching a partition to log or timber infill.

1) Figure 14–10 shows an alternative method for attaching a frame partition to a log or timber infill wall. This method is most frequently used in closets. First, the partition is plumbed and nailed to the log wall, using a spike and washer inserted through a slot cut with the chainsaw.

2) Then, run a chainsaw kerf down either side of the partition, providing a groove into which the finish material will fit. The Figure 14–10 inset shows the kerf cuts.

5. Attaching frame walls over log or timber walls.

Some builders prefer to attach a stud frame wall right over the log or timber wall in the kitchen or bathroom, so as to facilitate the installation of the plumbing, electrical wiring, cabinets, and counters. The easiest method for attaching a frame wall over a log or timber wall is to affix it to the vertical posts, top plate, and floor, leaving the infill pieces to settle unimpeded. The directions for such a procedure follow.

Tools: Eye and ear protection, chainsaw, adze, level, tape measure, chalkline, hammer, handsaw, chisel, pencil.

Materials: Stud wall material, 1″ × 4″ (19 × 89 mm) diagonal bracing, nails.

Procedure:

1) Flat-surfacing the posts to accept the frame wall can be done when the posts are being milled. If the decision to attach the frame wall is made after the walls are up, the posts can be flat-surfaced by making repeated vertical cuts with the chainsaw, and then removing the waste wood with an adze to produce a surface flush with the top plate face.

2) Construct the frame wall, as shown in Figure 14–11, and nail it solidly to the posts, top plate, and floor.

3) Put in place any electrical or plumbing rough-in, and apply the finish material to the frame wall.

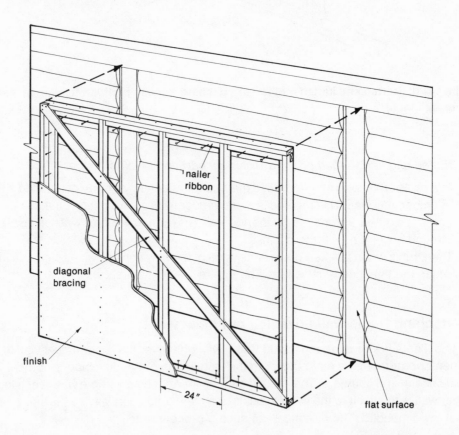

Figure 14–11. Attaching a frame wall over a log or timber wall.

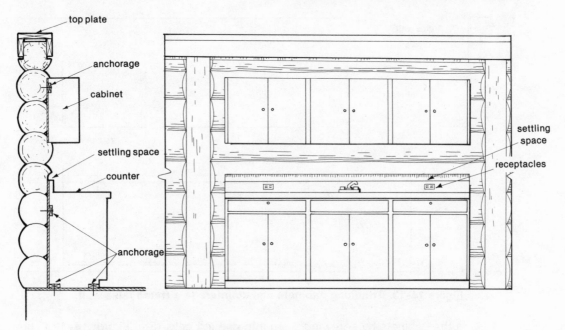

Figure 14–12. Attaching cabinets and counters to a log or timber wall.

6. Installing cabinets and counters.

There are two methods for adding cabinetry. The first method involves slightly recessing the cabinets and counters into the log wall. In this case, the electrical wiring and plumbing are hidden behind the counters, with the main stack contained within a stub wall located in the kitchen or bathroom.

The second method involves building a frame wall over the log wall. Then the cabinets and counters are attached directly to the false wall, with the wiring and plumbing hidden in its cavity.

Tools: Eye and ear protection, chainsaw, adze, level, handsaw, hammer, electric drill with wood bits, Robertson screwdriver (red), tape measure, chalkline, pencil.

Materials: Cabinets and counters, framing materials, drywall, common nails, drywall nails, #10 Robertson wood screws.

Procedure:
1) Figure 14–12 shows the cabinets and counters recessed into the log wall. Begin the layout on the log wall where the cabinets and counters will be situated.
2) Recess the cabinets and counters by making vertical chainsaw cuts 2″–3″ (50–75 mm) deep into the log. Remove the waste wood with an adze.

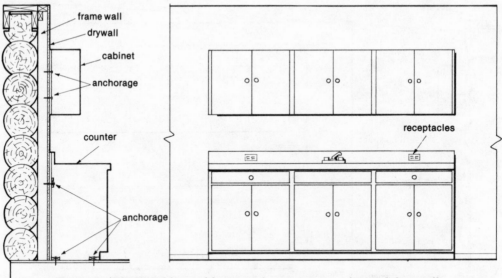

Figure 14-13. Attaching cabinets and counters to a frame false wall.

3) Hang the cabinets by screwing them into one log only. (See Figure 14-12.) The counters are screwed to the floor and wall. Allow for a settling space above the counter splash board.

4) Locate a stub wall near the sink to contain the main plumbing stack. Attach it to the log wall using one of the methods described in section **4,** above.

5) Figure 14-13 shows the cabinets and counters attached to a false frame wall. Attach this frame wall using the method described in section **5,** above.

6) Sheath the frame wall with drywall, placing wiring and plumbing in the cavity.

7) Attach the cabinets and counters to the frame wall, as shown in Figure 14-13.

7. Stair construction.

In building a staircase several safety factors must be taken into account. In order to effect safe passage there must be no deviation in tread or riser sizes. There should be adequate headroom, and guard rails with balusters must be installed on at least one side of each run on all stairs.

The construction of a stairway is greatly affected by the nature of its attachment to the wall. Affixing stairs to a horizontally laid-up log or timber infill wall, both of which are subject to settling, will result in an altered stair angle. However, compensatory measures can be taken to deal with these settling effects. (Such measures must also be taken when installing stairs in a long log notched corner building.) On the other hand, the method for affixing stairs to the stable vertical posts or top plate of a post and beam house is almost identical to the methods widely used with conventional frame buildings.

In planning the stair design, keep in mind that the stairway should not detract from the architectural style of the house, while still providing maximum utility within the space available. Figure 14-14 shows the components of a typical staircase.

8. Making calculations for a straight run staircase.

The optimum height for a riser is between 7"–8" (178–203 mm) and the optimum width of a tread between 9"–10" (228–254 mm). The slope of the stairs will vary with the proportion of riser height to width of the tread. If the riser height is increased, the stairs become steeper. A comfortable stair slope is achieved if the sum of the riser and tread equals 17" (432 mm). (These measurements do not include the tread nosing projection.)

There must also be adequate headroom with a minimum of 80" (2032 mm), and adequate stair width with a minimum of 36" (1 m). The stairway's approach and landings should also be a minimum of 36" (1 m). As well, there must be ample clearance around corners for the movement of people and furniture. The directions which follow are for a straight run staircase, the fundamentals of which can be applied to other stair configurations. See section **15,** below, for instructions on how to construct a timber spiral staircase.

Tools: Tape measure, pencil and paper.

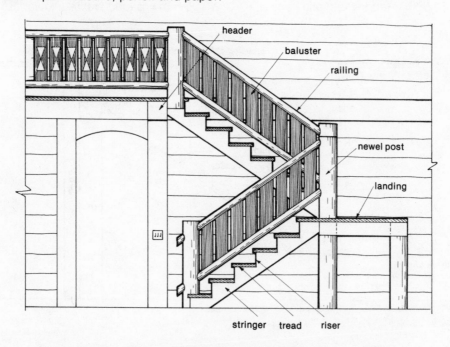

Figure 14-14. Parts of a staircase stairwell (120" minimum).

Procedure:

1) Establish the total rise by measuring the distance between the two finished floors (eg., 102″, or 2590 mm.)
2) Calculate the number of stair risers by dividing the total rise by an optimum riser height. For example: 102″ ÷ 7 = 14.57 (2590 mm ÷ 178 mm = 14.55) risers.
3) Since the number of risers must be a whole number, assume the number of risers to be 14 and redivide this number into the total rise to find the exact riser height: 102 ÷ 14 = 7.28 or 7¼″ (2590 ÷ 14 = 185 mm).
4) Calculate the tread width by subtracting 7.28″ (185 mm) from 17 (432 mm) which equals 9.72 or 9¾″ (247 mm).
5) To find the total run of the stair refer to Figure 14–15. Note that the second floor landing constitutes the 14th tread. Therefore the total run is 13 treads long or 13 × 9.72 = 126.36 or 126½″ (13 × 247 mm = 3211 mm).
6) Before proceeding further check to see if a staircase of these dimensions will fit within the space and headroom available. Adjust if necessary.
7) Calculate the length of the stair's stringers by using Pythagoras's theorem: $a^2 + b^2 = c^2$, where c is the stringer.

Example with standard measures

$$\sqrt{102^2 + 126.5^2} = c$$
162.5″ = c (add waste allowance)

Example with metric measures

$$\sqrt{2590^2 + 3211^2} = c$$
4125 mm = c (add waste allowance)

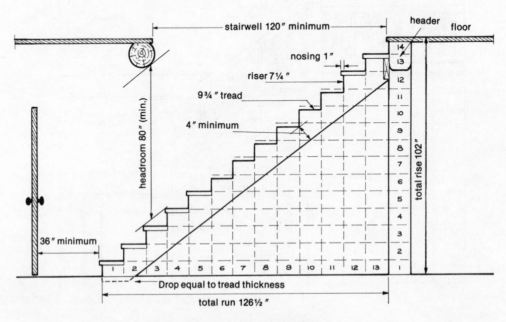

Figure 14–15. Stair calculations.

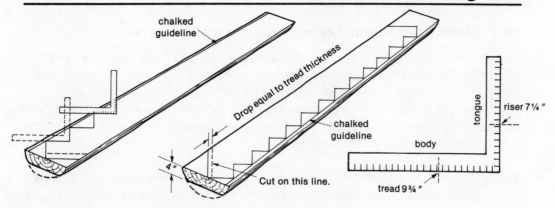

Figure 14–16. Layout for a log stringer.

9. Laying out a log stringer.

Begin by selecting a dry, straight grained log of substantial size and length. Mill the two opposite sides flat. Once this has been done, the log is cut lengthwise in half to produce the two stringers on which the layout work can begin.

Tools: Tape measure, sharp pencil, chalkline, steel square, circular saw with combination blade, cross-cut handsaw.

Materials: Log stringer pieces.

Procedure:
1) Prepare the log for layout as explained above.
2) Chalk a guide line along the outside edge of each stringer. This line will represent a straight edge from which to work. It will also serve to prevent confusion and the production of two right or left stringers.
3) Starting at the bottom (butt) of the stringer, align the steel square so that the 9¾ " (245 mm) tread mark on the body and the 7¼ " (185 mm) riser mark on the tongue are touching the guide line. (See Figure 14–16.)
4) Lay out the tread and riser by stepping-off 13 times along the stringer, carefully beginning each new tread at the ending of each riser mark.
5) After the desired number (13 in this example) of treads and risers are marked out, square off the ends as shown in Figure 14–16. (Note that in the example, the 14th tread and riser are at the second floor.)
6) Repeat this procedure for the other stringer. When they are matched up they should be identical.
7) Whatever the thickness of the tread material, it will be necessary to cut this amount from the bottom of each stringer. This is called the "drop" allowance.
8) Using the circular saw and a sharp blade, carefully cut out the stringers.
9) Level them, and attach the stringers solidly to the header.

10. Fastening dimensional or log treads to the stringers.

With the stringers securely fastened in place, the placing of the treads can begin. If housed treads are desired it will be necessary to rout the dado grooves with the stringers detached form the heads. (See Figure 14–17.)

Whether you are using dimensional or log slab treads the material should be dry and relatively defect-free. For easy passage of both people and furniture, the minimum stair width is 36″ (1 m) clear of the handrail.

Tools: Eye and ear protection, chainsaw, scriber, 1¼″ (32 mm) gouge chisel, mallet, electric drill with ⁵/₈″ (16 mm) bit and ¾″ (19 mm) countersink, cross-cut hand-saw, socket wrench.

Materials: Tread material, ¾″ (19 mm) hardwood dowels and wedges, lag screws, wood glue.

Procedure:
1) Cut all pieces of the tread material to equal lengths. (For example: 36″ + 2″ (1 m + 50 mm) overhang on either end.)
2) Stretch a taut string line down the length of one of the stringers. The string line should extend 2″ (50 mm) past the outer edge of the stringer. Lay the treads in place so that each touches the string. This will bring them all into alignment.
3) Mark out and drill countersink and pilot holes for screws, or dowel holes, depending on which is to be used to fasten the treads to the stringers.
4) If using log slab treads, level the treads in both directions, then scribe them into place. The depth of scribe will be the tread thickness minus the 1″ (25 mm) tread exposure. (See Figure 14–17.)
5) When the positioning and drilling are completed, glue should be applied to the joining surfaces, and the tread securely screwed or dowelled in place. The countersunk screwheads can be concealed with wood plugs.

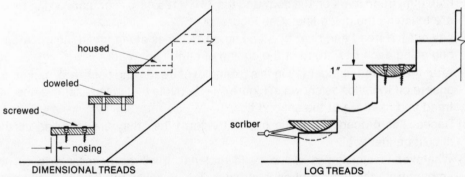

Figure 14–17. Fastening dimensional or log treads to the stringers.

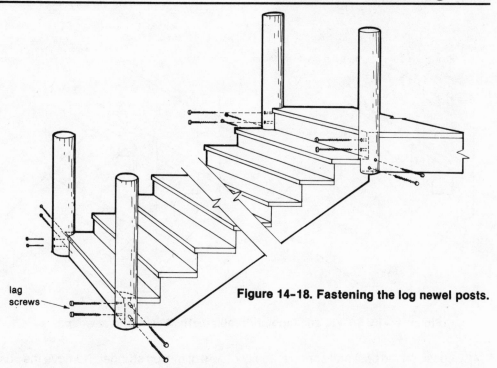

lag
screws

Figure 14-18. Fastening the log newel posts.

11. Fastening the log newel posts.

The newel posts are primary structural elements in the balustrade. For this reason it is very important that they are fastened securely in position. They will, however, only acquire their full structural potential when the railings and balusters are in place.

There are a multitude of design and joinery options for newel posts. The example described below has the newel post attached directly to the staircase.

Tools: Eye and ear protection, chainsaw, tape measure, scribers, level 1½ " (38 mm) chisel or slick, electric drill with ¾ " (19 mm) and ½ " (12 mm) bits, pencil, socket wrench.

Materials: Lag screws, newel posts, ¾ " (19 mm) wood plugs, wood glue.

Procedure:
1) Position the newel post to sit on the corner of the staircase. Then block and plumb it. (See Figure 14–18.)
2) Trace the corner of the staircase onto the underside of the post, then extend vertical lines up at the corners to equal the depth of the riser and tread.
3) Remove the newel post and cut out the waste wood. In this example, the post rests firmly on the floor.

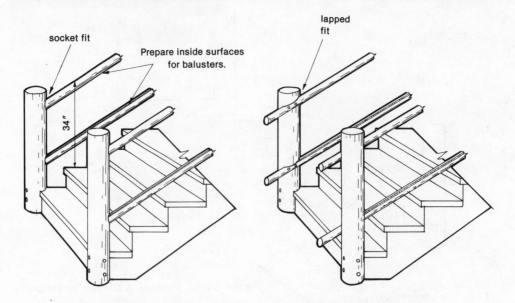

Figure 14-19. Socket and lapped fit railing attachments to newel posts.

4) Reposition the post and scribe to the contours of the log stringer. Remove the post to cut waste wood.
5) Reposition the post, lay out the lag screw holes, then countersink and drill the pilot holes. Apply a generous amount of glue to the joining surfaces and screw the post firmly in place.
6) Plug the countersink holes.
7) Repeat the above procedure for all newel posts.

12. Fastening the railings to the newel posts.

The material used for railings should be dry and relatively free of defects. The tree species jack pine, or banksian pine (*Pinus banksiana*), makes excellent stair railings, as it is quite common to find poles which hold to a uniform thickness of 4" (100 mm) or so.

There are many possible ways of joining the railings to the newel posts. Two common methods are described below. The only important criteria are the height at which the top handrail is placed (34", or 864 mm) and, the secure fastening of the railings.

Tools: Eye and ear protection, chainsaw, tape measure, chalkline, stringline, electric drill with ¾" (19 mm) and ½" (12 mm) bits, 1½" (38 mm) chisel or slick, socket wrench, pencil, router with ¾" (19 mm) straight bit (optional).

Materials: Lag screws, railings, ¾" (19 mm) wood plugs, wood glue, hardwood wedges.

Procedure:

1) Prepare the railings to receive the balusters. (See section **13,** below, then sand to remove rough edges and splinters.) Figure 14–19 shows the two methods of railing attachment.

2) Stretch a taut stringline between the two newel posts to determine the height and positioning of the two railings.

3) Mark out the appropriate joinery for either a socket or lapped fit.

4) Remove the waste wood for the joint.

   Note: If you are fastening the railings with a socket fit, the mortise waste wood can be removed with a router or drill.

   Drive a hardwood wedge part way into the end grain of the tenon end of the railing. Then, when the railing is driven into the mortise, the wedge will spread the end and prvent loosening of the joint.

5) Apply glue to the surfaces of the joint before final assembly.

13. Fastening the balusters to the railings.

Balusters provide vertical support to the railings, while at the same time providing a partition which will keep children from falling off the stairs. The design of the balusters is important, as it can enhance or detract form the house's design as a whole. Below are four methods for fastening balusters to the railings.

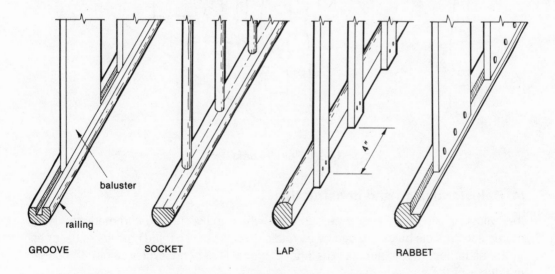

GROOVE   SOCKET   LAP   RABBET

Figure 14–20. Fastening balusters to railings.

Tools: Eye and ear protection, chainsaw, tape measure, chalkline, cross-cut handsaw, hammer and nail set.

For the groove method: rout with a ¾ " (19 mm) straight bit. For the socket method: use a 1½ " (38 mm) hand auger.

Materials: Baluster material, wood glue, finishing nails.

Procedure:
1) Prepare the balusters by sanding and staining them. (See section **14,** below.)
2) Fasten balusters between the railings, with one of the methods shown in Figure 14–20.

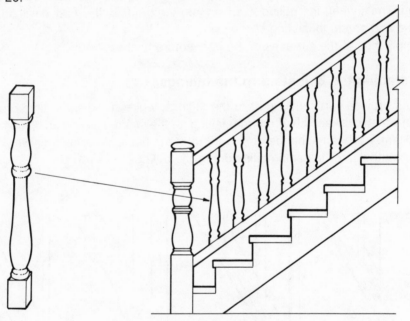

Figure 14-21. Spindle balusters.

14. Baluster design and construction.

The balusters are the parts of the staircase which make the most immediate visual impression. Spindle balusters can be as rustically simple as peeled pole saplings, or as ornate as lathe-turned columns. The final choice will depend largely upon the design and decor of the entire house.

The board baluster with cut-out patterns is simple to construct, yet offers a great deal of design flexibility. This type of baluster provides more design opportunities for utilizing the negative space (where the wood is cut away) than does the spindle baluster.

Tools: Spindle baluster: Eye protection, table saw with combination blade.
Board baluster: Eye protection, router with ³/₈″ (9 mm) straight bit and template guide.

Materials: Baluster material, ¹/₈″ (3 mm) hardboard template material.

Procedure:
1) Make up the hardboard templates to your design.
2) Tack-nail the template to the baluster board as shown in Figure 14–22. Ensure there is extra material for the bevel cut for attachment to the top railing.
3) Secure the baluster board and rout the design as shown.
4) Attach balusters between the railings.

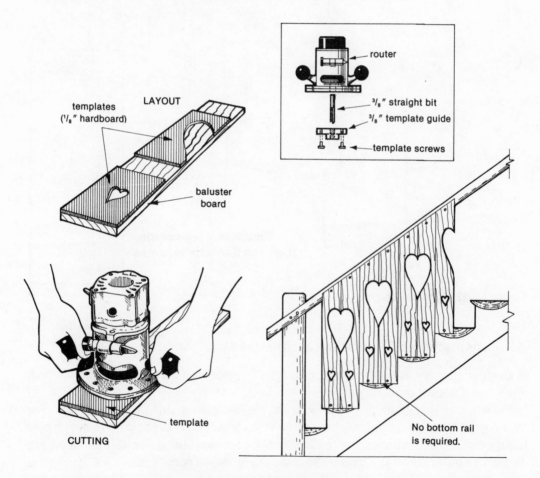

Figure 14-22. Making board balusters.

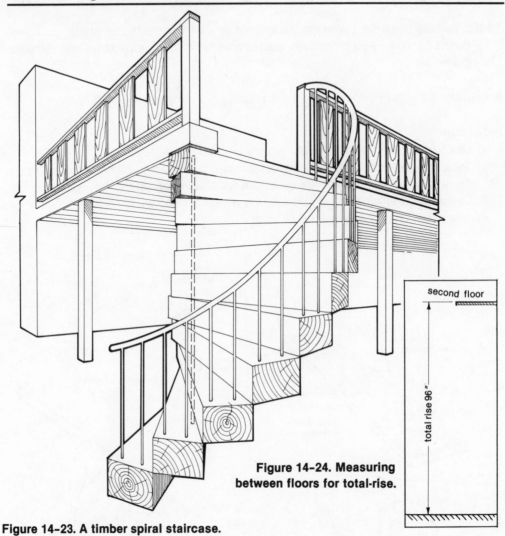

Figure 14–24. Measuring between floors for total-rise.

second floor

total rise 96″

Figure 14–23. A timber spiral staircase.

15. Constructing a Timber Spiral Staircase.

A circular stairway affords the opportunity of transforming the common stairway into the interior's most dramatic feature.

Constructing a circular stairway with curved, laminated stringers is both complex and costly. A fan-type, circular stairway in which treads are spread out around an axis pivot simplifies construction and reduces costs. Common fan-type spiral staircases are fabricated out of steel. The timber spiral staircase shown here (Figure 14–23) uses the same basic approach of fanning the treads around an axis. This is done with a quick and simple method which allows the builder to construct an impressive circular staircase with a minimum of experience, tools, and materials.

In an average house with an approximate 8′ (2400 mm) total rise between floors, the timber circular staircase will need approximately 180° or half of a circle (semi-circle) to complete its total run. It is recommended that the radius of this semi-circle be between 42″–54″ (1066–1370 mm), so that two people may pass each other comfortably on the stairs. For a still greater passage space, increase the radius. Timber tread materials must be dry, since green wood will shrink, causing a reduction of the stair's height.

A.   Determining the total rise, total run, and tread size.

1) Determine the total rise by measuring the distance between the finished floors of the two storeys. For example: 96″ or 2400 mm. (See Figure 14–24.)

2) Determine the number of risers and treads by dividing the total rise by the optimum riser height. For example, 8″, or 200 mm.

   96″ (2400 mm) ÷ 8″ (200 mm) = 12 risers and treads.

   There will actually be 11 risers and treads, since the second floor landing forms the 12th tread riser.

3) Determine the total run by multiplying the number of treads by the optimum tread width. For example, 12″, or 300 mm. These timber treads are designed to be wider than usual to allow for more usable exposed tread.

   11 treads × 12″ (300 mm) = 132″ (3300 mm) total run.

4) When this has been done, proceed with the subfloor layout, the directions for which follow.

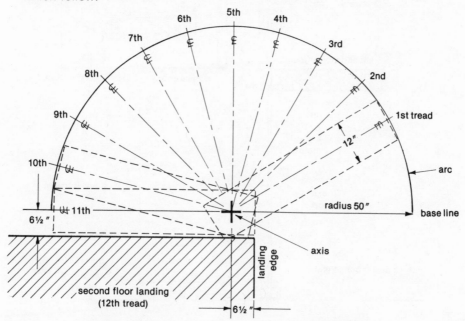

Figure 14–25. Spiral stair layout on the subfloor.

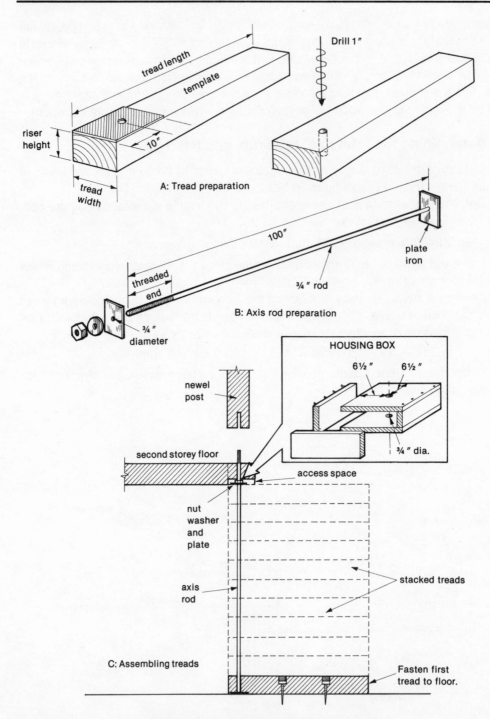

Figure 14-26. Constructing the staircase.

B. Layout on the subfloor.

1) Begin the layout on the main floor by establishing the location of the second storey landing. Lines can be chalked on the floor to represent the landing, as shown in Figure 14–25.

2) Next, chalk a parallel line 6½″ (165 mm) from the landing representation as shown. The 6½″ allow for the last stair tread to run parallel with the landing with ½″ (12 mm) clearance. This parallel line then forms the base of the semi-circle. Locate the axis point as indicated, so that the tread will be flush with the edge of the landing.

3) Draw the semi-circle arc. This can be done by embedding a nail at the axis and then, using a length of wire and pencil to scribe an arc equal to the radius. (In this case, 50″/1270 mm.) (See Figure 14–25.) The total run of the staircase is along the arc of this semi-circle. To determine if more than a semi-circle is required for the total run of 132″ (3300 mm), it is necessary to calculate the circumference of the semi-circle. The formula for a semi-circle is:

π (Pi) times radius. Pi is a constant equal to 22/7 or 3.1416.

3.1416 $\times$ 50″ (1270 mm) = 157″ (3990 mm)

Since the total run is only 132″ (3300 mm), the staircase will fit within the semi-circle.

(The formula for a circle is Pi times diameter.)

4) Lay out the tread centers along the arc line, remembering that the landing constitutes the last tread. Begin from the base line (the center of the 11th tread), and step off eleven 12″ (300 mm) units around the arc, as shown in Figure 14–25.

5) Proceed with an actual stair construction, as described below.

C. Stair construction.

Tools: Electric drill with 1″ (25 mm) and ⅝″ (16 mm) auger bits, level, tape measure, crescent wrench, pencil.

Materials: Iron rod ¾″ × 100″ (19 × 2540 mm) long threaded 16″ (400 mm) at one end; two pieces of plate iron, ³/₁₆″ × 4″ × 4″ (4 × 100 × 100 mm), ¾″ (19 mm) nut and washer, 10″ (250 mm) lag screws (2), tread material (dry).

Procedure:

1) Mill eleven treads to the dimensions 8″ × 12″ × 56″ (200 × 300 × 1422 mm). See Figure 14–26A.

2) Using the template as shown in the diagram, locate, and then drill a 1″ (25 mm) hole in one end of each tread. Plane and sand the tread surfaces.

3) Fabricate an axis rod by welding one plate iron piece to the end of the rod as

shown in Figure 14–26B. The second plate must have a ¾ ″ (19 mm) hole drilled through its center.

4) Position the rod and first tread on the axis mark located on the subfloor, as in Figure 14–26. With the first tread placed in its correct location, secure it to the floor with countersunk lag screws.

5) Stack the remaining treads on the rod as shown, then cinch down the nut with plate and washer to firmly hold the stacked treads.

6) Anchor the rod to the second floor landing. One way of doing this is to install a housing box like the one shown in the inset of C. An access space must be left under the housing box to permit tightening of the nut if the treads loosen as a result of shrinkage.

7) Fan the treads out to their respective center marks then firmly tighten the nut. Use a plumb bob or straightedge and level to match the treads to the layout marks. The completed spiral staircase should look like the one in Figure 14–23.

8) The railing and baluster will help to secure the ends of the treads. A curved storage closet can be made by framing in the space under the stairs, using the arc line for reference.

CHAPTER FIFTEEN

Wood Finishes

"Weathering" is the very slow breakdown and wearing away of the wood's surface fibers, a change in color, and roughening of the wood's surface. As long as wood is sheltered and protected from rot, due to ongoing damp conditions, it is only for aesthetic reasons that weathering may be considered undesirable. Wood is visibly affected by mold and mildew. Mold and mildew fungi can begin to grow and discolor a newly peeled log within forty-eight hours if conditions are warm and humid. Such an early fungal attack requires an initial treatment with a fungicide such as pentachlorophenol, or toxic metallic salts, such as zinc naphthenate. (Copper naphthenate stains wood green.) They, however, tend to leach out with rain, depending upon the carrier used. (See discussion of preservatives, below.) If mildew growth has already begun, it can be removed by cleaning the log with a detergent and bleach (1:1 ratio) solution. The design of the building should include wide roof overhangs to protect the exterior walls from rain.

Exterior finishes

Once the walls and roof of the building are complete, an exterior finish may be applied. Exterior finishes fall into two categories, the penetrating type, such as stains and preservatives, or the surface type, such as paints and varnishes. Surface finishes should be avoided on wood with a high moisture content, as blistering will result from trapping of moisture between the wood and its painted surface. Even those good quality exterior varnishes which contain ultra-violet absorbers are limited in their effectiveness and suffer from early cracking and peeling.

Penetrating Finishes

Preservatives

These types of exterior finish are recommended for coastal and other damp regions where mildew and decay are likely. Water repellent preservative finishes contain waxes, oils, resins, preservatives, and optionally, pigments. The waxes, oils, and resins cause the wood surface to repel water, while the preservatives impart mildew and decay resistance. Pigments add color and protect the wood surfaces from deterioration caused by ultra-violet light. The finish's life is related to its pigment, ranging from two to four years. One application of a preservative finish is usually sufficient. Maintenance is also simple. The surface is cleaned and washed with soap and water before another coat of finish is applied.

Note: Repellents could cause additional finishing problems unless another repellent finish type is applied over top. The preservatives used in this type of finish are the same fungicidal chemicals described earlier. The water repellent carriers will prevent rain leaching out the initial fungicidal treatment on freshly peeled logs. Since fungicides and mildewcides are extremely toxic they must be handled with great caution.

Pigmented stains

Pigmented stains are a popular finish, being easy to apply, attractive, and easy to maintain. Most pigmented stains are oil-based. This type of finish is recommended for drier regions, but also works well in wet areas if a fungicide is added.

Semi-transparent stains are most often used on wood surfaces as they do not hide the natural grain and texture of the wood. Opaque stains hide the grain and should be avoided. Depending on climatic conditions, a stain finish can be expected to last up to five years. Because the surface film is thin and flexible, stain will not peel, crack or blister.

Stain finishes are easy to maintain. The surface is washed down with soap and water and a new coat applied about every two years.

Oils

Most contractors tend to blanket the house, both inside and out, with an oil finish. Oils, however, tend to darken the wood. Most oil finishes perform best in dry areas. Boiled linseed oil, the favorite of many builders, often remains softer and tacky so that insect and dirt particles will stick to it. This is even more true of raw linseed oil, and mildew may form as well. Stains will offer the same protection while providing a better appearance.

All three of these penetrating finishes are best applied by brush, and the wood's surface must be clean. A maintenance coat of finish should be applied before the old finish has deteriorated badly.

The Madison formula

The Madison formula is a modified, semi-transparent, oil based stain developed by the Forest Products Laboratories of the Canadian Department of the Environment and the U.S. Department of Agriculture. The mixture is intended to produce the color of western red cedar. A formula for other woods can be mixed by altering the type of pigment. (See Appendix I for a pigment chart.)

Basically, the Madison formula is an all-around exterior finish which incorporates all the qualities of a preservative, a stain, and an oil. It contains paraffin wax to increase the linseed oil's water-repellency, and pentachlorophenol to inhibit mildew. Because the formula includes wax, no finish can be successfully applied over it which does not also contain wax.

Madison formula for natural cedar color

Boiled linseed oil	3.1 gal (U.S.)	12 L
Mineral spirits	1 gal	4 L
Burnt sienna color-in-oil	1 pt	0.5 L*
Raw umber color-in-oil	1 pt	0.5 L*
Paraffin wax	14 oz	0.4 kg
*Pentachlorophenol concentrate 10:1	2 qts	2 L
Zinc stearate (keeps wax in suspension)	1¾ oz	50 g

Pour the mineral spirits into an open-top 7 gal (25 L) can. Heat paraffin and zinc stearate in the top of a double boiler and stir until the mixture is uniform. Pour this into mineral spirits, stirring vigorously. *This should be done outside to avoid the risk of fire.*

Add pentachlorophenol and linseed oil to the cooled solution. Stir in the colors until the mixture is uniform.

One quart (liter) covers 350–450 sq. ft. (8–10 sq. meters) on a smooth surface and 175–225 sq. ft. (4–5 sq. meters) on a sawn-textured surface, depending on how porous the wood is.

* As pentachlorophenol is a highly toxic ingredient the builder may wish to substitute it with the less toxic zinc napthenate.

Interior Finishes

The purpose of interior wood finishes is to add depth, warmth, and character with a clear finish or a slightly pigmented stain. In addition, interior finishes give protection against scuffs and scratches. Once a fungicide has been applied to the freshly peeled logs the interior of the house should not be treated with any further toxic preservatives. Indeed, with an inside air moisture content of less than twenty percent no mildew will grow.

Interior finishes are categorized as either pigmented stains or clear finishes.

Pigmented stains

Pigmented stains are classified by the solvent carrier in which they are dispersed. The most common solvents are water, alcohol, and oil. Water stains perform satisfactorily. Spirit (alcohol) stains give good service, but they dry very rapidly, making them more difficult to apply. Oil stains are slower in drying and easier to apply evenly.

Clear finishes

Waxes used to be popular as flat, interior wood finishes, but have been largely replaced by synthetic varnishes which have high water and abrasion resistance. Furthermore, a wax finish is virtually impossible to remove, as well as being difficult to refinish with other products.

Polyurethane varnishes are available in a full range of glosses. They produce a hard, tough finish that is resistant to oil, water, alcohol, and heat. The long drying time that was a problem with the traditional varnishes has been elimited in the polyurethanes. To allow greater penetration into the wood and reduce the possibility of a poor finish due to a wood's excessive moisture content, the first coat of varnish should be thinned with 15%–20% of solvent. The second coat can then be applied in full concentration.

Boiled linseed oil is a favorite finish for many builders, but its worth is questionable. Its slow drying time makes it susceptible to marking. It has a tendency to collect dust and to darken the wood. The oil should be spread evenly with a brush or rag, and must be given 24 hours drying time between coats.

General interior formula

⅓ turpentine
⅓ boiled linseed oil
⅓ varnish

Mix thoroughly and apply with brush. Allow to dry until surface finish is hard to the touch. This general interior formula gives a pleasant, yet hard oil finish.

Appendix I

Mixing Desired Pigments

This chart may be used in coordination with any of the finishes listed in Chapter 15.

Color Desired	Pigment required	Quantity for 5 gallons (19 liters)	
Cedar	burnt sienna	1 pint	(.5 L)
	raw umber	1 pint	(.5 L)
Light Redwood	burnt sienna	1 quart	(1 L)
Chocolate Brown	burnt umber	1 quart	(1 L)
Fruitwood Brown	raw sienna	1 pint	(.5 L)
	raw umber	1 pint	(.5 L)
	burnt sienna	½ pint	(.25 L)
Tan	raw sienna	1 quart	(1 L)
	burnt umber	3 fluid oz.	(85 cl)
Green Gold	chrome oxide	1 pint	(.5 L)
	raw sienna	1 pint	(.5 L)
Forest Green	medium chrome green	1 quart	(1 L)
Smokey Gray	white house paint	1 quart	(1 L)
	raw umber	6 fluid oz.	(170 cl)
	lamp black	2 fluid oz.	(57 cl)

Appendix II

Tree Species and Wood Properties: The softwood and hardwood tree species identified in this chart list the geographical sources, physical properties of the wood, and the parts of a post and beam building for which each species is best-suited.

Letter Grade Key
E = Excellent
G = Good
M = Moderate
P = Poor
N/A = Not available

Tree Species (geographical source)	Roof members	Floor members	Walls	Top plates	Posts	Ground sills	Workability	Checking resistance	Movement resistance (lack of spiral grain)	Decay resistance	Strength
Ash, Silvertop (*Eucalyptus fastigata*); Australian states of N.S.W., Victoria, and Tasmania.	G	G	G	G	G	M	G	G	G	N/A	G
Ash, White Mountain (*Eucalyptus regnans*); Australian states of N.S.W., Victoria, and Tasmania.	E	E	G	E	G	G	G	G	G	M	E
Blackbutt (N/A); Australian states of N.S.W. and Queensland.	G	G	G	G	G	M	G	G	G	M	G
Cedar, Atlantic White (*Chamaecyparis thyoides*); eastern U.S.	P	P	E	P	G	E	G	G	G	E	P
Cedar, Eastern Red (*Juniperus virginiana*); eastern U.S. and Canada.	P	P	E	P	G	E	G	G	G	E	P
Cedar, Western Red (*Thuja plicata*); western U.S. and Canada.	P	P	E	P	G	E	G	G	G	E	P
Cottonwood, Black (*Populus trichocarpa*); western Canada, northwestern U.S.	M/P	M/P	G	M	G	P	G	G	M	M/P	P
Cottonwood, Eastern (*Populus deltoides*); middle and eastern U.S. and Canada.	M/P	M/P	G	M	G	P	G	G	M	M/P	P
Elm, White (*Ulmus americana*); middle and eastern U.S. and Canada.	G	G	G	G	E	M	G	M	M	M	E
Fir, Amabilis (*Abies amabilis*); Pacific coast of Canada and northern U.S.	M/P	M/P	G	M	E	M	G	G	M	M	M/P
Fir, Balsam (*Abies balsamea*); middle and eastern Canada.	M/P	M/P	G	M/P	M	M	G	G	M	M/P	M/P
Fir, Douglas (*Pseudotsuga menziesii*); western U.S. and Canada.	E	E	G	E	E	E	G	G	M	M	E
Fir, Grand (*Abies grandis*); Pacific coast of U.S. and southern Canada.	M	M	G	M	E	M	G	G	G	N/A	M
Gum, Blue (*Eucalyptus globulus*); Australian states of Tasmania and Victoria.	G	G	G	G	E	G	M	M	M	G	G
Gum, Spotted (*Eucalyptus maculata*); Australia coast of New South Wales and Queensland.	G	G	G	G	G	G	G	M	G	E	E
Hemlock, Eastern (*Tsuga canadensis*); southeastern Canada to middle eastern U.S.	G	G	G	G	G	M/P	G	M	G	M/P	M/P
Hemlock, Western (*Tsuga heterophylla*); western U.S. and Canada.	M/P	M/P	M/G	M	M	M/P	G	G	M	M/P	G
Jarrah, Curly (*Eucalyptus marginata*); western Australia.	G	G	G	G	M	G	M	M	M	G	E

A letter grade (see key) is given for the wood's properties and suitability. For example, the three species of cedar shown have excellent decay resistance but are poor in strength. Hence cedar would be well-suited for a building's ground sills which are exposed to repeated wet conditions, but would not be suitable for top plates and floor or roof structural members, unless the member is made sufficiently large to support the load.

Species										
Karri (NA); western Australia.	E	M/P	M	M	M	M	M	M	G	G
Kauri, New Zealand (*Agathis australis*); New Zealand.	G	G	E	G	G	G	G	G	G	G
Larch, European (*Larix decidua*); Alps, western Poland into Russia and Carpathian mountains.	E	E	E	G	G	E	E	E	E	E
Larch, Japanese (*Larix leptolepis*); Shinano province in Japan.	E	E	E	G	G	E	E	G	E	E
Larch, Tamarack (*Larix laricina*). Throughout northeastern U.S. and Canada to eastern British Columbia.	G/E	E	E	M	G	E	E	G	G/E	G/E
Larch, Western (*Larix occidentalis*); northwestern U.S. and eastern British Columbia.	E	E	E	M	G	E	E	G	E	E
Oak, White (*Quercus alba*); eastern U.S. and Canada.	E	M/G	G	G	G	M/G	E	E	E	E
Pine, Eastern White (*Pinus strobus*); eastern Canada and northeastern U.S.	M	M	M/P	G	G	M	M	M/P	M/P	M/P
Pine, Lodgepole (*Pinus contorta*); western Canada and northwestern U.S.	M/G	M	M/P	G	G	M	G	M/P	M	M
Pine, Ponderosa (*Pinus ponderosa*). Scattered throughout western Canada and U.S.	M/G	M	M	G	G	M	G	G	G	G
Pine, Red (*Pinus resinosa*); northeastern U.S. and eastern Canada.	M/G	M/G	G	G	G	M/G	G	G/E	G/E	G/E
Pine, Scots (*Pinus sylvestris*). Throughout Europe and England.	G	M	G	G	G	M	G	G	M	M
Pine, Western White (*Pinus monticola*); southwestern Canada and western U.S.	M	M	M	G	G	M	G	M/P	M	M
Poplar, Balsam (*Populus balsamifera*). Throughout Canada and northern U.S.	P	M/P	M/P	M	M	M/P	M	M/P	P	P
Spruce, Black (*Picea mariana*). Northeastern U.S. and throughout Canada, except the Southwest.	G	M	G	G	G	M	M	G	G	G
Spruce, Engelmann (*Picea engelmannii*). Along North American Rocky mountain range from western Canada to New Mexico, U.S.A.	G	M	G	G	G	M	G	G	G	G
Spruce, Norway (*Picea abies*). Extending eastward from England to the Alps, Carpathians, and Russia.	G	M	G	G	G	M	G	G/E	G	G
Spruce, Sitka (*Picea sitchensis*); Pacific coast of U.S. and Canada.	G	M	G	G	G	M	G	G/E	G	G
Spruce, White (*Picea glauca*). Throughout Canada and northeastern U.S.	G	M	M/G	G	G	M	G	G/E	G	G
Tallowwood (NA); western Australia.	E	G	G	G	G	G	G	G	G	G

Note: As species wood properties vary in accordance with different locales, this chart is intended as a general guide. Builders should consult local information sources for more detailed information on species properties and suitability.

Appendix III

Structural Beam Loading and Sizing

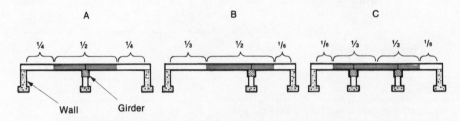

Figure III-1. —Proportions of floor weight carried by girders.

Before one can determine the size of the support beam needed to carry a load, it is first necessary to determine the proportion of load the beam carries. Figure III-1 shows floor support girders. In A, the single girder provides a center support and carries half the weight of each floor joist resting on it. Thus, the girder carries half the weight of the floor, while the two foundation walls carry the other half.

In B, a single girder is placed slightly off-center to support a bearing partition. Again, the girder carries half the floor weight, and only the proportion of weight carried by the foundation walls changes.

In C, there are two support girders, and each beam carries a third of the floor weight, while the foundation walls carry a sixth each, or a total of a third of the floor weight.

The girder serves to bisect the floor joist into two or three sections, depending on the number of girder supports. The support beams of a roof operate in the same manner.

A roof is like a floor with its middle pitched up to form a peak and with its sides sloped. The rafters function in the same manner as the floor joists, and the ridge pole and purlins function like floor girders. The proportion of roof weight these beams carry is determined in the same way as for floor girders. In Figure III–2A the ridge pole beam carries half the weight on the roof, while the walls carry the other half.

In B, a purlin beam is included on each slope. Here the ridge beam carries an eighth of the weight of each roof slope, or a quarter of the weight of the roof, while the purlins each carry a quarter of the weight of the roof. The side walls carry the other quarter of the roof weight, or an eighth of the weight each.

Defining loads

The loads carried by floors and roofs are broken down in the following manner.
Dead load: The weight of the building alone.
Floors: 10 lbs per sq. ft. or .48 kilonewtons per sq. meter (kN/m²).
Roofs: 20 lbs per sq. ft. or .95 kilonewtons per sq. meter (kN/m²).

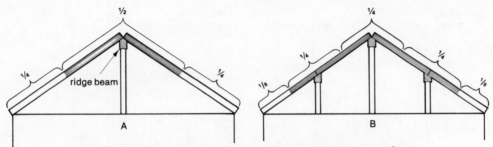

Figure III-2. Two ways of distributing roof weight on rafters.

Live load (on the floor only):   Occupants and furnishings.

Main floor: 40 p.s.f. or 1.9 kN/m²

Second floor: 30 p.s.f. or 1.43 kN/m²

Snow load (on the roof only):   This varies with geographic area: check with building authorities.

Note: Sloped roofs hold only a percentage of the total ground snow load. Apply the weight reduction as follows:

Metric roof slope	Standard roof slope	% of Ground snow load
0/250	0/12 (Flat roof)	100 (no weight reduction)
80/250	4/12	80 (20% weight reduction)
165/250	8/12	70 (30% weight reduction)
210/250	10/12	60 (40% weight reduction)
250/250	12/12	50 (50% weight reduction)
295/250	14/12	40 (60% weight reduction)
375/250	18/12	30 (70% weight reduction)

Calculating beam size

Once the proportion of the floor and roof load that the beam will carry has been determined, it is easy to calculate the size of the beam needed. Below is an example house with steps shown on how to calculate the size of floor girder and roof ridge and purlin beams.

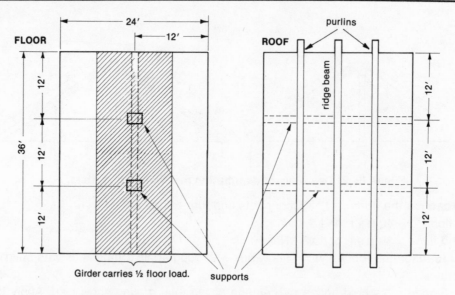

Figure III-3. Calculating beam size of example house.

Example house data: Single storey 24′ × 36′ (7.315 × 11 m)
Single floor girder supported at two equal spacings.
8/12 pitch roof (165/250 cut of the roof)
Ridge pole and purlins supported at two equal spacings.
Local snow load 30 p.s.f. (146 kg/m²) (variable upon
geographic location)

A. Determining floor girder size

		Standard measures	Metric measures
1)	Determine the total floor load per sq. ft. (sq. meter). (Refer to page above.)	Dead load = 10 p.s.f. Live load = 40 p.s.f.* Total load = 50 p.s.f.	Dead load = .48 kN/m² Live load = 1.9 kN/m²* Total load = 2.38 kN/m²
2)	Determine proportion of joist floor load carried by the girder. (Refer to page 262.)	Span = 24 × ½ = 12′	Span = 7.315 × ½ = 3.658 m
3)	Find the distance between the girder supports (given).	(given) = 12′	(given) = 3.658 m)
4)	Find the linear foot (meter) load on the girder by multiplying the proportion of girder load carried by the total floor load.	12′ × 50 p.s.f. = 600 p.l.f.	3.658 m × 2.38 kN/m² = 8.70 kN/m
5)	To find the total load of the girder, *multiply the linear foot (meter) load on the girder by the span between the girder supports*, as in the example.	600 p.l.f. × 12′ = 7,200 lbs	8.70 kN/m × 3.658 = 31.8 kN

6) Find the beam size needed from the beam size table, below. In the column *Span in Feet/meters* locate 12′ (3.6 m) and follow the figures down until the number approximating 7,200 lbs (31.8 kN) or the next largest number appears. (E.g., 8,537 lbs, or 38.0 kN.) Now move horizontally to the left, till you are under the heading *Solid Beam Size*, where the dimensions are given. In this case an 8″ × 10″ (200 × 250 mm) girder or 9″ (230 mm) diameter log is needed. (Note beam dimension in relation to strength explained below.)

Girder size needed = 8″ × 10″ (200 × 250 mm) timber
9″ (230 mm) log

*main floor

B. Determining roof ridge and purlin beam sizes

		Standard measures	Metric measures
1)	Total roof load	Dead load = 20 p.s.f. Snow load (8/12 pitch = 70% of 30 p.s.f.) = 21 p.s.f. Total load = 41 p.s.f.	Dead load = .95 kN/m² Snow load = 165/250 = 70% of 1.43 kN/m² = 1.0 kN/m² Total load = 1.95 kN/m²
2)	Proportion of roof load carried by the ridge beam or purlin (See Figure III–1.)	Span = 24 × ¼ = 6′	Span = 7.315 m × ¼ = 1.828 m
3)	Distance between supports (given)	= 12′	3.658 m
4)	Linear foot (meter) load on the ridgebeam or purlin.	6′ × 41 p.s.f. = 246 p.l.f.	1.828 m × 1.95 kN/m² = 3.56 kN/m
5)	Total load carried by the ridgebeam or purlin	246 p.l.f. × 12′ = 2,952 lbs.	3.56 kN/m × 3.658 = 13.0 kN
6)	Ridge beam and purlin size needed (see beam size, below, under Span in Feet/meters) (e.g., 12′, or 3.6 m) then left locate beam size	= 4″ × 8″ timber or 6″ log	100 × 200 mm timber or 150 mm log

Beam Size in Relation to Span and Total Load*

Assumed no material defects: Allowable Fiber Stress 1400 p.s.i. (9.6 Megapascal, MPa)

Solid Beam Size in Inches/millimeters	Span in Feet/meters						
	6 (1.8 m)	7 (2.0 m)	8 (2.4 m)	10 (3.0 m)	12 (3.6 m)	14 (4.2 m)	16 (4.8 m)
2 × 6 (50 × 150 mm)	1318/5.9	1124/5.0	979/4.4	774/3.4	636/2.8	536/2.4	459/2.0
3 × 6 (75 × 150 mm)	2127/9.5	1816/8.1	1581/7.0	1249/5.6	1025/4.6	863/3.8	740/3.3
4 × 6 (100 × 150 mm)	2938/13.1	2507/11.2	2184/9.7	1726/7.7	1418/6.3	1194/5.3	1023/4.5
6 × 6 (150 × 150 mm)	4263/19.0	3638/16.2	3168/14.1	2504/11.1	2055/9.1	1731/7.7	1483/6.6
2 × 8 (50 × 200 mm)	1865/8.3	1865/8.3	1760/7.8	1395/6.2	1150/5.1	973/4.3	839/3.7
3 × 8 (75 × 200 mm)	3020/13.4	3020/13.4	2824/12.6	2238/10.0	1845/8.2	1560/6.9	1343/6.0
4 × 8 (100 × 200 mm)	4165/18.5	4165/18.5	3904/17.4	3906/17.4	2552/11.4	2160/9.6	1802/8.0
6 × 8 (150 × 200 mm)	6330/28.2	6330/28.2	5924/26.4	4698/21.0	3873/17.2	3277/14.6	2825/12.6
8 × 8 (200 × 200 mm)	8630/38.4	8630/38.4	8078/35.9	6406/28.5	5281/23.5	4469/19.9	3851/17.2
2 × 10 (50 × 250 mm)	2360/10.5	2360/10.5	2360/10.5	2237/10.0	1848/8.2	1569/7.0	1356/6.0
3 × 10 (75 × 250 mm)	3810/17.0	3810/17.0	3810/17.0	3612/16.1	2984/13.3	2531/11.2	2267/10.1
4 × 10 (100 × 250 mm)	5265/23.4	5265/23.4	5265/23.4	4992/22.2	4125/18.4	3500/15.6	3026/13.5
6 × 10 (150 × 250 mm)	7990/35.5	7990/35.5	7990/35.5	6860/30.5	6261/27.9	5312/23.6	4593/20.4
8 × 10 (200 × 250 mm)	10920/48.6	10920/48.6	10920/48.6	9351/42.0	8537/38.0	7244/32.2	6264/27.9
2 × 12 (50 × 300 mm)	2845/12.7	2845/12.7	2845/12.7	2845/12.7	2724/12.1	2315/10.3	2006/8.9
3 × 12 (75 × 300 mm)	4590/20.4	4590/20.4	4590/20.4	4590/20.4	4394/19.6	3734/16.6	3234/14.4
4 × 12 (100 × 300 mm)	6350/28.3	6350/28.3	6350/28.3	6350/28.3	6075/27.0	5165/23.0	4474/19.9
6 × 12 (150 × 300 mm)	9640/42.9	9640/42.9	9640/42.9	9640/42.9	9220/41.0	7837/34.9	6791/30.2
8 × 12 (200 × 300 mm)	13160/58.6	13160/58.6	13160/58.6	13160/58.6	12570/55.9	10685/47.5	9260/41.2
2 × 14 (50 × 355 mm)	3595/16.0	3595/16.0	3595/16.0	3595/16.0	3595/16.0	3199/14.2	2776/12.3

*Total load in body of table is expressed in pounds and kilonewtons. This table is calculated for Douglas fir, southern pine or an equivalent. Sound round logs approximating square beam sizes are assumed to be 20 percent stronger than square timbers.

Beam dimensions and relative strength

 = x load.

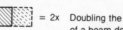 = 2x Doubling the *width* of a beam doubles its load carrying capacity.

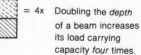 = 4x Doubling the *depth* of a beam increases its load carrying capacity *four* times.

Appendix IV

Common Rafter Lengths

Degree of Roof Slope	Metric Roof Slope	Standard Roof Slope	Constant	×	Building Run		= Rafter Line Length
15°	60/250	3/12	1.03	×		=	Rafter Line Length
20°	81/250	4/12	1.05	×		=	
23°	103/250	5/12	1.08	×		=	
26.5°	123/250	6/12	1.12	×		=	
30°	144/250	7/12	1.16	×		=	
33.5°	166/250	8/12	1.20	×		=	
37°	188/250	9/12	1.25	×		=	
40.5°	210/250	10/12	1.30	×		=	
45°	250/250	12/12	1.41	×		=	
49.5°	295/250	14/12	1.54	×		=	
53°	335/250	16/12	1.67	×		=	
56.5°	375/250	18/12	1.80	×		=	
59°	415/250	20/12	1.95	×		=	
61.5°	460/250	22/12	2.09	×		=	
63.5°	500/250	24/12	2.24	×		=	

The line length of a rafter can be determined from this table by locating the roof slope (in degrees/ metric/ or standard) in one of the three lefthand columns. Then, on the same line to the right, the constant number is obtained. Multiply this constant with the building run measurement to find the rafter length. To this figure add wastage and overhang allowance.

Example: Find the rafter line length for a 45° (250/250, 12/12) slope, whose building run is 15′ (4572 mm).

Standard (12/12) 1.41 × 15′ = 21′2″ rafter line length

Metric (250/250) 1.41 × 4572 mm = 6446 mm rafter line length

Appendix V

Truss Specifications

When fabricating dimensional frame trusses, the gusset placement is important. The information given below is intended to supplement the conventional trussed roof system described in Chapter 13, section **2.**

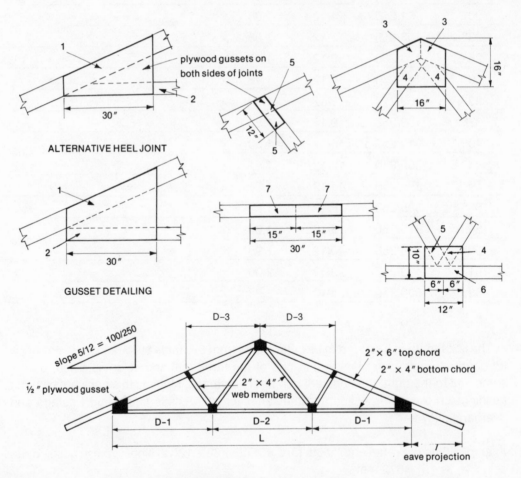

Note: 2″ × 4″ (38 × 89 mm) top chord may be used for a 22.5 p.s.f.. snow load.

Figure V–1. A nailed "W" truss.

Nailed 'W' Truss:

Slope: 5/12 (100/250) only
Spans: 28′4″ to 34′4″ (8.64 to 10.46 m)
Gusset materials: ½″ (12 mm) plywood

Nailing procedures

Roof Snow Load	Slope	Span "L"		Joint Location						
		ft in	1	2	3	4	5	6	7
		30 4 (9.24 m)	12	12	4	4	3	4	8
22.5 lbs/ft²	5/12	32 4 (9.85 m)	13	12	4	4	3	4	8
1.07 kN/m²	100/250	34 4 (10.46 m)	14	13	5	5	4	5	9
		30 4 (9.24 m)	15	14	5	5	4	5	10
30 lbs/ft²	5/12	32 4 (9.85 m)	16	15	5	5	4	5	11
1.43 kN/m²	100/250	34 4 (10.46 m)	17	16	6	6	5	6	12
		28 4 (8.64 m)	17	16	5	5	4	5	12
37.5 lbs/ft²	5/12	30 4 (9.24 m)	18	17	5	5	4	5	12
		32 4 (9.85 m)	19	18	6	6	5	6	13
1.79 kN/m²	100/250	34 4 (10.46 m)	20	19	7	7	6	7	13

Dimensions

Span		L = 28′4″ = 8.64 m	L = 30′4″ = 9.24 m	L = 32′4″ = 9.85 m	L = 34′4″ = 10.46 m
Dimensions	D–1	10′1″ 3073 mm	10′10″ 3302 mm	11′7″ 3530 mm	12′4″ 3759 mm
	D–2	8′2″ 2489 mm	8′8″ 2641 mm	9′2″ 2794 mm	9′8″ 2946 mm
	D–3	6′4″ 1930 mm	6′9″ 2057 mm	7′2″ 2184 mm	7′7″ 2311 mm

Materials

Lumber

No. 1 Grade Spruce or equivalent for top and bottom chords.
No. 2 Grade Spruce or equivalent for web members.

Nails

Use 3″ (75 mm) common steel wire nails.

Nails should be in staggered rows and clinched perpendicular to the direction of the plywood face grain.

Solid blocking should be used under gusset plates during nailing.

Plywood

½″ sheathing grade Douglas Fir or equivalent throughout.

The plywood's grain direction should face parallel to the bottom chord except for plates joining web to top chord at quarter points.

Directions:

a) To ensure maximum stiffness, the upper chords must be in good bearing contact at the peak.

b) Trusses with spans whose sizes fall between those listed must be nailed in a way that is not less than that shown for the larger span.

Note: Roof snow load = 80% of ground snow load (for example, 5/12, 100/250 roof slope).

Trusses are spaced 24″ (600 mm) on center.

Appendix VI

Log and Frame Dimensions

Table 1: Log–Frame Conversion

3¼ ″ (82 mm) diameter log = 2″×4″ (38×89 mm) or 2″×5″ (38×114 mm).
4¼ ″ (108 mm) diameter log = 2″×6″ (38×140 mm).
5¼ ″ (133 mm) diameter log = 2″×8″ (38×184 mm).
6 ″ (152 mm) diameter log = 2″×10″ (38×235 mm).
7 ″ (178 mm) diameter log = 2″×12″ (38×286 mm).

Table 1 gives log to frame conversion equivalents. A given diameter log equal in strength to the corresponding dimensional material given. This conversion table can be used for quick reference in sizing floor joist equivalents. Increasing the width of the frame material corresponds with an increase in log diameter size.

Table 2 gives the minimum log diameter size needed for a given span and spacing. This table can also be used as a quick reference to determine the size of log floor joist members.

Table 2: Log Floor Joist Sizes (40 p.s.f., or 1.90 kN/m², main floor)**

Joist Diameter	Spacing	Span
4¼ ″ (108 mm)	24″ (610 mm)	8′ (2.4 m)
5¼ ″ (133 mm)	24″ (610 mm)	11′ (3.3 m)
6 ″ (152 mm)	24″ (610 mm)	14′ (4.3 m)
7 ″ (178 mm)	24″ (610 mm)	17′ (5.2 m)

*Assumed no major log defects
**Assumed 2″×6″ (38×130 mm) tongue & groove flooring

Bibliography

Design Books

Itoh, Teiji, and Futagawa, Yukio. *The Classic Tradition in Japanese Architecture.* New York, Tokyo: Weatherhill/Tankosha, 1971.

————. *The Elegant Japanese House.* New York, Tokyo: Weatherhill/Tankosha, 1967.

Itoh, Teiji, and Takai, Kiyoshi. *Kura: Design and Tradition of the Japanese Storehouse.* Seattle: Madrona Publishers, 1981.

Kern, Ken. *The Owner Built Home.* New York: Charles Scribner's Sons, 1972.

McHarg, Ian. *Design with Nature.* New York: Doubleday/Natural History Press, 1969.

Olgyay, Victor. *Design with Climate.* Princeton, N. J.: University Press, 1963.

Walker, Les, and Milstein, Jeff. *Designing Houses.* New York: Overlook Press, 1976.

History Books

Barbeau, Marius. "The House That Mac Built." *The Beaver Magazine Quarterly* (December 1945): 10–13.

Bugge, Gunnar, and Schultz-Norberg, Christian. *Stav Og Laft.* Oslo: Byggekunst, 1969.

Callen, Mary K. *History of Fort Langley 1827–96.* Ottawa: National Historic Parks and Sites Branch, 1979.

Cook, Kathleen, trans. *North Russian Architecture.* Moscow: Progress Publ., 1972.

Hansen, Hans Jurgen. *Architecture in Wood.* New York: Viking Press, 1971.

Kavli, Guthorm. *Norwegian Architecture Past and Present.* Oslo: Dreyers Forlag, 1958.

Lindholm, Dan, and Roggenkamp, Walther. *Stave Churches in Norway.* London: Rudolf Steiner Press, 1969.

Moogk, Peter N. *Building a House in New France.* Toronto: McClelland and Stewart Ltd., 1977.

Peeps, Calder. "Fort Langley in ReCreation." *The Beaver Magazine Quarterly* (Autumn 1958): 30–39.

Shurtleff, Harold R. *The Log Cabin Myth.* Glouchester, Mass.: Harvard University Press, 1939.

West, Trudey. *The Timber-frame House in England.* New York: Architectural Book Publishing Co., 1971.

Log Building Books

Janzen, Vic. *Your Log House.* Gardenvale, Quebec: Muir Publishing Co., 1981.

Langsner, Drew. *A Logbuilder's Handbook.* Emmaus, Pa.: Rodale Press, 1982.

Mackie, Allan B. *Building with Logs.* Prince George, B.C.: Log House Publ. Co., 1972.

————. *Log House Plans.* Prince George, B.C.: Log House Publ. Co., 1979.

Mann, Dale, and Skinulis, Richard. *The Complete Log House Book.* Toronto: McGraw-Hill Ryerson Ltd., 1979.

Phleps, Hermann. *The Craft of Log Building.* Ottawa: Lee Valley Tools Ltd., 1982.

Stonework Books

Kern, Ken; Magers, Steve; and Penfield, Lou. *Stone Masonry.* Oakhurst, Calif.: Owner Builder Publications, 1976.

Schwenke, Karl, and Schwenke, Sue. *Build Your Own Stone House.* Charlotte, Vt.: Garden Way Publishing Co., 1975.

Timber Frame Books

Benson, Tedd, and Gruber, James. *Building the Timber Frame House.* New York: Charles Scribner's Sons, 1980.

Elliott, Stewart, and Wallas, Eugene. *The Timber Framing Book.* Kittery Point, Maine: Housesmiths Press, 1977.

Nakahara, Yasuo. *Japanese Joinery.* Vancouver: Hartley & Marks Publishers, 1983.

Tool Books

Arcand, R. D. *Log Building Tools & How to Make Them.* Sorrento, B.C.: R. D. Arcand, 1976.

McDonnell, Leo P. *Hand Woodworking Tools.* New York: Delmar Publishers, 1962.

Newberry, Bill. *Handbook for Riggers.* Calgary: Commercial Printers, 1967.

Tree and Wood Books

Constantine, Albert, Jr. *Know Your Woods.* New York: Charles Scribner's Sons, 1959.

Findlay, W. P. K. *Timber Properties and Uses.* London: Crosby Lockwood Staples Publ., 1975.

Hoadley, Bruce R. *Understanding Wood.* Newton, Conn.: The Taunton Press, 1980.

Hosie, R. C. *Native Trees of Canada.* Ottawa: Ministry of Environment, 1973.

Lloyd, C. *Australian Carpenter.* Melbourne: The MacMillan Company of Australia PTY Ltd., 1965.

Pinces Risborough Laboratory. *A Handbook of Softwoods.* London: Dept. of Environment, Millbank Tower, 1957.

Glossary

Anchor fastener: A bolt, bar, or spike protruding from the foundation, used to anchor the sill.

Backcut: The final felling cut in felling a tree.

Backfilling: Replacing the excavated soil around a foundation wall.

Baluster (also Bannister): An upright support of a handrail on a staircase.

Bar (or blade): The part of the chainsaw on which the cutting chain travels.

Bay: A uniform division of a building, such as the spaces between a series of four posts.

Beam: A principal horizontal support member in the building's floor or roof frame.

Bearing partition: A wall which carries second storey or roof loads.

Bent (framework): A framework of vertical posts and horizontal beams.

Birdsmouth: A V-shaped joint resembling a bird's open beak, used to join a rafter to the top plate.

Blade: See Bar.

Blockwork: A method of horizontal notched corner log and timber construction.

Brace: A diagonal support member used to stiffen unstable walls or frames.

Bucking: To saw a felled tree into log lengths.

Bulhuse: A sixteenth-century Danish term, referring to post and beam construction methods.

Butt: The large end of a log or tree sawn from the stump.

Butt joint: Any joint made by fastening two members together without overlapping.

Camber: An upward arch given to a beam or girder to prevent its becoming concave due to its own weight or the weight of the load it must carry.

Cantilever (beam): A projecting beam that supports a structure such as a balcony or overhang.

Carrier: Water, oil, or a solvent used to disperse a preservative or finish on a wood surface.

Caulk: To make tight against wind and water using a sealing material.

Chamfer: A sloping or beveled edge for decoration of a timber. Also used for tenon joints for easier insertion into a mortise.

Check: A longitudinal crack in a log or timber caused by too rapid seasoning.

Chinking: The process or materials used to fill gaps between horizontal wall logs or half timbers.

Chipper chain: The cutting teeth of a chainsaw chain whose round backs allow for planing and curved cuts.

Chisel chain: The cutting teeth of a chainsaw chain whose straight-edged backs prevent planing or curved cuts, and allow only straight cuts.

Collar-tie: A horizontal member connected at the midpoint between two rafters to reduce spreading or sagging of the rafters.

Common rafter: One of a series of support members extending from the top of an ex terior wall to the ridge of a roof.

Compression: A pressing or crushing type of force.

Conduction: Movement of heat through a material.

Cord: The principal top or bottom member of a truss.

Cordwood: Round pieces of wood 12"–16" (300–400 mm) long and 1"–6" (25–150 mm) in diameter, used in stackwall construction.

Countersink: Burying the head of a pin, screw, or bolt into an enlarged hole, which is then usually plugged.

Course: The tiered layers of logs or half-timbers used in solid wood construction.

Crawl space: A shallow space between the lowest floor of a house and the ground beneath.

Cross grain: Grains that run perpendicular to the straight grain of wood. In wood joinery it is more difficult to work the cross grain.

Cross-cut saw: A saw designed to cut across the wood grain.

Crown: Convex side of lumber or timber.

C.R.M.S.: Cold rolled mild steel, harder than H.R.M.S. (hot).

Cull: A tree or log considered unmarketable because of defects.

Cut (of a roof): The metrically measured angle of incline of a roof.

Dado: A rectangular groove in wood which runs perpendicular to the grain, usually cut with a dado plane or router.

Dado groove: See Dado.

Darby: A plasterer's float made of a narrow piece of wood or metal with two handles, used to smooth a stucco surface.

Dead load: Total weight of the building's structure (floor, walls, roof, etc.).

Defect: A fault or irregularity in wood materials which reduces strength, durability, or appearance.

Depth: The vertical thickness of a beam.

Diagonals: Used in the squaring procedure for establishing right-angle accuracy when laying out a foundation, or testing frame accuracy.

Dogs, chainsaw: Pointed metal teeth located between the blade and motor of the chain saw. Used when felling, bucking, or flat-surfacing wood when pivoting the saw to maintain position while sawing.

Dovetail: A tenon and mortise shaped like a dove's fantail; a locking joint.

Dowel: A wooden peg used to aid in fastening two pieces of wood together.

Drift pin: A metal punch of slightly less diameter than the pin or spike, used to embed the pin or spike into a countersunk hole.

Drip cap: Flashing or molding placed to prevent rain water from entering the building. A groove in the underside of a sill or header serves the same purpose.

Drywall: Interior wall and ceiling finishing material similar in appearance to plaster.

Eave: The part of a roof which projects beyond the face of a wall.

Excavate: To dig a cavity, such as for the foundation.

Expansion joint: A joint in concrete or plumbing designed to permit expansion without damage to the structure.

Facia: A finishing board around the face of eaves and roof projections.

Felling: The process of tree cutting.

Fiber failure: Structural failure of wood resulting from excess loading.

Firmer chisel: A heavy duty chisel strong enought to be hit with a mallet.

Fish wire: A wire or string used to pull electrical wire through a service hole.

Flashing: Sheet metal or other material used to shed water away from the building.

Flush (cut): An even cut which is level with an adjacent surface.

Fork and tongue joint: A modified mortise and tenon joint used for joinery of timber rafters at the peak of the roof.

Frame: A structure comprised of vertical and horizontal members.

Framework: The braced frame timber construction method.

Framing square: A steel L-shaped metal layout tool used for laying out joinery and roof members which also doubles as a rafter square.

Furring: Wood nailing strips laid on a roof for the application of wood shakes, and on walls to support finishing material.

Gable: The triangular portion of the end wall of a building formed by the roof.

Gable roof: An A-shaped roof with two equal slopes meeting at the ridge.

Girder: A principal beam used to support loads.

Green (wood): Freshly cut wood which has not been seasoned.

Groove: A rectangular slot running parallel to the wood grain.

Gusset: A wood or metal plate attached to one or both sides of a joint to increase its holding power.

Half-lap: A joint in which half of the opposing wood of each member is removed and the connection lapped.

Half-timber: A log whose sides have been flat-surfaced while the top and bottom are left round. Used as a wall infill material in post and beam construction, where the rounded width portions may be scribed and fitted together.

Hardwood: Referring to broad-leaved deciduous trees, rather than to the hardness of the wood.

Header: The horizontal wood member above a window or door.

Hew: To square a timber or half-timber by hand using a scoring axe and broad-axe.

Holding wood: A portion of wood left uncut between the undercut and backcut of a tree, which acts as a hinge for controlled felling.

Housing: A mortise or cavity cut to receive the end of a beam, for example, a floor joist.

H.R.M.S.: Hot-rolled mild steel, which is softer than C.R.M.S. (cold).

Hudson's Bay frame: An English term referring to the short log post and beam construction methods of early Canada.

Hypotenuse: The sloping side of a right-angle triangle.

Infill (panels): The material, such as log, half-timber, or stackwall, which is placed between the bays of a post and beam frame.

Jamb: The side member of a door way or window lining.

Jig: A device used to hold work during the manufacture of an assembly, such as a panel.

Joinery: The craft of joining wood to form a structure with the use of various joints.

Joint: A connection between two wood members.

Joists: The horizontal wood members used to support a floor or ceiling.

Kerf: A saw cut.

Kick-back: An uncontrolled jerk of the chainsaw bar which is a common cause of cuts.

King-post: The vertical member in the center of a truss.

Knee brace: A timber member placed diagonally between a post and beam, used to stiffen a frame.

Laft work: A Norwegian term for the blockwork method of construction.

Lag screw: A heavy wood screw with a square head and coarse thread.

Layout: The process of drawing a joint's dimensions in preparation for cutting.

Linear dimension: Measurement along a line.

Live load: The occupancy weight added to a building (people, appliances, furnishings, etc.).

Lofting: A layout process in which graphic representation, as of the roof truss, is drawn full scale.

Main stack: The main vent pipe of a house's plumbing system.

Mallet: A 2½ lb (1 kg) hardwood hammer used to drive a chisel.

Member: A building component, such as a log, timber, or half-timber.

Moisture barrier: A material used to prevent the passage of moisture.

Mortise: A female socket designed to receive a male tenon to form a joint.

Nominal size: The dimensions of undressed lumber.

Notch: The groove in a log or timber to receive another log or timber.

Oakum: Tar-impregnated hemp used for caulking joints.

On center: Identified by the center line symbol, it represents the center of a member, and is used to take measurements from when laying out spacings for joists, rafters, etc.

Overall length: The total length of a member, including tenons, overhang allowance, etc.

Overhang: Projection of the roof beyond the wall.

Partition: A wall which separates rooms.

Perimeter: The outer boundary of a structure.

Pièce-sur-pièce: A French term for the all wood post and beam building methods of early Canada; also called pièce-en-pièce.

Pin: A steel peg or spike used in fastening two pieces of wood together.

Pitch: A roof's angle of incline expressed in standard measurement.

Plumb: Vertical; or to test for the vertical plane.

Pocket: Similar to a mortise or housing.

Pony wall: A short partition often used instead of a girder beam to support a floor.

Post: The vertical log or timber posts of a post and beam frame.

Post and beam: A term referring to a log or timber frame of posts and beams historically built with log or half-timber wall infill.

Purlin: A horizontal, structural roof member spanning between the gable ends, which may be supported midway depending on the span distance.

Pythagorus' theorem: In a right-angle triangle, the sum of the squares of the sides is equal to the square of the hypotenuse: $a^2 + b^2 = c^2$. Used in calculating foundation, roof, and knee-brace lengths.

Rabbet: A long, step-shaped groove cut along the edge of a board or timber, which may be cut to receive a window or door.

Rafter: A sloping support member of the roof frame which extends from the top plate to the ridge.

Red River frame: The English term for the all wood and post and beam building methods of early Canada.

Reiswerk: A Norwegian term in reference to the vertical posts of early post and beam construction.

Ridge beam: The topmost horizontal roof member spanning between the gable ends; also ridge board and ridge pole.

Rip saw: A saw designed to cut parallel to the wood grain.

Rise: The vertical height measured from the top plate to the ridge of a building.

Roof slope: The roof's angle of incline; termed ''pitch'' when expressed in standard measurement and ''cut of the roof,'' in metric measurement.

Rough-in: Enclosing the electrical and plumbing lines in the floors, walls, and ceilings.

Rough opening: An opening framed or cut to receive a window or door.

Round: See Course.

Run: The horizontal distance from the building's outside wall to the ridge line; half the span distance.

Sash: The framework which holds the glass in a window.

Scarf joint: A joint for splicing two wood members end to end.

Scribe: The process of duplicating the contours and dimensions of one surface onto another for the purpose of joinery.

Scriber: A common tool used in log building for scribing two irregular surfaces for the purpose of joinery.

Seasoning: The drying of wood to reduce its dimensional shrinkage.

Settling factor: A calculated amount of shrinkage based on ½ ″ (12 mm) per vertical 12 ″ (300 mm) of horizontally laid green wood.

Settling space: The space, based on the calculated settling factor, which is left above a window or a door that has been installed within a solid wood infill wall.

Shakes: A defect in wood showing a partial or complete separation between the wood's growth rings.

Shear: A force causing slippage between layers of wood fibers.

Sheathing: A covering of plywood, boards, or waterproof material on the exterior of a building.

Shim: A thin tapered material, such as a cedar shingle, used in leveling a window or door frame.

Sill: The horizontal member that rests on the foundation; also the lowest horizontal member of a window's rough opening.

Skids: Poles which elevate wood materials above the ground. Also used to provide a stable work surface.

Skirting board: A board used to conceal a settling space.

Slip joint: An attachment to a log wall designed to permit the natural, unimpeded settling of the wall.

Sod roof: A roof whose covering includes two layers of grass turf, originating in northern Europe.

Soffit: The materials attached to the underside of a roof overhang.

Softwood: Refers to needle-leaved coniferous or evergreen trees, rather than to the softness of the wood.

Solid wood construction: A term referring to the methods of all-wood post and beam or blockwork construction.

Span: The horizontal distance between a building's side walls. Also the distance between supporting members, such as beams, rafters, and joists.

Spiral grain: A corkscrew-shaped grain pattern most often found in woods such as Tamarack and Black Spruce. Excessive spiral grain can cause posts or beams to twist out of position.

Spline: A rectangular strip of wood which, when fitted into grooves in two adjoining members, locks them together.

Squaring-off: To cut wood at a right-angle. Also refers to the process of taking the diagonals of a rectangle to establish right-angle corners.

Stackwall: A wall infill using stacked cordwood embedded in mortar. (Usually a double wall system with an insulated middle cavity.)

Stave construction: See Reiswerk.

Stav og laft: A Norwegian term for combined reiswerk and laft construction which became true post and beam construction.

Stress: The internal force of a material which resists change in shape or size caused by external forces.

Structural trim board: The load supporting boards which also serve to conceal a settling space.

Strut: A structural member whose placement in a structure such as a truss serves to resist loading forces by acting in compression.

Stub wall: See pony wall.

Stucco: A cement-like material used as an exterior wall covering, similar to plaster in its properties and appearance.

Stud frame: A framework of dimensional studs (2″, or 50 mm, nominal thickness) using external sheathing to provide rigidity.

Sway brace: To temporarily strengthen a wall which might otherwise be unsafe.

Template: A full-size pattern made of a hard material used in layout and checking joints.

Tenon: The male projection of a wood member formed to join with the female mortise.

Tension: The stress that resists two forces pulling away from each other.

Thermal mass: A body of material which acts to store heat. The amount of thermal storage potential is relative to the quantitative mass.

Thermal resistivity: The ability of a material to resist heat conduction.

Tie-beam: A beam spanning between the two side walls of a building and locking them in place to prevent spreading caused by forces exerted by the roof rafters.

Timber: A large four-sided wood member.

Timber frame: A braced frame infra-structure using timbers joined and doweled together.

Tongue and slot: A traditional method of joining solid woodwall infill to the posts, where the infill pieces are fashioned with tongues which fit into a slot or groove in the post.

Top plate: The top horizontal member in the building's wall system which serves to tie the walls together and forms a level, flat surface to support the roof.

Truss: A structural framework designed to withstand external loading, such as a roof truss.

Undercut: A wedge section cut from the base of a tree to cause it to fall.

Vapor barrier: See Moisture barrier.

Wall channel: A vertical groove removed from a log wall to allow connection with a slip joint and a partition.

Wane: The rounded edge of a square sawn timber.

Waste wood: The portion of wood cut away to reveal the joint.

Width: The horizontal thickness of a beam or post.

Wood lath: A thin, narrow piece of wood used as a base for applying plaster or stucco.

Index